MATCHING BOOKS AND READERS

SOLVING PROBLEMS
IN THE TEACHING OF LITERACY
Cathy Collins Block, Series Editor

Recent Volumes

How to Plan Differentiated Reading Instruction:
Resources for Grades K–3
Sharon Walpole and Michael C. McKenna

Reading More, Reading Better
Edited by Elfrieda H. Hiebert

The Reading Specialist, Second Edition:
Leadership for the Classroom, School, and Community
Rita M. Bean

Teaching New Literacies in Grades K–3:
Resources for 21st-Century Classrooms
Edited by Barbara Moss and Diane Lapp

Teaching New Literacies in Grades 4–6:
Resources for 21st-Century Classrooms
Edited by Barbara Moss and Diane Lapp

Teaching Reading: Strategies and Resources for Grades K–6
Rachel L. McCormack and Susan Lee Pasquarelli

Comprehension Across the Curriculum: Perspectives and Practices K–12
Edited by Kathy Ganske and Douglas Fisher

Best Practices in ELL Instruction
Edited by Guofang Li and Patricia A. Edwards

Responsive Guided Reading in Grades K–5:
Simplifying Small-Group Instruction
Jennifer Berne and Sophie C. Degener

Early Intervention for Reading Difficulties:
The Interactive Strategies Approach
Donna M. Scanlon, Kimberly L. Anderson, and Joan M. Sweeney

Matching Books and Readers: Helping English Learners in Grades K–6
Nancy L. Hadaway and Terrell A. Young

Children's Literature in the Classroom: Engaging Lifelong Readers
Diane M. Barone

Matching Books and Readers

*Helping English Learners
in Grades K–6*

Nancy L. Hadaway
Terrell A. Young

THE GUILFORD PRESS
New York   London

© 2010 The Guilford Press
A Division of Guilford Publications, Inc.
72 Spring Street, New York, NY 10012
www.guilford.com

Printed in the United States of America

This book is printed on acid-free paper.

Last digit is print number: 9   8   7   6   5   4   3   2   1

Library of Congress Cataloging-in-Publication Data

Hadaway, Nancy L.
   Matching books and readers : helping English learners in grades K–6 / Nancy
L. Hadaway, Terrell A. Young.
       p. cm. — (Solving problems in the teaching of literacy)
   Includes bibliographical references and index.
   ISBN 978-1-60623-881-3 (pbk.: alk. paper)–ISBN 978-1-60623-882-0
(hardcover: alk. paper)
   1. English language—Study and teaching—Foreign speakers.   2. English
language—Study and teaching (Elementary)   3. Bilingualism.   4. Language
acquisition.   5. Reading (Elementary)   I. Young, Terrell A.   II. Title.
   PE1128.A2H244 2010
   428.2′4—dc22
                                                                                       2010020422

About the Authors

Nancy L. Hadaway, PhD, is Professor of Literacy Studies in the College of Education at the University of Texas at Arlington. Her scholarly interests have focused on the literacy issues of English learners. Dr. Hadaway has served on various state and national committees of professional literacy organizations; presented at numerous state, regional, national, and international conferences; and received grants from the Adolescent Literature Assembly of the National Council of Teachers of English and the Association of Colleges and Universities. She has been a committee member for several children's book awards, including the Orbis Pictus Award, the Notable Books for a Global Society, and the Outstanding International Books. Dr. Hadaway's articles have appeared in *Book Links, The Reading Teacher, Journal of Adolescent and Adult Literacy, Language Arts, The English Journal, Childhood Education, Ethnic Forum,* and *Equity and Excellence in Education,* and she has written chapters in books on literacy and multicultural education issues. She is coauthor or coeditor of *Literature-Based Instruction with English Language Learners, K–12; Supporting the Literacy Development of English Learners: Increasing Success in All Classrooms;* and *Breaking Boundaries with Global Literature: Celebrating Diversity in K–12 Classrooms.*

Terrell A. Young, EdD, is Professor of Literacy Education at Washington State University. He is a member of the International Reading Association (IRA) Board of Directors for 2009–2012; received the IRA's Outstanding Teacher Educator in Reading Award in 2006; and was president of the Washington Organization for Reading Development, the Washington State IRA affiliate, from 2000 to 2001. Dr. Young also served as president of the IRA Children's Literature and Reading Special Interest Group from 2004 to 2006 and the National Council of Teachers of English Children's Literature Assembly from 2006 to 2008. He has been a committee member for many children's book awards, including the IRA Children's Book Awards, the Notable Books for a Global Society, the Notable Children's Books in the Language Arts, the Orbis Pictus Award for Outstanding Nonfiction in Children's Literature, and the Washington Children's Choice Picture Book Award. Dr. Young's scholarly interests include literature-based practices, English language learners, and the creative process of authors and illustrators. His articles have appeared in *Book Links, Childhood Education, Language Arts,* and *The Reading Teacher.* He is coauthor or coeditor of *Caught in the Spell of Writing and Reading: Grade 3 and Beyond; Supporting the Literacy Development of English Learners: Increasing Success in All Classrooms; Happily Ever After: Sharing Folk Literature with Elementary and Middle School Children; Literature-Based Instruction with English Language Learners, K–12;* and *Creating Lifelong Readers through Independent Reading.*

Poem and Essay Authors

Jorge Argueta is the author of several children's books. He is the winner of the Americas Award for Latin American Literature and the Independent Publishers Book Award for Multicultural Fiction for Young Adults for his book *Xóchitl and the Flowers* (*Xóchitl, la Niña de las Flores*), among many other awards. Mr. Argueta is a San Francisco Library Poet Laureate. His heartwarming, bilingual English–Spanish stories and poetry are the favorites of Latin American children and adults from all cultures.

Yangsook Choi grew up in Korea and moved to New York to study art. She was selected as one of the most prominent new children's book artists by *Publishers Weekly*. Ms. Choi has written and illustrated many children's books and is the recipient of several awards, including the International Reading Association's Children's Book Award, a California Young Reader Medal, and the Oppenheim Toy Portfolio Gold Award.

Lulu Delacre has been writing and illustrating children's books since 1980. Her Latino heritage as well as her own life experiences inform her books, among them *The Bossy Gallito, Arrorró mi niño: Latino Lullabies and Gentle Games*, and *The Storyteller's Candle*—all winners of the Pura Belpré Honor Award. *Alicia Afterimage* is her latest work. For further information, visit *www.luludelacre.com*.

Maya Christina Gonzalez is an award-winning multicultural children's book artist, author, and educator. She has illustrated 20 children's books and written two. The first book Ms. Gonzalez both illustrated and wrote, *My Colors, My World*, received the 2008 Pura Belpré Honor Award. She recently began Reflection Press with her husband to support educators in bringing creativity as a tool of empowerment into classrooms.

Uma Krishnaswami is the author of picture books including *Chachaji's Cup* and *Monsoon*, early readers (*Yoga Class, Holi*), and a middle-grade novel, *Naming Maya*. Another middle-grade novel, *The Road to Sunny Villa*—a Bollywood-style joyride with a determined young protagonist supported by a cast of larger-than-life eccentrics—is forthcoming in 2011. Ms. Krishnaswami is on the faculty of the Vermont College of Fine Arts MFA Program in Writing for Children and Young Adults.

J. Patrick Lewis is the author of 65 children's poetry and picture books to date. His recent titles include *Kindergarten Cat, Mr. Nickel & Mrs. Dime, Skywriting: Poems in Flight, First Dog's First Christmas*, and *Self-Portrait with Seven Fingers: A Life of Marc Chagall in Verse* (with Jane Yolen).

Asma Mobin-Uddin is a pediatrician who decided to write about the Muslim American experience because she had difficulty finding good books in this area to read to her children. She was born and raised in the United States and is of Pakistani descent. Dr. Mobin-Uddin is the author of three award-winning children's books: *My Name Is Bilal, The Best Eid Ever*, and *A Party in Ramadan*.

Pat Mora is a popular speaker and the author of award-winning books for children, teens, and adults, including *Zing!: Seven Creativity Practices for Educators and Students*. A literacy advocate excited about sharing what she calls "bookjoy," Ms. Mora founded the family literacy initiative El día de los niños/El día de los libros, Children's Day/Book Day ("Día"), now housed at the American Library Association. For further information, visit *www.patmora.com*.

Janet S. Wong is the author of 21 books, from picture books for toddlers (*Buzz*) to poetry for teens (*Behind the Wheel: Poems about Driving*). Several books highlight her Chinese and Korean heritage, such as *This Next New Year, A Suitcase of Seaweed, Apple Pie Fourth of July*, and *The Trip Back Home*. When she is not writing, Ms. Wong keeps busy by speaking at schools, libraries, and conferences. For further information, visit *www.janetwong.com*.

Preface

The Beginning of a Book

The seed for this book was planted many years ago when we and our friend and colleague Sylvia Vardell all taught at the same university. We were convinced that children's trade books—not textbooks or leveled text—were the perfect resource for helping English language learners develop language, literacy, and content. As we worked in schools with teachers and students and made presentations to K–6 teachers, we explored our ideas and approaches with them. Our work eventually led to the publication of *Literature-Based Instruction for English Language Learners, K–12* (Hadaway, Vardell, & Young, 2002c). In that book, we introduced the idea of criteria for helping teachers select literature for their English learners. As we continued to explore the issue, we published "Matching Books and Readers: Selecting Books for English Learners" in *The Reading Teacher* (Vardell, Hadaway, & Young, 2006). This book is an extension of the ideas we have developed over the years, including our work in *The Reading Teacher* article. We gratefully acknowledge Sylvia Vardell's ideas and influence that have helped us shape this project.

Whom Is This Book For?

In our dealings with classroom teachers, many have expressed the need for a resource to help them find appropriate books for their English learners. This book addresses that need. There are many books published about matching books to readers. The majority of them focus on using leveled text while a few deal with genuine literature. Yet, none of them address the particular needs of English learners. This book addresses that need by providing K–6 teachers with a background about English learners and the many benefits of using literature to help them develop language and literacy. More specifically, it provides teachers with criteria and guiding questions for selecting books for their students learning English. The criteria consider both the student in terms of language proficiency level and the text in regard to language and conceptual load and potential text support features. We also consider cultural issues related to texts and whether a book is a good cultural fit to the learner. In short, we make a case for providing English learners with ready access to books that are appropriate to their language and literacy development.

Organization of the Book

The basic question we explore in this book is "How can teachers select and use children's literature to foster the literacy development of English learners?" The first section of the book offers an overview of English learners and language acquisition while also proposing specific criteria for matching literature to English learners. The second section of the book features chapters for the major genres of children's literature, fiction, poetry, and nonfiction. Each chapter presents the value of the genre to meeting the needs of English learners and suggested books to support English learners' language and literacy development.

In addition, children's authors who write books that are especially suited to English learners were invited to share their reflections about language, literature, and culture, and these essays and poems are interspersed throughout the book. These pieces provide further insights to the value of using real literature with students learning English as a new language.

Part I: Getting to Know English Learners

Chapter 1, "English Learners," provides an overview of English learners, the fastest growing group in U.S. schools today, and highlights some of their special needs. We explain the process of language acquisition, provide an overview of how students develop literacy, and make a case for the role of using literature in helping students learn English while improving their reading and writing.

When matching English learners with books, educators must consider specific language factors that influence comprehension. The more the book material deviates from these criteria, the more teaching support will be needed to assist English learners with the obvious language and structural difficulties. Thus, Chapter 2, "Matching Books to English Learners," presents four specific criteria with guiding questions that teachers can use when selecting books for their elementary English learners.

Chapter 3, "English Learners' Academic and Social Language: Moving from Surviving to Thriving," highlights two types of language proficiency needed by English learners, social and academic language. Social language is needed for socializing on the playground and in the lunchroom. This language may take up to 2 years to develop. Academic language deals with the language of the curriculum. Such language is often not a part of students' everyday vocabulary and takes from 5 to 7 years to develop (even longer for children who immigrated to the United States without previous schooling). This chapter provides teachers with the necessary support to help English learners develop the social language needed to interact socially and to move beyond that to the academic language needed for school success.

Part II: Selecting and Using Books with English Learners

Reading fiction dominates the elementary language arts curriculum, so Chapter 4, "Selecting and Using Fiction with English Learners in Grades K–6," deals with issues in selecting and using fiction for English learners. Next, many teachers assume that poetry is too difficult for English learners, but poetry offers a unique format that can foster oral language development and reading fluency. Therefore, Chapter 5, "Selecting and Using Poetry with English Learners in Grades K–6," examines the issues in selecting and using poetry with English learners. Finally, nonfiction is the preferred reading of many children, and it also provides students with the academic language they need to unlock the content areas. Thus, Chapter 6, "Selecting and Using Nonfiction Literature with English Learners in Grades K–6," highlights the critical issues in selecting and using nonfiction with English learners.

Appendices and Children's Book Lists

There are four helpful resources in the Appendix to this book. Appendix A, mentioned in Chapter 1, includes suggested books for both teachers and students to expand their understanding of English learners. This is not an exhaustive list, but the suggested titles offer an opportunity to explore issues related to English learners. Appendix B takes the four text selection criteria introduced in this book and matches those to the five TESOL proficiency levels, noting specifics to keep in mind at each step of the text selection process. Appendix C suggests social ("survival") language topics with examples of books matched to those. And, to help teachers choose book pairs or text sets for each of the narrow reading formats presented in Chapter 3, Appendix D has an extensive list of recommendations.

Finally, we offer a complete bibliography of the children's books cited in the text. These books span a wide variety of genres and themes that effectively meet the needs of both language and content instruction across the curriculum and elementary grades. At the end of each entry (as well as in the text citations), we have coded each book as a guide to help teachers choose books best suited for their classrooms, considering Teachers of English to Speakers of Other Languages (TESOL) proficiency level of the students and the general grade level (primary, intermediate, all grades, K–6). We have also coded each book with an indication of the broad genre of the book (fiction, nonfiction, poetry). We chose this system because grade-level reading indications are not necessarily helpful or accurate when working with English learners. Among English learners, we can have children at any of the five proficiency levels, and we have beginning readers at every grade level. Our coding scheme is merely an approximation; many of these books can be used across the K–6 curriculum depending on the objective of the lesson and the amount of support provided by you, the teacher.

Coding scheme for books cited in the text and in the bibliography

Teachers of English to Speakers of Other Languages (TESOL) Proficiency Level is indicated by TL 1, 2, 3, 4, 5; generally a range of levels is indicated.

1 = Starting

2 = Emerging

3 = Developing

4 = Expanding

5 = Bridging

Grade Level

P = Primary grades, K–2

I = Intermediate grades, 3 –6

A = All grades K–6

S = Secondary or adult (this level is for the resource books listed in Chapter 1)

Type of book is indicated by P, F, NF.

P = Poetry

F = Fiction

NF = Nonfiction

Coding Scheme Example: TL1, P, F = TESOL Level 1 proficiency; Primary grades, K–2; Fiction

Acknowledgments

The contributions of many people have made this book a reality. We first wish to recognize the support we received from the editorial staff of The Guilford Press. We are grateful for the time, skills, and guidance they devoted to this project. We also want to thank the reviewers who read our initial proposal and made helpful suggestions.

In addition, we would like to acknowledge the nine authors who shared their personal insights about English learners, language learning, multiculturalism, and literature in the essays and poems included in this book.

Finally, on a personal note, we want to express our appreciation to our families. In particular, Nancy wishes to dedicate this book to the memory of her husband, Art Sikes. Terry wishes to thank his wife, Christine, and their children for their unwavering support.

Without all of these partners, this book would not have been possible.

Contents

PART II. SELECTING AND USING BOOKS WITH ENGLISH LEARNERS

Pizza

JANET S. WONG

My grandmother came from Korea last week.
She will be here for one month.
She doesn't know English.
Only "Hello, how are you?"
And numbers. Prices.

Today we are at Disneyland.
She does not want anything to drink.
She points to the soda. Five dollars.
"Pi-sah" she says over and over,
"expensive" in Korean.

I buy a slice of pepperoni and hand it to her.
"Pizza," I say.
She nods like a bobblehead doll.
"Pi-SAH!" she says,
and pushes the plate away.

PART I

GETTING TO KNOW
ENGLISH LEARNERS

How to Say Thy Name

YANGSOOK CHOI

"Bucket, come over here, the ceiling is leaking!" My parents would call out to me when the almighty rain drops pelted on our shingle-roofed house. Their chuckles would follow. I was only a little child in a small town in Korea, yet I could be the hard-working bucket who saved my house from a flood, just because my name, Yangsook, is pronounced similar to the word for a nickel bucket. At school once, a teacher asked me to stand by, while she was demonstrating a proper way to mop our classroom.

While friends, teachers, and even my parents who gave me my name joked around about *Yangsook*, I was proud to have a name that I could live up to. *Yang*, my first name, means kind and gentle-spirited. *Sook*, a generational name given to all my female cousins, means pure and beautiful. Once I hit high school, the era of my name banter was over. Or I thought.

When I crossed the Pacific Ocean after college, 10,493 km away from home for a land called America, little did I expect to enter a new era of name banter. This time, I've turned out to be a banterer myself. While most people do a good job pronouncing my name correctly, I feared countless foreign names that mingle in this country.

Everyone I know is at war of one sort or the other, perhaps against finance, sickness, or career, but it had never occurred that a language would stand against me. I found myself in a battlefield where I have to consistently fight off miscommunication. Even with a weapon of an electronic dictionary or thesaurus, there are things that could only come after years of training to be a language warrior.

In the early years of speaking English, my American classmate once asked me, "How come?" I replied, "By bus." One day I fed my classmates with my home-made Korean curry dish, then asked, "Do you want some snakes?" My brain meant to say snacks, but my tongue said otherwise. They understood me, though. They knew I wasn't running a snake farm in my tiny apartment.

But expressions, nuances, and metaphors prickle my brain like tiny needles. And genders are a different level of biology as I could never comprehend the concept behind why a ship is a female. Articles are mind-boggling, still to this day.

If all this syntax is too much for my brain to juggle, English pronunciation of names are outside of my brain beyond measure. Intonation can be quite tricky, but when it comes to pronunciation, some names make me stutter and spit. Names are ferocious, baffling, and deceptive at times.

My throat would do a better job distinguishing a viral sore throat from a bacterial sore throat than the "r" and "l" sound, which are nonexistent in Korean. I would call Lane as Rain, Wale as the sea whale, not (wa-il-y). Ms. Rice came out as Ms. Lice from my hard-twisted tongue. For a while I wished to meet no Hall, the most challenging name. I would pronounce it hail, or hell, but never the right Hall.

At least people knew who I was talking about when I said Hairy Belly, not to insult Halle Berry. But the cab driver had no idea what street I asked him to take me when I said Houston, (hjstn) like Whitney Houston whom I used to listen to growing up as Pop Songs were a source of learning English. I later found out that the street in downtown Manhattan is pronounced (Ha-oo-sten).

My English has become much stronger over the years. I dream in English when I sleep. My brother in Korea asks me if the Americans understand my broken English. I told him that my English is not broken, it's poetic. I certainly do not want to break a language, nor a name.

As I have gotten a habit of asking people to teach me how to say their name right, I often get to learn about traditions, cultures, or interesting things behind a name. I still butter my tongue to say names correctly. But once I drop my barriers and begin to build bridges, the battleground disappears. English becomes a tool to communicate with. My fear is gone, my horizons are broadened, and I humbly receive grace from many who show me patience.

CHAPTER ONE

English Learners

You're not going to understand
a lot of what we say at first, Ms. Hernandez says.
This is called ESL class.
You and your classmates
will be learning English together.
It means they won't always
understand you.
And you won't always
understand them.
—KATHERINE APPLEGATE, *Home of the Brave*
   (Feiwel & Friends, 2007)

English learners are the fastest growing population in the schools today. About 3.9 million public school students were reported to be limited English proficient (LEP) in 2001, a number that nearly doubled in less than a decade (Kindler, 2002). Data further indicated that the number and percentage of students with non- and limited English proficiency in the national enrollment continued to grow in 36 states, with 18 states experiencing more than 10% growth. English learners will represent 25% of the total student population by 2026 (Garcia, 2000).

Other than the label, English learner, and the shared challenge of learning a new language, however, these students may have very little in common. They differ in the languages they speak and their cultural backgrounds, the socioeconomic status they hold, the level of fluency in their home language and English, their prior schooling and home literacy experiences, and their immigration or residency status. From children of middle class urban backgrounds who are literate in their home language and comfortable with school routines to children from strife-ridden countries with little or no schooling, English learners arrive in U.S. schools with many different needs. Notwithstanding these differences and needs, Carola and Marcelo Suárez-Orozco (2001) have documented the remarkably positive social attitudes—toward schooling, authority figures, and the future—of immigrant English learners as they enter school.

Once in school, English learners, both immigrant and native born, encounter many challenges. While English learners at the primary level may be able to adjust to a new language and culture and make academic progress, the changing academic and cognitive demands of increasingly print-based instruction around the third or fourth grade present problems (Olsen, 2006). The volume and broad scope of academic language in discussions, reading, and writing may appear daunting to some native English speakers, but for students learning English, it can be overwhelming.

The quality of schooling can ease or complicate the transition to a new language for English learners and additionally, for immigrants, to a new country and culture. Unfortunately, English learners often find themselves in segregated, poor, and conflict-ridden schools. Further compounding the academic issues, many immigrant children face negative social mirroring that adversely affects their developing identities (Suárez-Orozco & Suárez-Orozco, 2001). Consequently, the educational progress indicators of the past decade continue to reflect a constant achievement gap between English learners and English-fluent students (Olsen, 2006).

This chapter provides an overview of the diverse group labeled English learners highlighting some of their educational and psychosocial needs. Central to addressing the range of differences and developing language abilities that English learners bring to school is coherent, culturally sensitive, and meaningful instruction and curricula. The premise of this book is to encourage the use of children's literature as an integral part of instruction and curriculum.

The Many Faces of English Learners

From refugees, immigrants, asylum seekers, and sojourners who move back and forth across borders to children who were born in the United States or who have lived here the majority of their lives, English learners are an incredibly diverse group. The first step in creating an effective learning environment is understanding the learner and looking beyond the single label, English learner (Olsen, 2006). As a quick reference, teachers should get to know their English learners by learning the following about them (Suárez-Orozco & Suárez-Orozco, 2001; Ovando, Collier, & Combs, 2003):

- Country of origin
- Age at immigration
- Length of residence in the United States
- Extent of ties with the home country
- Political and economic situation in the home country
- Reasons for immigration
- Other countries lived in prior to arriving in the United States
- Home language literacy
- English language knowledge
- Language exposure other than English and the home language
- Amount and quality of schooling in the home language
- Quality of schooling in the United States
- Residency status

Table 1.1 considers one organizational framework for thinking about different English learners based on their time in the United States and their previous schooling. For instance, English learners with consistent previous schooling in their home country, hence, instruction in their home language, tend to catch up academically as compared with English learners who bring a history of interrupted schooling from their home country.

TABLE 1.1. Types of English Learners and Their Characteristics

Newly arrived with adequate schooling	Newly arrived with limited formal schooling	Long-term English learner
• Recent arrival (less than 5 years in North America) • Adequate schooling in native country • Soon catch up academically • May still score low on standardized tests	• Recent arrival (less than 5 years in North America) • Interrupted or limited schooling in native country • Limited native-language literacy • Below grade level in math • Poor academic achievement	• Seven or more years in North America • Below grade level in reading and writing • False perception of academic achievement • Adequate grades but low test scores • ESL or bilingual instruction, but no consistent program

Note. Based on Freeman and Freeman (2007).

The age English learners arrive in United States classrooms and begin the process of learning their new language also plays a crucial factor in becoming fluent in English. Collier (1989) found that children who arrived in the United States before age 12 with at least 2 years of schooling in their native country reached the 50th percentile on reading, language arts, science, and social studies tests within 5 to 7 years in U.S. classrooms. Younger children, ages 4 to 6 with little or no schooling in their native language, had not reached the 50th percentile after 6 years.

Closely connected to any schooling in the native country is first-language literacy. Both the school and the home contribute to first-language literacy. "Parents who read to and talk with their children in their home language help their children develop language skills in ways that will facilitate their learning of English" (Bermúdez, 1994). For instance, children who have been read to and who read at home, whatever the language, bring a more developed knowledge of print and print conventions (Krashen, 1987). Without a firm foundation in their native language, younger children may confuse English language concepts with those in the first language. Indeed, "research in second-language acquisition suggests that the best predictor of success is the skill amassed in the child's first language" (Suárez-Orozco & Suárez-Orozco, 2001, p. 137).

While teachers need to capitalize on the home-language literacy that children bring to school, they must also be aware of the similarities and differences between English and the home language in order to understand potential roadblocks. The more a student's first language differs from English the greater the challenge. As a case in point, while there are many similarities between English and Spanish, there are differences. There are no contractions such as *don't, isn't,* and so on in Spanish, and Spanish dialogue is marked by dashes rather than quotation marks. Further, there are differences between English and Spanish with the following consonants: *d, v, ll, h, j, r, rr, z, ñ, x* (Helman, 2004; Colorín Colorado, 2007). The Spanish /d/ is more similar to /th/ as in *then* in English. Additionally, Spanish does not have the following sounds (Helman, 2004; Colorín Colorado, 2007):

- Vowel digraphs: *ou, ow, eigh, au, aw, oo*
- Consonant digraphs: *sh, th, wh, ph*
- Consonant blends: *sk/sc, sl, sm, sn, sp, st, sw, sts, scr, skw, spl, spr, str, tw*
- Initial sounds: *kn, qu, wr, sk*
- Final sounds: *ck, ng, gh*
- Endings: *-ed* (pronounced /d/ or /t/ or /ded/ or /ted/)

- Endings: *-s* (pronounced /s/ or /z/ or /ez/ or /es/)
- Endings without a vowel: *-ps, -ts*

From an instructional standpoint, teachers can assist English learners by integrating children's literature that authentically highlights certain phonemes or language differences and bringing these to students' attention (Yopp, 1998). Some excellent examples of books to share with English learners include the following: Nancy Shaw's *Sheep Take a Hike* (1994, TL1–2, P, F), *Sheep on a Ship* (1989, TL1–2, P, F), *Sheep Out to Eat* (1992, TL1–2, P, F), *Sheep in a Shop* (1991, TL1–2, P, F), *Sheep Trick or Treat* (1997, TL1–2, P, F), *Sheep Blast Off* (2008, TL1–2, P, F), *Sheep in a Jeep* (1986, TL1–2, P, F), and *Raccoon Tune* (2003, TL1–2, P, F) or Anna Dewdney's *Llama Llama Mad at Mama* (2007, TL1–2, P, F), *Llama Llama Misses Mama* (2005, TL1–2, P, F), and *Llama Llama Red Pajama* (2005, TL1–2, P, F).

Conversely, the more similar the home language is to English in terms of alphabet, the more easily these learners' writing skills will transfer to English (Odlin, 1989). Of over 400 languages spoken across the United States, Spanish is the predominant language with 79% of English learners speaking Spanish. The similarities between English and Spanish are many including the use of the Roman alphabet, a high percentage, 30–40%, of cognates (words in English with a related Spanish word), similar sentence structure except for a couple of word order exceptions, and finally, the same basic processes—phonemic awareness, decoding, fluency, comprehension, and writing mechanisms—are involved in learning to read and write (Colorín Colorado, 2007). Among other English learners, 2.0% speak Vietnamese, 1.6% speak Hmong, 1.0% speak Cantonese, and 1.0% speak Korean; followed by Haitian Creole, Arabic, Russian, Tagalog, Navajo, Khmer, Mandarin, Portugese, Urdu, Serbo-Croatian, Lao, and Japanese. Many of the languages in this group are distinctly different from English in terms of alphabet, sentence structure, and morphology.

Finally, English learners vary tremendously in terms of their family's socioeconomic status. Among immigrants, for instance, those who are highly skilled move into highly paid jobs affording them access to middle-class neighborhoods and schools. Low-skilled immigrants enter poorly paid jobs and settle in neighborhoods with limited contact with middle-class Americans. "This in turn will affect the kinds of English that the children will be exposed to … and the quality of schools they attend" (Suárez-Orozco & Suárez-Orozco, 2001, pp. 61–62).

To help teachers and children in the classroom understand the tremendous diversity of experiences and backgrounds of immigrant and native-born English learners and the many adjustments they face, a resource list at the end of this book in Appendix A provides suggested books for both teachers and students to expand their understanding. This is not an exhaustive list, but the picture books for teachers and students and the chapter books and novels for teachers offer a beginning opportunity to explore more contemporary issues related to diversity, not just language issues.

The Many Facets of Language Acquisition and Development

The next step, and a critical one, in more effectively meeting the needs of English learners is understanding the process of acquiring a second language (Fillmore & Snow, 2000; Hamayan, 1990). The connection between first- and second-language acquisition is supported by a wide body of research that indicates the similarity of linguistic and cognitive processes at play (Ravem, 1968; Milon, 1974; Natalicio & Natalicio, 1971; Dulay & Burt, 1974; Ervin-Tripp, 1974). For instance, children use a creative construction process to learn a second language, just as they do with their first language (Dulay & Burt, 1974). In addition, researchers have noted a striking similarity between the general stages of language acquisition. Since most teachers in the United States are monolingual—fully 80% of California teachers working with English learners are monolingual (Hass, 2002)—Table 1.2 serves as a beginning point for awareness with a comparison of the more familiar first-language acquisition stages and those for acquiring a second language. The amount of time noted for each stage of the process is approximate (Krashen & Terrell, 1983) as many factors influence the timeline of language acquisition.

Toddlers demonstrate their understanding and growing awareness of their first language during the preproduction phase by responding nonverbally. For English learners, regardless of their age, there is also a preproduction stage. This "silent" period (Krashen & Terrell, 1983) is just as critical in second-language acquisition as it is with one's first language. The silent period establishes a level of comfort with the language, so that learners feel confident to progress to the next step.

As children listen and become familiar with a language, they eventually move to the early production phase. In first-language acquisition, children generally progress to this stage between 9 months and 2 years of age. They begin to experiment by producing one- or two-word responses. For English learners, this process may last up to 6 months with an empha-

TABLE 1.2. Comparing First- and Second-Language Acquisition

Language acquisition stages	First-language acquisition timeline	Second-language acquisition timeline
Preproduction Listening, silent phase	Birth–9 months	Several hours–months
Early production Producing one- or two-word responses	9 months–2 years	6 months
Speech emergence Generating phrases and short sentences	2–5 years	1 year
Intermediate fluency Verbally negotiating their environment and accomplishing daily needs	5 years–on	1–2 years
Academic fluency Using the language of school for academic achievement	5 years–on	5–7 years

sis on basic survival needs. This can be a confusing period as the learner sorts through a great deal of "noise" to comprehend just the basics. Yet very little, if any, of that comprehension can be expressed. Part of this process is reflected in the thoughts of a young immigrant, Farah, while on the class field trip in *One Green Apple* (Bunting, 2006, TL3–5, A, F).

> Our teacher gathers us around her. She talks to the class. Then she looks at me in a kind way. "One," she says. She touches an apple, then picks it. "One," she says again. I am to take only one, as the other students have done. I nod. I want to say, "I understand. It's not that I am stupid. It is just that I am lost in this new place." But I don't know how to tell her. (p. 12)

The speech-emergence phase is a time of phrase and short-sentence generation. When learning a first language, this stage extends for several years from approximately 2 to 5 years of age. This is a time of great experimentation—trial and error—as children construct their knowledge base through hypotheses about the correct vocabulary and structure of language. For English learners, the speech-emergence stage may take up to 1 year and most of the emphasis is on basic social language.

By age 5, individuals learning their first language reach the stage of intermediate fluency. At this point, they are able to verbally negotiate their environment. English learners take 1 to 2 more years to reach intermediate fluency once the earlier stages have been mastered. Academic fluency is the last stage of language acquisition and is the phase most closely associated with formal schooling.

The general language acquisition stages noted earlier map to the process of developing language within the school setting as noted in Table 1.3. English learners' language develops through five stages. These stages and the associated learner characteristics are described in the Teachers of English to Speakers of Other Languages (TESOL) PreK–12 English Language Proficiency Standards. Table 1.4 provides an overview of the characteristics.

According to TESOL PreK–12 English Language Proficiency Standards (2006), Level 1 English learners initially have limited or no understanding of English as is the case with Mari in *Marianthe's Story: Painted Words and Spoken Memories* (Aliki, 1998, TL3–5, A, F) when she "reads" the nonverbal cues of her teacher and classmates in order to participate in class. Level 1 students rarely use English for communication; instead, they respond nonverbally to simple commands, statements, and questions. As English learners become more comfortable with their new language, they venture out of their silent period and try to speak. As their oral comprehension increases, English learners at this stage imitate others, repeating after the teacher, peers, or other speakers. They also use gestures and facial expressions to indicate the meaning of what they are saying. In terms of constructing meaning from print sources, Level 1 learners need strong visual and graphic support. Daily read-alouds using simple picture books that provide explicit cues to meaning with one-to-one correspondence of print to illustration give learners at this level a jump-start on English language development. Teachers can choose alpha-

TABLE 1.3. Language Acquisition Stages Mapped to TESOL Language Proficiency Levels

Language acquisition stages	TESOL language proficiency levels
Preproduction	Level 1, Starting
Early production	Level 2, Emerging
Speech emergence	Level 3, Developing
Intermediate fluency	Level 4, Expanding
Academic fluency	Level 5, Bridging

Note. Data from TESOL (2006).

**TABLE 1.4. TESOL Language Proficiency Levels
and Learner Characteristics**

Proficiency levels	Learner characteristics
Level 1, Starting	*Initially*: • Limited or no understanding of English • Seldom uses English to communicate • Responds nonverbally to simple commands, statements, and questions • Visual literacy ("reading") through pictures and environmental print *Later*: • Begins to repeat and imitate others by using single words, simple phrases • Begins to use English spontaneously • Reads familiar words, phrases, and very simple sentences with support • Writing consists of copied letters, words, phrases
Level 2, Emerging	• Understands phrases and short sentences • Shares limited information in simple everyday and routine situations • Uses memorized phrases, groups of words, and formulaic language • Uses simple structures correctly but still produces basic errors • Uses general academic vocabulary and familiar everyday expressions • Reads familiar phrases and sentences and simple academic vocabulary with support • Makes writing errors that often interfere with communication
Level 3, Developing	• Understands more complex speech but still may require repetition • Uses English spontaneously but has difficulty expressing all of his or her thoughts due to a limited vocabulary and lack of command of language structure • Speaks in simple, comprehensible, and appropriate sentences, still frequently marked by grammatical errors • Proficiency in reading varies considerably • Comprehends texts for which he or she has background knowledge
Level 4, Expanding	• Language skills are adequate for most daily communication needs • Communicates in English in unfamiliar settings with occasional difficulty with complex structures and abstract academic concepts • May read with considerable fluency • Able to locate and identify specific facts within the text

(cont.)

TABLE 1.4. *(cont.)*

Proficiency levels	Learner characteristics
Level 4, Expanding *(cont.)*	• Has problems with texts with concepts presented in a decontextualized manner • Has problems with complex sentence structure, abstract vocabulary, or vocabulary with multiple meanings • Reads independently with occasional comprehension problems, especially with grade-level information
Level 5, Bridging	• Able to use fluent and spontaneous communication on a range of personal, general, academic, or social topics in a variety of contexts • Interacts with native-speaking peers with minimal language support or guidance • Has good command of technical and academic vocabulary as well as idiomatic expressions and colloquialisms • Produces clear, smoothly flowing, well-structured texts of differing lengths and degrees of linguistic complexity • Errors are minimal, difficult to spot, and generally corrected when they occur

Note. Data from TESOL (2006).

bet, counting, and concept books with their simple language and focus on vocabulary and key concepts to provide direct linguistic support.

There are numerous alphabet, counting, and concept books that teachers can choose. The most basic counting books, for instance, present the numbers 1 to 10 with phrases or simple sentences as in the bilingual counting book, *Counting Ovejas* (Weeks, 2006, TL1, P, F), appropriate for Level 1 English learners. When the young boy in this book is unable to sleep, he counts sheep. With each two-page spread, sheep of varying colors appear and then on the opposite page are bid farewell ("Una oveja blanca./ One white sheep./ Adios, oveja blanca!/ Good-bye, white sheep!"). *Island Counting 1 2 3* (Lessac, 2005, TL1–2, A, F) is another good choice with simple sentences: "Seven beach umbrellas soaking up the sun." *Zoo Flakes* (Howell, 2002, TL1–3, A, NF) is a basic alphabet book with different animals for each letter; for example, "C is for camel." *What Color Is Nature?* (Swinburne, 2002, TL1–2, P, NF) helps English learners master the colors in English with a straightforward question–answer format, or for a bilingual option, teachers can use *Spicy Hot Colors/ Colores Picantes* (Shahan, 2004, TL1–5, A, NF). There are many concept books to help develop vocabulary in the early stages of language development. One choice that is both a concept and an alphabet book is *Add It, Dip It, Fix It: A Book of Verbs* (Schneider, 1995, TL1–2, P, NF). English learners encounter 24 verbs in alphabetical order in simple two-word entries.

In terms of picture books to engage Level 1 English learners, one interesting possibility is *Niwechihaw, I Help* (Nicholson, 2008, TL1–2, P, F), a bilingual book in Cree and English. Each two-page spread shows the grandson following his grandmother and doing what she does: "Kohkom gets ready./ I get ready." In *The Zoo* (Lee, 2007, TL1–2, P, F), a young girl goes to the zoo with her parents but then wanders off, falls asleep, and dreams about the animals while her parents frantically search for her. The dream sequences are in color and wordless and can spark discussion in the classroom. Another book that takes advantage of wordless picture sequences is *How to Heal a Broken Wing* (Graham, 2008, TL1–3, P, F). In the city, young Will sees a pigeon collide with a tall building and fall to the pavement. He and his family take the bird home and nurse it to health. The simple sentences are often broken into phrases and clauses on separate pages. Interspersed throughout are multiple boxed pictures with a sequence of events and wordless pages that could lead to discussion for oral language development. These elements make this book accessible to Level 1 English learners.

At Level 2, English learners understand phrases and short sentences, and they communicate limited information in simple everyday and routine situations by using memorized phrases, groups of words, and formula such as paired statements for greetings: "Hi! How are you?/ I am fine." They use selected simple structures correctly and can engage in basic retelling of information (what, where, when), but they still systematically produce basic errors. At this proficiency level, English learners begin to use general academic vocabulary and familiar everyday expressions. Errors in writing are present that often hinder communication. Books with high-frequency vocabulary and predictable text are understandable to English learners at this stage of language development. Alpahabet, counting, and concept books can continue to be used at this proficiency level because they range in language and information from very basic to more complex. For instance, *Capital! Washington D.C. from A to Z* (Melmed, 2003, TL2–5, A, NF), has one to two sentences as the main text for each entry and then other sentences surrounding multiple illustrations. This type of alphabet book has possibilities for Level 2 and 3 English learners. The simple presentation in Cathryn Sill's series of books including *About Amphibians* (2000, TL2–4, A, NF) or *About Fish* (2002, TL2–4, A, NF) are ideal for introducing content concepts to Level 2 English learners. Another chance to emphasize content concepts and vocabulary is offered by Ann Morris's simple nonfiction concept books about the more familiar topics of food (*Bread, Bread, Bread*, 1993, TL1–4, A, NF), clothing (*Shoes, Shoes, Shoes*, 1998, TL1–4, A, NF or *Hats, Hats, Hats*, 1993, TL1–4, A, NF), or lifestyles (*Weddings*, 1995, TL1–4, A, NF) with photographs and examples from around the world. For opportunities to read along and have English learners join in on familiar words or recurring phrases, teachers can use the humorous predictable book, *Look Out, Suzy Goose!* (Horácek, 2008, TL2–3, P, F), that features onomatopoeia and strong verbs. Suzy goes into the woods for some peace and quiet. She is not alone, however, "Tiptoe, Tiptoe, padded the hungry fox. 'I spy goose for dinner.' He followed Suzy into the woods."

Level 3 English learners understand more complex speech but still may require some repetition. They use English spontaneously but may have difficulty expressing all their thoughts due to a limited vocabulary and command of language structure. They speak in simple sentences that are comprehensible, appropriate, and more regular grammatically but are still frequently marked by errors and some interference from their first language. Moving beyond basic retelling of information, English learners can now explain how and why. English learners also experiment more with writing at this level; they can convey more information and organize their thoughts into some logical sequence. However, their concern is more with communication, so instances of translation or first-language interference are still common. Proficiency in reading may vary considerably. Students are most successful constructing meaning from texts for which they have background knowledge. The survey books of Jim Arnosky and Gail Gibbons are excellent choices for English learners at this proficiency level as are some informational storybooks with a blended format (discussed in more detail in Chapter 6) such as the Magic School Bus series or *Oscar and the Bat: A Book about Sound* (Waring, 2008, TL2–3, A, F). As a means of helping English learners discuss their personal adjustments, *I Hate English* (Levine, 1995, TL3–5, A, F) is a picture book that depicts the struggle of a young girl from Hong Kong who is new to the United States and reluctant to learn a new language. As she begins to acquire more and more English, she worries that she will lose touch with her native heritage, culture, and language. Many English learners may identify with her situation.

At Level 4, English learners' language skills are adequate for most day-to-day communication needs. They communicate in English in new or unfamiliar settings but have occasional difficulty with complex structures and abstract academic concepts. English learners at this level can read independently and may do so with considerable fluency. They are able to locate and identify specific facts within the text. However, they may have occasional comprehension problems, especially when reading grade-level information and expository text. In particular, they may not understand texts where concepts are presented in a decontextualized manner, the sentence structure is complex, or the vocabulary is abstract or has multiple meanings. A wonderful example of multiple meanings and word play that some authors use is seen in *Art's Supplies* (Tougas, 2008, TL3–5, A, F): "Then the pastels arrived. They blended in smoothly./ Ink arrived with a splash and left a lasting impression./ The scissors were cutting jokes all night long. They really had the tape rolling." In Mini Grey's *Traction Man Meets Turbo Dog* (2008, TL4–5, I, F), humor, fantasy, and British vocabulary (trash bin) combine to potentially confuse English learners when Traction Man loses his pet, Scrubbing Brush, and then discovers him in the trash bin: "Traction Man squirts the Bin-Things with Germo and they hiss and wither./ Run and don't look round! Whatever you do, don't listen to the tormenting cries of the Bin-Things!" Humor and word play, as in these examples, are still difficult to comprehend for English learners at this level. On the other hand, more literal literature that addresses academic concepts with simple technical language can help pave the way to both English language development and content knowledge. The photo essays of George Ancona and Diane Hoyt-Goldsmith are an excellent mechanism for linking to the content curriculum or textbook and providing a personal view of many topics within the social studies. Also, using text sets with books that have content and language at different reading levels and content depth are a means of supporting English learners. The process of creating text sets is discussed in more detail in Chapter 3 and again, in Chapter 6 with nonfiction books.

Finally, at Level 5, English learners can express themselves fluently and spontaneously on a wide range of personal, general, academic, or social topics in a variety of contexts. They are poised to function in an environment with native-speaking peers with minimal language support or guidance. These students have a good command of technical and academic vocabulary as well as idiomatic expressions and colloquialisms. They can produce clear, smoothly flowing, well-structured texts of differing lengths and degrees of linguistic complexity. Errors are minimal, difficult to spot, and generally corrected when they occur. At this stage, English learners are closing in on native English-speakers in the grade level classroom. This level of proficiency or academic language proficiency is the ability we most closely associate with achievement in school. Guidance may be needed with figurative language, symbolism, and archaic vocabulary. For English learners in our schools, acquiring this level of academic fluency may take 5 to 7 years or longer (Thomas & Collier, 1995). This may not appear to be such a hardship to English learners entering American schools in prekindergarten or kindergarten. However, native English speakers already have a firm grasp of language when they enter school whereas children learning English as a second language must also juggle the content of their classes "so that by the time they can function in English they are not hopelessly behind in their other subjects" (Suárez-Orozco & Suárez-Orozco, 2001, p. 142).

Given the linear presentation of the stages of language acquisition and emerging language proficiency, teachers may assume that language acquisition is an orderly and predictable process. Nothing could be farther from the truth. While teachers can expect a progression in terms of the language characteristics displayed along the way from a silent period to one- or two-word utterances and then short sentences, the timing and depth of language development depends on many variables. As mentioned earlier, one factor in language acquisition is the quality of instruction. Yet, many English learners attend schools hypersegregated by poverty and race (Suárez-Orozco & Suárez-Orozco, 2001). Moreover, they are more likely to be taught by teachers with limited training in second-language acquisition. Such training could help teachers understand the diverse needs of English learners and select and implement effective curriculum and instructional strategies.

The Many Factors in Choosing Curriculum and Instruction for English Learners

Current debate about the best curriculum and instructional techniques for literacy instruction has centered on the issue of scripted instruction or "commercial reading programs that have highly structured lessons, often specific time allotments for teaching specific skills, and often word-for-word scripts of what the teacher is to say" (Cassidy & Cassidy, 2004–2005, p. 1). Such programs are frequently touted as necessary to providing teachers the essential elements of effective reading instruction and critical to filling in gaps and building a firm foundation for literacy skills among struggling learners, particularly minorities and English learners. Yet, critics are concerned that such programs limit teachers' ability to address the complex nature of literacy and provide for the diverse needs of many classrooms since teachers must execute the plan of the commercial program without making adjustments (Cassidy & Cassidy, 2004–2005). Indeed, in research conducted with English-only children in urban school settings, Moustafa and Land (2002) found scripted reading instruction to be less effective than reading instruction where teachers are allowed to exercise their professional judgment and match instruction to instructional needs.

The debate over the best curriculum and instructional techniques to support English learners in acquiring academic language on the level of their native English-speaking peers has been hampered by issues such as limited experimental evidence and some common misconceptions about effective instruction for English learners (Harper & de Jong, 2004). Understanding these misconceptions and their implications can help all educators create a strong program to support the language development and school achievement of English learners.

Topping the list of misconceptions about English learners is that their needs "do not differ significantly from those of other diverse learners" (Harper & de Jong, 2004, p. 152). Stemming from this is the belief that "exposure and interaction will result in English-language learning" (p. 153). Indeed, some children's picture books intended to create an awareness of the difficulties in language adjustment, may actually contribute to misconceptions. For instance, Unhei in *The Name Jar* (Choi, 2001, TL4–5, A, F) leaves Korea and enters an American school 1 week later. Throughout the story, little mention is made of any struggle related to understanding English although Unhei's mother asks at the beginning of the book, "Did you understand the teacher?" When Unhei nods, her mother responds, "I'm glad you are learning English well...." Unhei is able to understand and interact with her peers, and the only source of concern, as the title seems to indicate, is her name. She debates whether she should adopt an American name that is easier to pronounce and may lead to less teasing at school. In another picture book, *Hannah Is My Name* (Yang, 2004, TL4–5, A, F), readers meet a young Chinese girl who enters first grade and the only English she knows is "Hannah is my name." She makes rapid progress, however, and after a brief period of time—what appears to be a semester or less—Hannah is able to read one of the *Curious George* books independently when she and her father visit the books and periodicals section of the Woolworth's store. Finally, in *The Upside Down Boy* (Herrera, 2000, TL3–5, A, F), Juanito moves in record time from non-English speaking, struggling to understand words such as *recess* and *beautiful*, to writing a poem in English complete with metaphorical images as a result of his teacher reading a new poem aloud to the class each day for only a week.

Krashen (1987) and others have advocated the importance of comprehensible input for language learning, yet, we know that the progression of grade-level classrooms, textbooks, and standardized assessments require students to negotiate increasingly complex and abstract concepts (Lightbown & Spada, 1990; Spada & Lightbown, 1993). Therefore, teachers must provide targeted instruction, modeling the academic language needed to perform the required tasks. Fillmore (2002, n.p.) explains that academic English tends to

- Be more precise and specific in reference (personal, object, concepts, time, place, relational, etc.) than everyday English.
- Make greater use of vocabulary that is Latin or Greek in origin.
- Be more complex syntactically.
- Be more dependent on "text" than on "context" for interpretation.
- Be more cognitively demanding than everyday English.
- Use distinctive grammatical constructions and devices, vocabulary, rhetorical conventions, and discourse.
- Be learned in school—but not without instructional attention.

Related to the misconception that exposure alone will provide for language acquisition is the idea that the interaction between English learners and their peers in group work provides adequate input and practice for English language development. On the one hand, research indicates that small-group learning activities in cooperative learning can be an effective vehicle for learning content and learning in a second language (Klingner & Vaughn, 1996). For instance, Muñiz-Swicegood (1994) found that by working in small cooperative groups learning how to generate and answer questions about what they were reading, students scored better on reading comprehension measures than students using basal reading approaches. Calderon suggests that "cooperative learning is effective when students have an interesting well-structured task such as a set of discussion questions around a story they just read, producing a cognitive map of the story, or inventing a puppet show to highlight character traits" (2001, p. 280). Conversely, others stress that even with a highly structured cooperative learning activity, English learners may not possess the proficiency needed to participate effectively in the task by using language skills such as questioning, agreeing, disagreeing, interrupting, presenting an opinion, or asking for clarification or assistance (Pica, 1994; Swain, 1985, 1995). Therefore, teachers must consider both the task structure *and* the linguistic demands of classroom activities including the language of classroom discourse and small-group participation.

Closely linked to the misconception of homogeneity across groups—
that the needs of English learners are not that dissimilar from other
learners and that the process of language learning, be it a first or another
language, is not that different—is the idea of within-group similarity.
In other words, all English learners develop their new language "in the
same way and at the same rate" (Harper & de Jong, 2004, p. 154). Nothing could be farther from the truth; the diversity among English learners
in the classroom is quite challenging. And, while there are identifiable
stages of language development as highlighted in the preceding section,
there are a variety of family, cultural, and language factors that can assist
or cause difficulties for language acquisition. For instance, more rapid
progress in language learning can occur depending on the literacy foundation brought to school. As noted earlier, language acquisition research
indicates that an individual's knowledge and ability in the first language
is the best predictor of success for second-language acquisition (Snow,
1993), and as children's first teachers, parents help to lay that foundation.
In several children's picture books, readers are afforded glimpses of family literacy in the home language or in English. For instance, in *Good-
bye, 382 Shin Dang Dong* (Park & Park, 2002, TL4–5, A, F), Jangmi
writes letters in Korean to her friend, Kisuni, back home, and Jangmi's
father is obviously proficient in English as he reads an American news-
paper and teaches Jangmi the meaning of her name in English, "Rose."
Similarly, Yoon's father (*My Name Is Yoon*, Recorvits, 2002, TL3–5, P,
F) teaches her to print every letter in the English alphabet before she
attends her first day of school. Lastly, in *My Diary from Here to There*
(Perez, 2002, TL4–5, A, F), Amada doesn't yet know English, but her
literacy in Spanish is evident as she lovingly fills her journal with writing.
These examples represent linguistic competence that can assist in learning a new language. A different type of family issue that can influence
language acquisition is depicted in *The Color of Home* (Hoffman, 2002,
TL4–5, A, F), as Hassan, a young Somali, has to work through difficult
emotional issues he has brought with him to America because his uncle
was killed by soldiers before his family fled Somalia.

A final point that Harper and de Jong (2004) offer is that teachers
must examine the role of language in teaching and learning. Indeed, one
of the pervasive suggestions for working with English learners has been
to combine the teaching of language and content. This issue has important implications for content teachers who do not view themselves as language teachers and who are largely unaware of the language demands
of their discipline. As a general rule, content teachers view their role as

providing the conceptual background for a specific discipline such as science or math. Further, because they have a specialization in that content area, they tend to forget the distinctive literacy demands of the curriculum in their field. Recent research has also questioned the effectiveness of combining content and language teaching noting that invariably this led to sacrifices in the area of language development (Gersten & Baker, 2002). Echevarria, Vogt, and Short (2008) attempt to address these criticisms with the SIOP (Sheltered Instruction Observation Protocol), which requires significant teaching skills in both English language development and content instruction along with clearly defined language and content objectives, modified curriculum, supplementary materials, and alternative assessments.

In order to effectively address language and content objectives, teachers must carefully consider both the language and the cognitive "load" of instruction (Meyer, 2000). In terms of language load, content teachers should take into account the vocabulary of the discipline including the specific terms, both technical and common words, as well as the language of classroom interaction and instructions. The cognitive load refers to the difficulty of the concepts presented in class and the level of the materials used to convey the material. A primary example of cognitive load is the content textbook that often drives subject area instruction in the intermediate grades and beyond. The organization of a text can be classified as considerate (reader-friendly) or inconsiderate (Armbruster & Anderson, 1985). A reader-friendly, considerate text presents information so that even a reader with limited background knowledge feels that the information will be relatively easy to learn. Unfortunately, most content textbooks are not considerate; thus, they increase the cognitive load for the learner. Children's literature, on the other hand, offers a perfect solution to the problems of inconsiderate texts with a variety of books with reader-friendly characteristics. The many genres of literature accompanied by the array of formats, subjects, and authorial styles provide a rich source of meaningful input for English learners and serve to push students beyond the normal limits of both home and school language. Such a range of topics and language afford the flexibility to meet the diverse linguistic proficiency levels and cultural backgrounds found in today's classroom.

In terms of planning content, Gersten and Baker (2002, n.p.) argue, "effective teachers intentionally vary cognitive and language demands to achieve specific goals. In short, when cognitive demands are high, language expectations are simplified." There is after all "a profound difference between having a superficial conversational ability in a language and having the deeper level of competence required to understand difficult new subjects, to express subtleties of meaning, and to write a well-argued and well-phrased term paper" (Suárez-Orozco & Suárez-Orozco, 2001, p. 138). As an example, Figure 1.1 presents a view of curriculum and instruction in relationship to language demands. The left two quadrants (Quadrants I and II) focus on informal or social and less academic language that makes fewer demands on English learners. Quadrant I involves language that is both easy to understand as well as highly contextualized through teacher and peer as well as text support while Quadrant II addresses social language with less of the face-to-face context or

	Nonacademic or Lower-Cognitive-Load Activities	Academic or Higher-Cognitive-Load Activities	
CONTEXTUALIZED LANGUAGE	**Quadrant I** • Developing survival vocabulary/ social language • Following demonstrated directions and classroom routines • Playing simple games with visual cues • Engaging in face-to-face interactions • Answering lower-level questions	**Quadrant III** • Developing academic vocabulary • Understanding academic presentations accompanied by visuals, demonstrations, etc. • Participating in hands-on content activities and academic discussions • Making brief oral presentations, e.g., debriefing from group work • Understanding written texts through discussion, illustrations, and visuals • Writing simple science and social studies reports with format provided	**LOWER-LANGUAGE LOAD**
CONTEXT-FREE LANGUAGE	**Quadrant II** • Following simple verbal instructions • Developing initial reading skills: decoding and literal comprehension • Reading and writing for personal purposes • Writing answers to lower-level questions	**Quadrant IV** • Understanding academic presentations without visuals or demonstrations • Making formal oral presentations • Engaging in inferential and critical reading • Writing compositions and reports in content subjects • Solving math word problems without illustrations • Taking standardized tests	**HIGHER-LANGUAGE LOAD**

FIGURE 1.1. Curriculum and instruction planning framework. Based on Chamot and O'Malley (1987).

text support that can enhance understanding. To the right, Quadrants III and IV focus on academic language that is more challenging to English learners but essential to their success in school. However, the tasks in Quadrant III involve language that is more contextualized. In other words, academic content is introduced through hands-on or highly visual instruction and materials with text support that provides the scaffolding to master the concepts. Quadrant IV focuses on the most challenging language for *all* learners. The presentation of academic content without visuals or demonstrations to assist understanding is very demanding. When working at the Quadrant IV level, teachers need to build the appropriate background knowledge for students prior to the lesson and text assignment. In Chapter 2, this same framework is presented again with children's literature recommendations for each quadrant.

Conclusion

In summary, educators need to "guard against a 'one-size-fits-all' mindset, looking for the one best program for all [English learners]. Instead, the focus must be on implementation of optimal programs in local schools for local communities" (Christian, 2004, p. 5). Teachers must focus on the students' needs to determine the best fit for the materials used. Literature offers the flexibility and strong support to fit the range of English learners' language development.

"The real challenge for schools today is not the growing number of [English learners], but the school's continuing need to do a far better job of delivering instruction to them in English" (Christian, 2004, p. 5). A committed teacher with a beginning understanding of English learners' family background, issues in cultural adjustment, and some basic principles of language acquisition is a foundation that can make all the difference to a child's success in school. The next chapter examines criteria for choosing wisely from the tremendous variety of available children's literature and selecting materials that match the proficiency levels of English learners.

Writing the
Muslim American Experience

ASMA MOBIN-UDDIN

As a pediatrician, I have always encouraged new parents in my practice to introduce books to their infants very early in life. When I had my first child, I was excited to do the same. I bought wonderful books for my daughter— fuzzy chicken books, alphabet board books, mommy-loves-you-so-much-she-can't-stand-it books, and together, we shared them all. But there was one type of book I searched and searched for but could not find: books that accurately reflected our cultural and religious experience being a Muslim American family.

My children and I were all born in and grew up in America as Muslims. We are not alone in combining this national and religious identity. "There are more American Muslims than there are American Episcopalians, Jews, or Presbyterians," Harvard professor Diana Eck noted on the website about her book, *A New Religious America.* Yet, I found very few children's books in America's libraries or bookstores that authentically represented the experience of this community.

So I had two main reasons for starting to write books for children. I wanted to introduce accurate books about the Muslim American experience to the general community, and I wanted to write books that Muslim American kids would see themselves in.

My first book, *My Name Is Bilal*, is about a Muslim American boy, Bilal, who is afraid to let his classmates know that he is Muslim. Trying to hide his religious identity, he tells his class that his name is Bill. His sister, who wears the traditional Islamic headscarf, is being harassed, and Bilal is feeling guilty about not standing up for her. As he learns more about his religious heritage and the beloved figure in Islamic history for whom he is named, Bilal grows more comfortable with his religious identity and finds the courage to be himself.

Part of Bilal's struggles for self-acceptance reflects the struggle for identity that I went through growing up as a Muslim child in a small Ohio town that had few Muslim families. The specifics of the story in *My Name Is Bilal* reflect struggles in the Muslim American experience. I hope that by encouraging kids and adults to discuss issues relating to religious and ethnic diversity, the book will lead to greater tolerance, understanding, and respect in our communities. However, my overall purpose in writing this book was not limited to raising awareness about this community. I wanted the book to inspire children in general to be true to themselves and to learn to accept and cherish their own identity, instead of being afraid of what others might think about them. *My Name Is Bilal* won the Paterson Prize for Books for Young People, grades 4–6.

My second book, *The Best Eid Ever*, is about a Muslim American girl on Eid al-Adha, the biggest holiday of the Muslim year. Aneesa's parents are away at the Hajj pilgrimage and her grandmother from Pakistan has come to spend Eid with her. Initially, she misses her parents and feels sad that she has to spend the holiday without them. After meeting a refugee family at the morning prayer service, Aneesa and her grandmother carry out a plan to make sure the family's holiday is special. The themes in this book are ones that resonate with most children, regardless of cultural background. These themes include facing a holiday without a loved one, the special relationship between a child and her grandparent, and the realization that what makes a holiday special is not how much you get but how much you give. *The Best Eid Ever* was recognized with a 2008 Skipping Stones Honor Award, a 2009 Storytelling World Resource Award, and the 2008 Middle East Outreach Council Book Award Honorable Mention.

In *A Party in Ramadan*, young Leena is excited about fasting during the upcoming month of Ramadan with her family. Then she faces a challenge when she is invited to a classmate's party during the time she is not supposed to eat or drink anything during the day. How Leena negotiates being true to her faith and having fun with her friends is the basis of this story. This book was selected for a 2009 Parents' Choice Award (Approved category).

Children's books have always been an important way that kids have learned about others. Books and education about other cultures can help children from diverse backgrounds connect with each other on a human level, bypassing the walls of mistrust, anger, and ignorance that adults sometimes build. Educating children about other cultures early in life lays the groundwork for a lifetime of acceptance, respect, and understanding.

During my entire childhood growing up in Ohio, I never once read a book that had a Muslim girl character in it. To be able to share these types of stories with my own three children today is especially important to me. I really enjoy seeing my children's delight when they identify with the characters and recognize themselves, their traditions, and their heritage in the books we read.

CHAPTER TWO

Matching Books to English Learners

Slowly like clouds lifting, things became
clearer.
Sticks and chicken feet became letters.
Sputters and coughs became words.
And the words had meanings.
Every day Mari understood more and more.
Misapeechi became Mr. Petrie.
Waisha became Rachel, Kista became Kristin,
Ahbe became Albert, and Patik became
Patrick.
  —ALIKI, *Marianthe's Story: Painted Words*
   and Spoken Memories
   (Greenwillow, 1998)

English learners do not have the luxury of an extended time frame to acclimate to their new language. They experience heavy cognitive demands when asked to quickly learn both language and content to participate fully in the school curriculum. Placing comprehensible materials in English learners' hands helps them develop and practice as readers and writers in a new language. Research underscores the importance of time spent reading *and* time spent reading appropriate texts. "There is considerable evidence that providing access to books results in more reading and better reading and considerable evidence that providing time to read results in better reading" (Krashen, 2003, p. 26). Further, readers who practice the reading process often with textual material matched to their abilities become fluent, build their vocabulary, and increase their skills while children who read less or do not have books matched to their abilities increasingly fall behind their peers (Stanovich, 1985).

The process of matching text to reader is complex, however. Many teachers are uncertain about the factors that influence readability and consequently, may choose books that are too easy or too hard. The aim is to find books that are in a reader's "zone of proximal development" (Vygotsky, 1978) or that furnish optimal input for the English learner (Krashen, 1985). In other words, learners need texts that are fine-tuned, slightly beyond their independent reading level, but not so far beyond that they are not able to handle them without teacher support. Texts that are too easy will not contribute to English language development, and texts that are too hard will be beyond the student's grasp and lead to frustration (Scarcella, 1990). As teachers select books of increasing difficulty, but within the zone of proximal development, they must support, or scaffold, readers so they continue to grow and attain higher levels of functioning.

To assist teachers, many tools for matching texts to readers have been developed including readability formulas, decodability, vocabulary control systems, and qualitative leveling (Mesmer, 2008). Each of these methods has strengths and weaknesses, but a critical missing variable is that they do not specifically address the growing population of English learners in schools. They provide general grade levels or indications of readability, in the case of readability formulas, or they are based on beginning reading needs, not necessarily those of English learners. Teachers working with English learners must consider some unique needs and additional language factors that influence literacy and language development. The goal, however, is always selecting quality reading text. Thus, this chapter considers current tools for matching texts to readers, the gap between what exists and what is needed, and important criteria teachers must consider when selecting books for English learners.

Tools for Matching Books to Readers

Readability formulas (e.g., Fry, Flesch–Kincaid) are among the oldest text analysis tools and represent an objective measure to estimate textual difficulty in terms of reading grade level. Such formulas examine word level and/or sentence difficulty. Longer, multisyllabic words and longer, more complex sentences are indicators of more difficult text. While readability formulas are reliable and offer an easy method to calculate a quantitative measure of difficulty, they have limitations. For instance, the grade-level estimates are not exact and can vary from one-half to several grade levels depending on the formula used, they are not sensitive enough for beginning readers, and perhaps, most importantly for English learners, they do not necessarily reflect readers' interests, background knowledge, content, or motivation (Mesmer, 2008). Readability formulas are an estimate—a beginning point, and teachers need to clearly understand that reading is a transactional process between the reader and the text. Therefore, they must consider not only the text but also the students and the educational context.

Basal collections, high-interest/low-readability materials, and materials written for struggling readers and English learners have routinely been adapted using readability formulas. To modify the text, authors employ "fractured and narrow" language that many students find unnatural (Goodman, Shannon, Freeman, & Murphy, 1988). These authors often write to the formulas restricting sentence length and word difficulty. "The text is narrowed by the process of revision. The revision may involve shortening sentences, substituting more frequent for less frequent words and phrases, using shorter words, simplifying syntax, eliminating or modifying plot features. Or it may be a synthetic text, one that is produced by the authors and editors of the basals to fit their scope and sequence criteria" (Goodman et al., 1988, p. 85). In general, students find this unnatural text difficult to understand. The language is less predictable, and it is difficult for them to apply their understanding of story structure and English syntax to their reading.

Lexiles and Degrees of Reading Power (DRP) are second-generation readability formulas (Mesmer, 2008). Using technology, Lexiles and DRPs have more comprehensive word difficulty lists, and they sample substantive portions of text. Based on these tools, the resulting readability is measured not in grade levels but in unique units. The Lexile Framework breaks text into hundreds of difficulty steps from 200 to 1,700 and the DRP from 15 to 85. While these tools allow for more sensitivity than grade-level measurements, teachers may not understand the Lexile or DRP units and again, they are measures focused on the text and not the reader. For instance, it is possible to have a text with fairly simple to decode but uncommon words that would receive a high readability score (easy to read) when in fact it is not.

Because readability formulas are not sensitive or precise enough to match texts to beginning readers, supports such as decodable text, vocabulary control, and qualitative leveling have been used. Decodable readers or phonics readers assist readers with letter–sound knowledge while vocabulary-controlled materials "pace the introduction of new words within and across stories" (Mesmer, 2008, p. 89). Qualitatively leveled books are ones that gradually increase in difficulty according to a text gradient (Mesmer, 2008). The leveling is holistic, based not on quantitative features such as number of words in a sentence as in readability formulas but on qualitative information about many text features. Qualitative leveling considers language issues (sentence complexity, organization, style, and predictability), content features (familiarity, genre, and vocabulary), and text format (length, print, layout, and illustrations). Each of these support systems can assist beginning readers; however, the first two methods in particular, with their single-criterion and controlled material often result in boring or stilted stories since they are "manufactured" text.

Matching Books to English Learners

The previously mentioned tools focus on the text, but the written word is just one part of the reading equation. The reader also influences the text-matching process. Teachers must consider factors such as readers' abilities (reading level, attention, memory), their motivation (purpose for reading, interests, self-efficacy), and their knowledge (first language, prior knowledge, and print and alphabetic understanding) (Mesmer, 2008). Understanding English learners' backgrounds and abilities helps teachers to select texts, shaped, of course, by language-acquisition research. Text selection should be based on an understanding of what English learners are learning about their new language, how they learn it, and the text features that can provide support for language and literacy development. In addition, decisions need to be related to the language and literacy strategies and skills that English learners are acquiring, and those that they are moving toward learning (Hiebert, 1998).

Unfortunately, teachers worry that English learners will not be able to handle authentic materials such as trade books given that they are often encountering the reading/writing process for the first time alongside learning English. And, even when English learners enter our schools later and have mastered the reading process, teachers frequently feel more secure with "special" materials adapted for this population. Thus, publishers have responded to these concerns by creating artificial text with vocabulary and sentence structure targeted at various reading levels and with adaptations through readability formulas or decodable or vocabulary-controlled stories. However, these "simplified" materials rob English learners of an authentic language opportunity and may contribute to boredom, frustration, and the feeling that they are being labeled "remedial." Hiebert (1998) further maintains that "engaging literature—

rather than—the highly controlled contrived texts invites children to reread, a primary way to learn about the relationship between oral and written language" (p. 199). Also, Johnson (1981) argues that students who read adapted materials may have difficulties transitioning to and reading materials of normal length and structural patterns that contain linguistic cues and low-frequency words. Finally, and perhaps most importantly in this age of accountability and high-stakes testing, various research studies (Rosenshine, Meister, & Chapman, 1996; Guthrie, Schafer, VonSecker, & Alban, 2000) have established "unequivocally that using abundant diverse texts for reading instruction produces higher achievement than using fewer, more constrained materials" (Guthrie, 2003, p. 124). So, just as the classroom reflects diversity, selected reading materials should be varied, cutting across the genres as noted in Figure 2.1.

Allen (1994, p. 112) recommends that selected texts should accomplish the following with English learners:

- Encourage them to choose to read.
- Help them discover the values and functions of written language.
- Permit them to use written language for a wide range of purposes.
- Be appropriate for their age and interest level.
- Take into account their cultural and conceptual background.
- Make use of their native languages when possible.
- Support their acquisition of English.

FICTION: PICTURE BOOKS	POETRY
• ABC and Counting Books • Concept Books • Wordless Picture Books • Predictable Books • Picture Storybooks	• Anthologies and Single-Topic/ Thematic Collections • Single-Author Collections • Poem and Song Picture Books
FICTION: TRADITIONAL LITERATURE	**NONFICTION**
• Folktales (Usually in Picture Book Form)	• ABC and Counting Books • Concept Books
FICTION: TRANSITIONAL READERS, CHAPTER BOOKS, NOVELS • Contemporary Realistic Fiction • Historical Fiction	• Survey Books • Photo Essays • How-To and Activity Books • Journals and Diaries • Biography (Including Picture Book Biographies)

FIGURE 2.1. Overview of genres.

- Offer a rich array of genres.
- Have text structures that support their understanding.

These recommendations are actually more complicated than they sound. Age suitability is typically linked to grade levels. However, English learners may enter school alongside their native English-speaking peers in kindergarten, or they may come to school later after immigrating to the United States On entering school, some English learners may have a firm grasp of their home language and may have been actively involved in reading and writing behaviors that precede and help to develop literacy. Other English learners may not come to school with well-developed oral language or early reading and writing experiences (e.g., visual literacy and scribbling), even in their home language. As a result, picture books, traditionally considered to be for younger children, may be the most fitting literature choice even with older English learners. Highly visual books help provide scaffolding as students begin by "reading the pictures." This can build confidence and independence, too. Fortunately, the sophisticated illustrations as well as the mature content and themes of some recently published picture books make them more suitable for older audiences. Despite the fact that many picture books are adaptable across grade levels, some themes may not be appropriate for younger readers. Conversely, older readers may believe they have outgrown picture books, but numerous illustrated trade books address relevant and mature content issues with multiple layers of meaning to explore. *Brothers in Hope: The Story of the Lost Boys of Sudan* (Williams, 2005, TL4–5, I, F) and *The Enemy: A Book about Peace* (Cali, 2009, TL3–4,I,F) are two picture books that deal with the difficulties and senselessness of war, and both are more appropriate for the intermediate grades and beyond.

While textbooks are "one size fits all," literature comes in different shapes and sizes—from picture books with just one word on each page to transitional readers, chapter books, and novels. Literature can fit all learners and provides flexibility for instructional purposes. In the next section, specific criteria for matching literature to English learners are presented.

Considering Criteria for Selecting Literature for English Learners in Grades K–6

To determine the criteria for text selection for English learners, research findings related to language acquisition and beginning reading were considered and several important points emerged. First and foremost, teachers need to choose instructional texts with features that promote language acquisition and literacy development for English learners. For instance, several features of whole texts support beginning English learners including the total amount of text, its predictability, imagability and familiarity of concepts, and word density (the ratio of different or unique words to total words) (Hiebert, 1998). Thus, Level 1 English learners need shorter texts with high-frequency words, phonetically regular words, and a repetition of word patterns. Over time as English learners move to a Level 2 or 3 language proficiency level, denser text with more unique words can be used. Teachers must also consider features of text that can distract English learners from attending to and applying key skills and strategies. The most common distractions or obstacles are text that is too dense or long and text that has unfamiliar concepts (Hiebert, 1998). Alternatively, illustrations and predictable syntax (repeated phrases and episodes) are supportive text features. Still, these supports should be varied because readers may over rely on illustrations and fail to develop word-recognition skills (Hiebert, 1998). Finally, English learners need numerous experiences with texts as this helps them to focus on critical features and to remember them (Juel, 1991), and they need exposure to a variety of texts so they learn to "associate oral and written language, to understand the functions and forms of written language, and to distinguish the language of books from typical speech" (Hiebert, 1998, p. 213).

Taking these findings from the research on language acquisition and literacy development, Table 2.1 highlights four criteria to guide book selections for English learners: (1) level of content familiarity or background knowledge, (2) level of language, (3) level of textual support, and (4) level of cultural fit, and poses guiding questions for each area that teachers can use to more effectively select books. These criteria and the accompanying guiding questions are developed more fully in the remainder of this chapter, and then they are applied to fiction, poetry, and nonfiction in the chapters that follow with examples of suggested books for K–6 English learners. Teachers should keep in mind that there is no rigid or "correct" sequence to the texts selected or the features in those texts, just as there is no fixed sequence of skills and elements that English learners must master as they learn their new language and develop literacy. English learners need to be involved in many texts to move to an advanced level of proficiency in English.

TABLE 2.1. Criteria and Guiding Questions for Selecting Literature for English Learners in Grades K–6

Criteria	Guiding questions
Level of content familiarity or background knowledge How close a fit is the text to the English learner's content knowledge or background experiences?	• What content and concepts are presented in the text? What is the content/conceptual load of the text? Basic and familiar? New but general? New and specialized? • Is this presentation an introduction to the content and concepts or is it continued conceptual development at a higher level? • What is the English learner's level of content familiarity or background knowledge related to the content and concepts? Is the concept very familiar, familiar, unfamiliar, or not common? • What content background knowledge does the learner have on the topic/focus of the text? • Has the topic/focus of the text been previously covered in the curriculum? When? At what level? What was the level of success of English learners? • Is the topic/focus of the text likely to be part of the readers' background experience? How so? How can the teacher best link English learners' previous experiences/understandings to the text?
Level of language How close a fit is the text to the English learner's vocabulary and syntactic knowledge and overall proficiency level?	• What is the vocabulary load of the text (e.g., basic and familiar, sophisticated/advanced and unfamiliar, concrete or abstract, general or technical/specialized, idiomatic, formal or informal, vocabulary with multiple meanings, figurative language)? • How many new vocabulary words are presented? • Does the text present new vocabulary in meaningful contextual language? • How likely is the English learner to encounter the vocabulary in this text in other reading? • What is the English learner's previous experience with the vocabulary of the text (completely new, some exposure, should be part of active vocabulary)? Is the vocabulary currently or likely to be part of the English learner's speaking vocabulary? Listening vocabulary? Reading vocabulary? Writing vocabulary? • If the text is predictable, what is the size of the predictable unit and what percent of the text does the predictable unit account for? • What is the syntactic structure of the text? Word level? Phrase level? Single simple sentences per page? Multiple simple sentences? Short paragraphs with simple sentences? Compound sentences? Complex sentences? Compound/complex sentences? Embedded clauses? • How familiar is the English learner with those syntax patterns? Does the English learner use that syntax pattern in speaking? Writing?

(cont.)

TABLE 2.1. *(cont.)*

Criteria	Guiding questions
Level of language (cont.)	• What types of text structure does the text use? Chronological? Sequential? Description? Listing? Cause–effect? Problem–solution? • How familiar is the English learner with this text structure pattern? Has the English learner encountered this pattern previously? • What is the genre of the text? • How familiar is the English learner with this genre?
Level of textual support What types of support does the text provide and how familiar is the English learner with these types of text support?	• Are there visuals (photographs or illustrations)? • Are the visuals clear and direct? One-to-one correspondence of visuals to text? General connection to text? Primarily for aesthetic purposes? • Are there graphic aids in the text (charts, maps, tables, graphs)? • How much does the English learner know about these types of graphic aids? Has the English learner successfully used these types of aids in previous reading? Is the general format of the aid new or familiar (e.g., different types of graphs, picture, bar, line, circle)? • What types of text features are used? Print style such as bold or italics? Headings and subheadings? Captions and labeling of visuals/graphics? Table of contents, index, glossary? • How familiar is the English learner with these types of text features?
Level of Cultural Fit How close a fit is the text to the English learner's cultural or experiential background (ethnic, language, geographic, religious, socioeconomic, gender)?	• Is the text culturally neutral (with general diversity portrayed but no focus on a specific group)? Culturally generic (with a group featured but less specific detail provided)? Culturally specific (with explicit details about a group portrayed)? • Does the text reflect the background and/or experiences of recent immigrants? U.S.-born English learners? • Are the characters similar or different than English learners in the classroom? • Have English learners had an experience like one described in the story? • Have English learners lived in or visited places like those in the story? • How far removed is the story from current times? • How close is the main character's age to English learners'? • Is the main character the same gender as the reader? • Do the characters talk like the English learners and their families? • Is this author/author style familiar to English learners?

Level of Content Familiarity or Background Knowledge

Level of content familiarity or background knowledge relates to the cognitive or conceptual load for the student as opposed to the text's language load, vocabulary, and syntax. All readers bring their background knowledge and previous exposure and understanding, or lack of knowledge, about concepts to a text. In comparing the different genres of literature addressed in this book, generally, nonfiction books have the highest cognitive, or conceptual, load for all learners as discussed in Chapter 6 on selecting and using nonfiction books. The content density of much informational writing makes this genre more challenging to English learners who will be learning new content and concepts via a new language. Of course, more universal or very familiar topics in any genre will be more accessible to the reader, and both poetry and fiction tackle content and concepts that may prove challenging, as in single-topic collections of poetry on math and science topics or picture books that explore different historical eras or cultures unfamiliar to the reader. As teachers examine text with this criteria in mind, they are considering the fit of the conceptual level of the text with the English learner's content knowledge or background experiences. A few questions can help the teacher with text selection in the area of content familiarity and background knowledge.

- What content and concepts are presented in the text? What is the content/conceptual load of the text? Basic and familiar? New but general? New and specialized?
- Is this presentation an introduction to the content and concepts or is it continued conceptual development at a higher level?
- What is the English learner's level of content familiarity or background knowledge related to the content and concepts? Is the concept very familiar, familiar, unfamiliar, or not common?
- What content background knowledge does the learner have on the topic/focus of the text?
- Has the topic/focus of the text been previously covered in the curriculum? When? At what level? What was the level of success of English learners?
- Is the topic/focus of the text likely to be part of the readers' background experience? How so? How can the teacher best link English learners' previous experiences/understandings to the text?

When students already know about a concept in their own language, transitioning to a book in English about the same concept is not so overwhelming as they can build on their current knowledge base. For Level 1 English learners, texts need to be related to basic or "survival" topics and concepts that are needed quickly by these students who are new to English and perhaps new to the United States. Books focused on basic concepts such as time, money (*The Coin Counting Book*, Williams, 2001, TL1–3, A, NF), school, colors (*Carlos Likes Colors*, Spanyol, 2003, TL1, P, F), clothing, days of the week, months of the year, signs and symbols, foods, weather (*Where Does the Wind Blow?* Rink, 2002, TL2–3, A, F), family, homes and houses, occupations, and animals furnish essential initial reading material. Ann Morris's concept book on transportation, *On the Go* (1994, TL1–4, A, NF), Taro Miura's books on measurement, *Ton* (2006, TL1–2, P, NF) and tools used in various jobs, *Tools* (2007, TL1–2, P, NF), Kathleen Krull's introduction to the *Supermarket* (2001, TL2–4, A, NF), and Jeff Smith's humorous book about getting dressed, *Little Mouse Gets Ready* (2009, TL1–2, P, F) offer minimal text, simple details, and clear illustrations as scaffolds so that English learners can master concepts.

As noted earlier, for all text selections, teachers need to consider features in the text that promote language acquisition along with literacy development, and for this specific criteria, conceptual development. For instance, authors use analogies or comparisons of new information to knowledge that readers may already possess. Single-topic poetry collections, or thematic poetry collections, on content subjects such as math, science, and social studies offer a focus on one topic with different poems that may allow for repetition of concepts or information. Also, many nonfiction authors use layers of information in their books, a type of spiral curriculum, that revisits the information with increasing depth. These layers of information are presented on the same page, but content presented within the main text may also be supplemented with additional content information and resources at the end of the text. Multilayer text is helpful for meeting the needs of English learners at different proficiency and conceptual levels. If multilayer books are not available on certain concepts, however, part of the process of text selection is to enable teachers to build collections of books, or text sets, that target different levels of content density, a practice discussed in Chapter 3 with narrow reading. Of course, teachers will support English learners and the content by selecting books related to classroom activities already going on—a lesson, a special event, or a shared experience. This provides for needed repetition and reinforcement of concepts encountered in the text.

Level of Language

The language load is related to word- and text-level issues. At the word level, teachers must consider the word density or the ratio of different or unique words to total words (Hiebert, 1998) along with the use of high-frequency words, phonetically regular words, and word patterns. Other word-level concerns take account of concrete versus abstract vocabulary, literal versus figurative language, the level of academic language, and the use of dialect or slang. At the text level, considerations center around the amount of text, the type of text from simple phrases or sentences to more complex ones, and the use of predictable, repetitive text. To select appropriate books for English learners, the teacher must judge how close a fit the text is to students' vocabulary and syntactic knowledge and their overall language proficiency level. Some guiding questions as teachers examine books for language include the following:

- What is the vocabulary load of the text (e.g., basic and familiar, sophisticated/advanced and unfamiliar, concrete or abstract, general or technical/specialized, idiomatic, formal or informal, vocabulary with multiple meanings, figurative language)?
- How many new vocabulary words are presented?
- Does the text present new vocabulary in meaningful contextual language?
- How likely is the English learner to encounter the vocabulary in this text in other reading?
- What is the English learner's previous experience with the vocabulary of the text (completely new, some exposure, should be part of active vocabulary)? Is the vocabulary currently or likely to be part of the English learner's speaking vocabulary? Listening vocabulary? Reading vocabulary? Writing vocabulary?
- If the text is predictable, what is the size of the predictable unit and what percent of text does the predictable unit account for?
- What is the syntactic structure of the text? Word level? Phrase level? Single simple sentences per page? Multiple simple sentences? Short paragraphs with simple sentences? Compound sentences? Complex sentences? Compound/complex sentences? Embedded clauses?
- How familiar is the English learner with those syntax patterns? Does the English learner use that syntax pattern in speaking? Writing?

- What types of text structure does the text use? Chronological? Sequential? Description? Listing? Cause–effect? Problem–solution?
- How familiar is the English learner with this text structure pattern? Has the English learner encountered this pattern previously?
- What is the genre of the text?
- How familiar is the English learner with this genre?

Beyond judging if the language of the text is accessible to the English learner, teachers should also take into account the potential of the text to develop language and literacy skills such as increasing word knowledge or introducing different sentence patterns that might contribute to growth in writing and speaking ability. While basic vocabulary and syntax assist beginning English learners to comprehend text, they need encounters with varied text, so that their language ability is constantly developing.

Comparing the language load of fiction, poetry, and nonfiction, all can vary from basic to complex, and each genre has factors that contribute to difficulties or distractions to the English learner. Nonfiction text can be challenging because of the academic language and technical and specialized vocabulary. Poetry and fiction, on the other hand, may be highly descriptive with intensity of feeling and use of abstract and figurative language. The issues related to the level of language in each genre are discussed in separate upcoming chapters.

As with content complexity, good authors use techniques that support beginning English learners with the language of the text. For instance, authors use words with high imagery, ones with clear and concrete images, such as nouns and actions, as these are more easily understood even without illustrations (Paivio, 1968; van der Veur, 1975). On the other hand, most high-frequency words (e.g., *the, of, and, a, to, in, is you, that, it*) are low-imagery words and must be memorized. Along with familiar, concrete terms, authors may use simple, direct phrases or sentences. Or, when more elaboration is needed, they may use multilevel text; a simple sentence to introduce and then multiple sentences to a paragraph or more of text for additional explanation. In addition, authors can present new vocabulary in meaningful context that supports comprehension of the key terms. An author's writing style influences the language level and readability of text. Some authors choose a conversational tone or voice even for nonfiction text, and English learners may find informal and personal informational text more engaging. A characteristic of expository writing is the use of organizational patterns or text structures such as chronological, sequential, description, listing, cause–effect, comparison–contrast, and problem–solution. These text structures are signaled by key terms to point out the pattern of organization. Finally, predictability is another way that authors support readers with the language load as how texts are structured influences meaning-making (Beck, McKeown, Omanson, & Pople, 1984). Hiebert (1998) notes two aspects of predictability that are particularly important to the reader: the size of the repeated unit and the proportion of the text accounted for by the repeated unit. The more that repetition is in the text, the more beginning English learners are able to apply their knowledge and to read fluently. As English learners develop their language proficiency and literacy ability, scaffolds such as high-imagery words and predictable, repetitive text are gradually withdrawn so that learners practice their skills and knowledge in their new language.

Level of Textual Support

"Interesting texts are well organized, illustrated, and aligned with the child's conceptual knowledge base" (Guthrie, 2003, p. 124). In fact, cognitive psychologists found that how texts are structured influences meaning-making (Beck et al., 1984; Stein & Glenn, 1979). In terms of organization, a text can be classified as considerate (reader-friendly) or inconsiderate (Anderson & Armbruster, 1986). A considerate text presents information so that even a reader with limited background knowledge feels that the information will be relatively easy to learn. For instance, visual layout is one organizational issue. As English learners turn from page to page, they know what to expect in alphabet and counting books and question–answer books as these books have a consistent and predictable organizational pattern that make them user-friendly. In terms of text selection, teachers try to find considerate books, ones with strong text support, for English learners. To evaluate the level of text support, teachers can ask the following questions:

- Are there visuals (photographs or illustrations)?
- Are the visuals clear and direct? One-to-one correspondence of visuals to text? General connection to text? Primarily for aesthetic purposes?
- Are there graphic aids in the text (charts, maps, tables, graphs)?
- How much does the English learner know about these types of

graphic aids? Has the English learner successfully used these types of aids in previous reading? Is the general format of the aid new or familiar (e.g., different types of graphs, picture, bar, line, circle)?

- What types of text features are used? Print style such as bold or italics? Headings and subheadings? Captions and labeling of visuals/graphics? Table of contents, index, glossary?
- How familiar is the English learner with these types of text features?

When word knowledge is limited, readers rely on other cues to help them "figure out" the meaning of text. The illustrations in children's books today are often ideal for this purpose. As Hiebert (1998, p. 212) notes, "Clear and salient illustrations of the key concepts in a book are a primary means whereby children are 'invited' into books." The concept books of Tana Hoban, in particular, are driven by vivid photographs that depict spatial relationships in *Over, Under, Through* (2008, TL1–3, A, NF) or antonyms in *Exactly the Opposite* (1997, TL1–3, A, NF). The use of large color photographs in Seymour Simon's many nonfiction books (*Wolves*, 2009; *Whales*, 2006; *Sharks*, 2006, TL3–5, A, NF) also help students unlock the meaning of the text. Lois Ehlert cleverly uses illustrations along with increasing page size to highlight the life-cycle stages of a butterfly in *Waiting for Wings* (2001, TL1–3, A, NF). In *Biggest, Strongest, Fastest*, Steve Jenkins (1995, TL1–4, A, NF) supplies the reader with helpful graphics to compare the size of various animals to familiar objects for the reader. This visual dimension of some books makes them especially helpful as a link to the more difficult content and concepts across the curriculum. To be useful, however, illustrations must connect to concepts and words that English learners are familiar with. For example, *On the Way to the Beach* (Cole, 2003, TL2–4, A, NF) appears to be a basic text about the plants and animals at the beach. The author offers a simple sentence: "I sat at the edge of the marsh and peered through the tall cordgrass. I saw ...." Readers turn the page and unfold it to display a list of all the animals (e.g., a snowy egret, a diamondback terrapin) in the marsh. There is no other support to directly link the animals in the illustrations to their names. Further, of the nine animals listed, none are common except the mosquito.

In comparing the genre, nonfiction literature and expository textbooks may have the most forms of textual support from photographs and captioned illustrations, bold and italicized print, graphic aids (e.g., charts, graphs, maps), and text features such as the index, glossary, and table of contents. These features support the conceptual load of nonfiction text helping the reader construct meaning. There is far less text support with poetry where the emphasis is more on the language itself. Poets use vivid description to create visual images or rhythm and rhyme to create a musical quality to the text. The poem picture book may be one exception as this is an illustrated version of a single poem as the text. The single-poem focus with accompanying illustrations supports English learners' comprehension.

Level of Cultural Fit

The multicultural nature of classrooms and schools calls for books that speak to diverse cultures, language groups, and lifestyles. Books with this cultural connection help students, both those new to this country as well as those born here, see that many cultures and experiences are represented and valued here. Looking for books that are culturally relevant to the lives of students is an important variable in text selection. For the purposes of the criteria for text selection, cultural fit is used to encompass ethnicity or cultural background, language, geography, religion, socioeconomic status, and gender. As teachers are thinking through issues of cultural fit, they are trying not to limit books to only those that reflect the children in their classrooms, although teachers should be concerned about selecting books with a range of cultural representations so that all children can see themselves reflected in literature. Instead, they are making decisions about the cultural accuracy and the depth of cultural detail as well as the type of background knowledge students, in particular, English learners, may need to comprehend the text. As teachers examine books for cultural accuracy and detail, they should take into account whether a book is culturally specific with explicit details about a group, culturally generic with a group featured but less specific detail provided, or culturally neutral with general diversity portrayed but without a focus on a specific group. Culturally specific books are the ultimate goal for cultural relevance, but for Level 1 and 2 English learners, culturally specific books about unfamiliar cultures and topics may be too challenging in terms of terminology and background knowledge needed for comprehension. Also, in terms of English learners, teachers can determine whether a book reflects the experiences of recent immigrants or U.S.-born English learners. Immigration, for instance, may not be a familiar topic for U.S.-born English learners. Too, teachers should not make assumptions about students simply because they are part of a cultural group. All Latino children are not familiar with quinceañeras or posadas celebrations nor are all Asian children acquainted with the lunar New Year festivities.

As teachers consider the issue of cultural fit, they can use these guiding questions, some suggested by Freeman and Freeman (2004). All of these criteria, characters, and settings for instance, may not apply if the text is nonfiction.

- Is the text culturally neutral (with general diversity portrayed but no focus on a specific group)? Culturally generic (with a group featured but less specific detail provided)? Culturally specific (with explicit details about a group portrayed)?
- Does the text reflect the background and/or experiences of recent immigrants? U.S.-born English learners?
- Are the characters similar or different than English learners in the classroom?
- Have English learners had an experience like one described in the story?
- Have English learners lived in or visited places like those in the story?
- How far removed is the story from current times?
- How close is the main character's age to English learners'?
- Is the main character the same gender as the reader?
- Do the characters talk like the English learners and their families?
- Is this author/author style familiar to English learners?

In comparing the genre, fiction, poetry, and nonfiction all have many culturally relevant texts that could be effectively used with English learners. Among the many culturally relevant nonfiction books, there are picture book biographies that depict historical figures as well as photo essays that provide a detailed snapshot of a cultural group. There are also bilingual and multicultural poetry collections including Francisco Alarcón's collections (1997, 1998, 1999, 2005, 2008, TL3–5, A, P), *Laughing Out Loud, I Fly: A Carcajadas yo Vuelo* by Juan Herrera (1998, TL4–5, I, P), and *My Mexico/ México Mío* by Tony Johnston (1996, TL3–5, I, P). And, in the fiction category, the many aspects of migrant work and Hispanic family life are beautifully depicted in *Tomás and the Library Lady* (Mora, 1997, TL4–5, A, F) while *How My Parents Learned to Eat* (Friedman, 1984, TL3–5, A, F) and *This Next New Year* (Wong, 2000, TL2–4, A, F) celebrate the rich traditions of families from different cultures. Just as with limited content knowledge, though, English learners may need additional support to access books with cultural information that is distant from their own experiences. In one research study, Johnson (1981) found that the cultural origin of a story had more effect on the comprehension of English learners than the level of syntactic and semantic complexity in both adapted versus unadapted text.

In the United States, there has been an increase in the number of bilingual books published for children in a variety of formats (Ernst-Slavit & Mulhern, 2003) from those with the complete text in two languages (Carmen Garza's *In My Family/ En Mi Familia*, 2000, TL3–5, A, NF) to those published in different versions, one book for each language (e.g., Gary Soto's *Too Many Tamales*, 1994, TL3–4, A, F, and *Que Monton de Tamales!*, 1996, TL3–4, A, F), as well as books in English interspersed with words and phrases from another language (Pat Mora's *Confetti: Poems for Children* 1996, TL2–5, A, P). While the majority of books with complete text in two languages are English–Spanish, many other languages are being used in children's literature as reported in the first Bilingual Books for Children Booklist from the Association of Library Services for Children (2005). This list of high literary quality books published from 1995 to 1999 includes selections in Chinese, Hopi, Inuktitut, Japanese, Khmer, Korean, Russian, Swahili, Thai, Tibetan, Vietnamese, and of course, Spanish.

Certainly, bilingual books can be a positive reflection of the linguistic diversity of the classroom. Such books support children's English acquisition by connecting the new language to the more familiar home language. In addition, children who are already literate in the first language don't need to "learn to read" in another language. English learners need exposure to their new language in meaningful formats, ones that affirm their cultural background and might possibly encourage language maintenance and not just a transition to English only. Bilingual books are not just for the culturally and linguistically diverse student, however. All children need opportunities to see the diversity of languages in the United States. While children will be aware of the prevalence of Spanish in this country (almost 80% of English learners in the schools are native Spanish speakers), they may be completely unaware of the many other languages used in their community or state.

The four text selection criteria—level of content familiarity or background knowledge, level of language, level of text support, and level of cultural fit—are just one part of the text selection process, however. The integration of selection criteria with language proficiency levels is the next part of the process and is presented in the following section.

Linking Language Proficiencies
to Text Selection Criteria

In Chapter 1, the proficiency levels are presented in Table 1.4 as a means of helping teachers understand the characteristics of English learners at the various language development phases. In the preceding section of this chapter, the four criteria for text selection are discussed and presented in Table 2.1. The next step in making sure that English learners' proficiency levels are considered as an integral part of the text selection criteria is to integrate the two tables as a type of checklist for teachers to use as they examine texts while always keeping in mind the English learners in their classrooms. The result is Appendix B, presented at the end of this book, that matches each of the five proficiency levels—Level 1, Starting; Level 2, Emerging; Level 3, Developing; Level 4, Expanding; and Level 5, Bridging—with the four text selection criteria noting specifics to keep in mind at each step of the process.

Teachers also need to consider the reading approach when matching books. English learners often need support to read books in their new language, so teachers need to read aloud the most difficult books. Reading aloud offers students the highest level of teacher support and is critical for helping students experience text they could not read on their own. Indeed, Capellini notes that books teachers read aloud to children can be "two or three grade levels above the children's reading level, with the children participating interactively or the teacher modeling reading strategies in think-alouds and the use of rich language" (2005, p. 60). Moderately challenging books are appropriate for English learners when they receive additional support either through teacher guidance (such as shared or guided reading) or in partner reading situations. Shared and guided reading approaches are critical in helping students develop skills and strategies they need in order to read independently. Reading with partners and group response are also critical in supporting students. The easiest books are best for independent reading and provide students with opportunities for what Allington (2009b) refers to as high-success reading. "High-success reading is accurate reading, fluent reading, and reading with understanding" (2009b, p. 51). Such reading requires that students read with 99% accuracy. Reading independently is the goal for all students. Indeed, teachers may be surprised to see that some of their English learners understand more of what they read than what they hear.

Linking Texts to Instruction with English Learners in Grades K–6

When selecting any reading material, teachers should consider instructional goals. Too often, the textbook drives instruction, and reading "real" books is reserved for free time. Although free reading time is certainly valuable, literature should not be relegated to that use alone. Moreover, textbook instruction often dominates the content areas outside the language arts—science, math, social studies—when literature could be so easily linked to any lesson or curricular theme within the traditional scope and sequence.

Instructional planning for the range of language proficiency levels among English learners, sometimes in the same classroom, can be a challenging task as noted in the last section of Chapter 1 with the discussion of the Curriculum and Instruction Planning Framework. Because the intent of this book is to help teachers incorporate literature throughout their instruction with English learners, Figure 2.2 extends the framework introduced in Chapter 1 by suggesting activities and literature matched to each of the four quadrants. The literature suggestions in the upper quadrants (Quadrants I and III) have more text support, and therefore less of a language load, to help English learners' comprehension while the lower quadrants have limited or no text support. The left two quadrants (Quadrants I and II) have literature suggestions with less academic language thereby lessening the cognitive load on English learners. With Level 1 English learners, in particular, time is needed to learn the basic language and routines of school. Yet, content concepts must not be forgotten, even with learners at the beginning proficiency levels, so the right quadrants (Quadrants III and IV) present literature suggestions that focus on developing academic language.

Conclusion

This chapter has outlined criteria that teachers can use to select books for English learners and then match those criteria to the TESOL PreK–12 English Language Proficiency Standards. This is an important process because placing meaningful materials in English language learners'

	Nonacademic or Lower-Cognitive-Load Activities	Academic or Higher-Cognitive-Load Activities	
CONTEXTUALIZED LANGUAGE	**Quadrant I** **Viewing/listening activities** **Follow a demonstration/directions.** Examples: • Teacher read-aloud of predictable book and students join in on repeated phrase • Total Physical Response lessons with literature; students follow actions **Literature Suggestions:** Books on universal/familiar topics with simple language and clear illustrations with text-to-visual correspondence including the following: counting books, concept and alphabet books, wordless books, poem and song picture books, predictable books with predictable unit accounting for significant portion of the text	**Quadrant III** **Participation activity** **Make a model, chart, graph.** Examples: • Participating in hands-on academic lessons: math manipulatives, discovery science, drawing maps • Participating in shared, guided, and partner reading • Making a timeline of events • Writing with structured support **Literature Suggestions:** Books on content-related topics or using academic language with illustrations with text-to-visual correspondence including the following: concept and alphabet books, survey books, life cycle books, photo essays, folktales in picture book format, picture book biographies, how-to and activity books, single-topic/theme poetry collections	**LOWER-LANGUAGE LOAD**
CONTEXT-FREE LANGUAGE	**Quadrant II** **Discussion activity** **Interaction is conducted in more informal language.** Examples: • Literature circles with personal response to reading • Writing personal response to reading **Literature Suggestions:** Books on familiar topics with simple language and limited illustrations or ones that are more general and aesthetic in nature including the following: counting books, concept and alphabet books on general topics, fiction and traditional literature, single-author poetry collections	**Quadrant IV** **Translation activity** **Transform the content from the previous activities into academic language to state the main idea of the lesson.** Examples: • Listening to academic presentations without visuals • Independent reading of texts for the content areas • Writing for the content areas **Literature Suggestions:** Books on a wide variety of topics including the following: chapter books without illustrations, journals, diaries, complete, partial, and collective biographies (not picture book biographies), traditional literature collections, poetry anthologies	**HIGHER-LANGUAGE LOAD**

FIGURE 2.2. Curriculum and instruction planning framework with literature suggestions. Based on Chamot and O'Malley (1987).

hands helps them develop and practice as readers and writers in a new language. However, the process should not stop at this point. Teachers need to call English learners' attention to the many options available for reading and language learning. This can be accomplished through a variety of techniques. Naturally, the teacher can begin by reading aloud regularly to provide a fluent model of reading as well as the implicit invitation to the "reading club" so essential to ongoing language and literacy development. In addition, teachers can draw attention to featured authors or books with bulletin board or center displays, and they can spotlight a book of the week through a book talk or by reading aloud selected portions. Further, according to Routman, "The availability of reading materials greatly impacts children's literacy development. The most effective reading programs are generally supported by large classroom libraries. The better the libraries, the better the reading achievement as measured by standardized tests" (2003, p. 64).

Once teachers have sparked student interest, they need to step back and provide a regular time and freedom of choice for English learners to enjoy the books and continue to make additional suggestions as students' language proficiency develops and their reading tastes mature. With variety and time to pore over these books, English learners notice the many powerful ways the written word can be used—to inform, to entertain, and to persuade. In short, they discover the power and pleasure of their new language through books.

The next chapter explores two different types of language proficiency that are important for English language development—social language and academic language—and how literature can be used to develop both types of language. While social language may be the beginning of the process of language learning, English learners must quickly move toward academic language for school success.

Only a Joke?

Humor as a Bridge between Cultures and Languages

UMA KRISHNASWAMI

In his exploration of humor, Berger (1997) writes that
in the everyday world humor is seen as a disruption of
routine, an intrusion into more important arenas of life.
For most of us, humor is an almost unnoticed part of an
average day. How often, however, does someone then say,
"But, seriously...," thus returning the conversation to
the previous, more earnest subject? According to Berger,
"The comic is posited as an antithesis to serious concerns"
(p. 6). The conventional formula by which we try to pull
back from a humorous observation that might offend, from
a joke that has "gone too far," is the apology, "But it was
only a joke!"

Only a joke. Naturally, when writers embark on
the serious business of crossing cultural and linguistic
boundaries in their work, they rarely start out with "only
a joke." Children's and young adult author Cynthia Leitich
Smith (2004) has written about the dearth of books with
cultural resonance that are also funny. Inquiring into the
challenges of publishing multicultural humor, she finds
"answers ... rooted in the writing itself, in the history and
politics, in often misguided perceptions, and perhaps most
of all in our grown-up psyches."

When I began writing and submitting work to publishers, I too wanted to be taken seriously. Knowing that
my understanding of the structure of story came from
traditional tales that I had heard as a child, I started
by retelling them. Luckily for me, I selected a character
whose power lies in his comic aspects—the elephant-

headed Hindu god Ganesha. Using this comic character to open the doors to a rich and complex tradition, I began to understand how humor itself opens doors that otherwise seem impassable. Without really meaning to be funny, I discovered the power of humor.

The Broken Tusk: Stories of the Hindu God Ganesha quickly raised linguistic challenges. It would have been easiest to use English approximations for the Sanskrit words common to the tradition that I sought to convey. That is what conventional writing instruction advises. But I wanted those words to add their unique rhythm and cadence, to serve as a kind of auditory background music to the story. Sometimes such terms, designated as "foreign" by style manuals, became critical to meaning. When Ganesha dances in the face of a possible curse, deflecting his antagonist's anger into amusement, nothing but the onomatopoeic "Tham—thakita—tham!" of south Indian classical dance instruction could possibly convey the particular nuance of flat-footed grace demanded by the scene.

Sometimes an inside joke can be used simultaneously as a nod to readers who know it and an invitation to those who don't. The word *hapa*, once a derogatory label derived from the Hawaiian word for *half*, has been adopted as a term of pride by many Asian Americans of mixed racial heritage. In Janet Wong's middle-grade verse novel, *Minn and Jake*, Jake's racial background is never mentioned. In the sequel, *Minn and Jake's Almost Terrible Summer*, we learn that Jake has a Korean grandmother. That makes him one-quarter Korean, or as he says, "Quarpa." By punning on such an insider's term, the author invites not only Minn to share in the joke, but the reader as well. In fact when Minn feels cheated because Jake never told her this important fact about himself, the reader understands what Minn does not. In reply, Jake continues half-jokingly, but with unmistakable intent, "And did I ever tell you that I like taking bubble baths and playing Halo 2 until midnight?" Here is the comic tackling serious matters indeed, of identity, identification, and the heart of knowing a person.

Finally, humorous narrative can be used to invite an exploration of language and its myriad permutations. In two of my picture books, *The Happiest Tree: A Yoga Story*, and *Bringing Asha Home*, Hindi words are woven into the text, their meaning made contextually clear. A character falls *gup-choop* silent in astonishment. Her parents refer to her affectionately as *rani*. The significance of a bracelet and the holiday bearing its name, is revealed in a scene in which the narrative camera is not directly focused on this cultural material. Instead the reader is diverted by the protagonist's friend, who complains that his new baby sister "cries all the time. She can't do anything."

In the world of young adult books, we have made some progress since Cynthia Leitich Smith quoted a young African American reader as asking, "Why is it that it's only the white kids in books who seem to laugh and have fun?" To some degree this is because satire as a form refuses to accept the dichotomy between laughter and the serious world. Gene Luen Yang's graphic novel, *American Born Chinese* and Sherman Alexie's *The Absolutely True Diary of a Part-Time Indian* both rely on humor to weave culture, language, history, and circumstance together in new ways for young adult readers.

In picture book and middle-grade multicultural books, however, the tilt remains toward serious and worthy. This is ironic, as children in general are much more open to laughter and playfulness than are we adults. We who write for children should be mining those joyful instincts for rich, evocative, culturally grounded material. When young readers are able to laugh while reading a story written in one language and containing the linguistic threads of another, they also become subliminally aware that it is possible to engage in play in all languages. Far from being "only a joke," this combination of laughter and understanding is no less than the heart of what makes us human.

References

Alexie, S. (2007). *The absolutely true diary of a part-time Indian* (E. Forney, Illus.). New York: Little, Brown.

Berger, P. L. (1997). *Redeeming laughter: The comic dimension of human experience*. New York: Walter de Gruyter.

Krishnaswami, U. (2005). *The happiest tree: A yoga story* (R. Jeyeveeran, Illus.). New York: Lee & Low.

Krishnaswami, U. (2006a). *Bringing Asha home* (J. Akib, Illus.). New York: Lee & Low.

Krishnaswami, U. (2006b). *The broken tusk: Stories of the Hindu god Ganesha* (M. Selven, Illus.). Little Rock, AR: August House. (Original work published 1996)

Leitich Smith, C. (2004). Multicultural humor, seriously. Posted to *cynthialeitichsmith.blogspot.com/2004/07/multicultural-humor-seriously.html*.

Wong, J. (2001). *Minn and Jake*. New York: Frances Foster.

Wong, J. (2008). *Minn and Jake's almost terrible summer*. New York: Frances Foster.

Yang, G. L. (2006). *American born Chinese*. New York: First Second.

CHAPTER THREE

English Learners' Academic and Social Language

Moving from Surviving to Thriving

Soon the thick of the monsoon would arrive, and a thousand
raindrops would hit our clay-tiled roof all at once. But I wouldn't
be here to listen to them. I would be halfway around the world
in a strange, foreign place called 112 Foster Terrace, Brighton,
Massachusetts, U.S.A.

—FRANCES AND GINGER PARK, *Good-Bye, 382 Shin
Dang Dong* (National Geographic, 2002)

Imagine that you are a child and you have just found out that your family
is moving. Not only will you leave your friends and many family members
behind, but you are about to enter a new place with a language and
customs that are completely unfamiliar. The sounds and symbols of this
new language are completely different. Yet, you attend school and try to
navigate and communicate in this new environment and make friends
among the strangers around you. It is challenging and sometimes frightening. The language demands intensify in the classroom, as you struggle
to pay attention to lesson after lesson and to find the right word in order
to respond in class. In addition, you sometimes feel overwhelmed as you
race to catch up to your peers who don't have to juggle new and complex
concepts in an unfamiliar language.

Moving to a new place or entering school for the first time requires
adjustments. Add to that, learning a new culture and a new language,
and the transitions become more complex. As individuals learn a new
language and culture, they are acquiring several different types of profi-

59

ciency. This chapter contrasts two types of language proficiencies needed by English learners in school—social and academic language. On moving to a new country or learning a new language, one's first need is to survive—to get basic needs met. Thus, the initial part of this chapter offers ideas for developing English learners' social or "survival" language so that they can interact and understand basic classroom instructions. Various categories of survival language are introduced with books matched to those topics as well as strategies to help English learners master this level of language. The next sections of this chapter provide guidelines for moving students beyond social language to the academic language needed for school achievement.

Social versus Academic Language

James Cummins (2003) has highlighted two types of language proficiency that individuals learning a language need—social and academic language. Social language does not require formal schooling to develop. It grows naturally out of everyday interactions. This is the language needed for socializing on the playground and in the lunchroom and hallways. Unfortunately, teachers sometimes mistake the social ability that English learners first develop for the fluency needed to succeed in the classroom. They may believe students are more fluent than they are based on their growing ease with everyday language. Research has shown that English learners acquire social language in 1 to 2 years as they interact socially (Collier, 1989; Cummins, 1981, 2003; Cummins & Schecter, 2003).

Academic language, on the other hand, is the focus of the curriculum, textbooks, and formal instruction. Such language is often not a part of students' everyday vocabulary and takes from 5 to 7 years to develop—even longer for children who immigrated to the United States without previous schooling (Collier, 1989; Cummins, 2001). Echoing the focus of high-stakes testing, accountability, and the No Child Left Behind Act (2001), an increased emphasis on academic content and language is clear in the newly revised TESOL PreK–12 English Language Proficiency Standards. Four of the five standards are devoted to the ability to communicate information, ideas, and concepts necessary for academic success in language arts, mathematics, science, and social studies, respectively, as highlighted in Table 3.1. Only the first standard is targeted at communicating for social, intercultural, and instructional purposes. Standard 1, however, is not devoted solely to social language. Communicating for instructional purposes can have different levels of complexity. The basic

TABLE 3.1. Comparison of Instructional Emphasis: Social versus Academic Language Based on TESOL English Language Proficiency Standards

Standards more focused on social language	Standards focused on academic language
• TESOL Standard 1: English language learners communicate for social, intercultural, and instructional purposes within the school setting.	• TESOL Standard 2: English language learners communicate information, ideas, and concepts necessary for academic success in the area of language arts. • TESOL Standard 3: English language learners communicate information, ideas, and concepts necessary for academic success in the area of mathematics. • TESOL Standard 4: English language learners communicate information, ideas, and concepts necessary for academic success in the area of science. • TESOL Standard 5: English language learners communicate information, ideas, and concepts necessary for academic success in the area of social studies.

Note. Data from TESOL (2006).

routines of the classroom (e.g., fold your paper, read pages 1–5, write your name on the first line, label the picture) can be classified as social language that helps English learners get along in the classroom. The other dimension of instructional language is more complex, more academic; for instance, understanding the language of cooperative learning roles (reporter, recorder, etc.) or the instructions for participating in literature circles (support your point of view with evidence from the reading).

Viewed as a continuum (WIDA Consortium, 2007), English learners in schools move from simple and informal social language in the initial language proficiency levels toward more complex and formal academic language in the later language proficiency levels as illustrated in Figure 3.1. From an instructional standpoint, the movement from social to academic language is not completely linear and does not exclude exposure to academic language as part of early lessons. Academic language cannot wait until social language is fully developed just as reading and writing cannot wait until oral language is fully developed (Pilgreen, 2006). While the initial need for English learners is vocabulary for social and instructional interaction, children in the primary grades have more time to develop both social and academic language. At the intermediate grades and beyond, however, English learners are in a more difficult race to catch up with their English-speaking peers. They need social and

Social Language	$\Rightarrow$ Academic Language
Tier I Vocabulary	$\Rightarrow$ Tier II and III Vocabulary
(Beck, McKeown, & Kucan)	$\Rightarrow$ (Beck, McKeown, & Kucan)
Initial Language Proficiency Levels	$\Rightarrow$ Later Language Proficiency Levels
Concrete ideas and concepts	$\Rightarrow$ Abstract ideas and concepts
Explicit meaning	$\Rightarrow$ Implicit meaning
Familiar situations	$\Rightarrow$ Unfamiliar situations
Informal registers	$\Rightarrow$ Formal registers
General vocabulary	$\Rightarrow$ Technical vocabulary
Single words and phrases	$\Rightarrow$ Extended discourse
Nonconventional forms	$\Rightarrow$ Conventional forms

FIGURE 3.1. A continuum of language development. Based on Gottlieb, Cranley, and Cammilleri (2007).

instructional language, yet, even more important is a focus on academic language. The older English learners are when they enter school, the less likely they will have enough time remaining in school to master the academic language proficiency for school achievement. The key, then, is making academic language comprehensible in the early stages of language learning by carefully considering the academic concepts taught and focusing on those that are more concrete and explicit.

Social Language

English learners may enter school with diverse proficiency levels. Those who begin school at Level 1 proficiency will have limited or no understanding of English. In the process of language acquisition, they move from the familiar, general, and concrete to the more unfamiliar, specialized, and abstract. Social language cannot be sidestepped. Just as with first-language acquisition, beginning English learners need basic vocabulary to interact with others and to understand how to negotiate daily routines in and out of school. As their oral comprehension increases, these learners begin to use their newly acquired language but their verbalizations consist of repeating what they hear and using memorized chunks of language—routines such as greetings.

Similar to social language is the vocabulary that Beck, McKeown, and Kucan (2002) refer to as Tier I, the most basic words of a language (e.g., *happy, clock*). These are the words that native English speakers come to school already knowing through their interactions in the home language in their early preschool years. These words are learned and reinforced through social interaction. While Beck et al. contend that Tier I words "rarely require instructional attention to their meanings in school" (p. 8), this may not be the case for all learners. English learners may not know Tier 1 words when they come to school, or they may know them in their home language but not have acquired the English label for the word. Indeed, a portion of the standardized placement testing done with English learners to determine their oral proficiency level in English when they first enter school is focused on social language (e.g., subtests such as Simon Says, Choose a Picture, What's in the House? Listening Comprehension targeted at understanding everyday conversations). For those English learners who do not have well-developed oral language, social language needs to receive explicit instructional attention since it is the foundation for academic language development (Schrank, Fletcher, & Alvarado, 1996).

Krashen and Terrell (1983) support the thematic presentation of vocabulary for English learners arguing that such a strategy offers the student an immediate network of relationships linking new words and concepts. One excellent resource for beginning vocabulary is *Maisy's Amazing Big Book of Words* (Cousins, 2007, TL1–2, P, NF). Grouped into thematic categories such as getting dressed, on the farm, things that go, and so forth, more than 300 basic vocabulary words are presented with each word accompanied by a bright illustration. The two- to four-page groupings of words by themes make word study easy for English learners, supportive family members, and teachers.

Building social language and Tier I vocabulary with English learners is similar to the oral language development that occurs during first-language acquisition. Unfortunately, some English learners do not have the opportunity to develop oral language proficiency in their new language before entering school, but many of them bring a wealth of oral language experiences in their home language. Oral language development plays a powerful role in both acquiring a language and providing a foundation for reading and writing (Lesaux, Geva, Koda, Siegel, & Shanahan, 2008). English learners who come from a home environment with ample opportunity for oral language development in the home language have the advantage when they enter school. They possess a wide vocabulary and conceptual background because they have participated in opportunities to talk about daily concerns and activities with care-givers, siblings, peers, and relatives. Through these chances to talk and listen, they gained many intuitive understandings about language and how it functions—how the language sounds in various circumstances from formal to informal, and how sentences are structured, how differ-ent words are used with different audiences and for different occasions. These understandings count when they enter school since they only need new English labels for the concepts and structures they already know in the home language. According to researchers, a firm background in the home language is a strong indicator of eventual success in learning another language (Collier, 1989; Cummins, 1980, 1981). Conversely, Eng-lish learners may not bring a well-developed oral language background to school. This lack of word knowledge is a chief indicator of the restricted amount of elaborated language that children experience at home (Wells, 1986), and these gaps can present problems in learning a new language.

Selecting Books and Instructional Strategies to Reinforce Social Language

Social and instructional language is routinely used throughout a normal day, but the vocabulary is often not made explicit. This is where teachers can make a difference for English learners. They can become aware of these vocabulary needs. What are the types of social language needed? Figure 3.2 provides a list of social or basic "survival" topics needed early in the language learning process.

Once teachers are aware of these topical areas for social language, they can collect books and plan activities to help English learners maxi-mize their vocabulary acquisition. In selecting books for social (survival) language, teachers need to also keep in mind the characteristics of Level 1 and 2 English learners who need to develop social (survival) language, and they can use the four criteria for text selection introduced in Chapter 2. First, in terms of the level of familiarity or background knowledge, the content/topic of the book should be related to universal or familiar concepts thereby lessening the conceptual load. Next, for the level of lan-guage, the vocabulary used needs to be basic, concrete, and/or familiar, and the whole text should be brief and written at the word, phrase, or simple sentence level. Like the conceptual load, the language load should not be challenging. Third, the level of text support should be significant.

• Basic directions and signs	• Movement
• Calendar	• Numbers to 100
• Clothing	• Parts of the body, actions
• Colors	• Recreation and activities
• Feelings	• Routines
• Food	• Safety
• Games	• School and classroom
• Greetings	• Self and family
• Home and household	• Shapes
• Hygiene	• Shopping
• Jobs	• Social behavior
• Letters of the alphabet	• Spatial relations
• Measurement	• Time
• Money	• Weather

FIGURE 3.2. Social language (basic "survival") topics.

The text should have support features such as clear labeling and/or visuals that are clear and direct and generally, have a one-to-one correspondence of visual to text. Finally, in terms of the level of cultural fit, the text needs to have a universal or familiar focus for all learners or it needs to closely reflect the background and experiences of the learner. Appendix C at the end of this book provides a list of social (survival) language topics and examples of books matched to those.

With help from their teachers and peers, English learners quickly learn English labels for concepts that are already known in their home language. To assist this process, teachers can use language-mediation strategies—basically adjusting language to facilitate comprehension and communication. As teachers share and discuss literature with the class, they can use the following language-mediation strategies (Olmedo, 2003) for the benefit of all learners, but particularly for English learners:

- Direct teaching of key vocabulary before, during, and after reading
- Labeling and using visuals and objects in lessons
- Using concept-building and vocabulary-building graphics
- Writing key words while reading
- Underlining key words on the whiteboard
- Rephrasing or restating
- Previewing and summarizing key points

- Simplifying key words
- Elaborating and extending key words
- Providing antonyms and synonyms for key words
- Demonstrating the meaning of a word
- Creating comparisons/similes
- Pointing out similarities and differences in key words/concepts
- Pointing out prefix/suffix
- Giving examples/non-examples
- Using clear intonation
- Repeating and emphasizing key words
- Simplifying grammar and vocabulary
- Adjusting the pace
- Actively involving students in doing something to reinforce learning

Linking appropriate literature with engaging instructional activities can aid the process of learning social language. Several techniques work well to highlight social language, and literature can be an integral part of these strategies. Again, these activities are helpful for all learners, whether they are just learning English or not.

Using Read-Alouds

Reading to students is "a supportive approach where a skilled reader, acting on the author's behalf, reads to a less skilled audience" (Mooney, 2004, p. 73). Teachers who read aloud to their students provide a model of fluent, expressive reading. Moreover, they share their passion for reading and demonstrate reading's many functions: reading for pleasure, gaining information, meeting personal needs, and solving problems. Reading to students plays a fundamental role in "inviting listeners to be readers" (Fisher, Flood, Lapp, & Frey, 2004, p. 8).

Unfortunately, many teachers do not see the value of reading aloud to students. Yet, many reasons exist for reading to students. Indeed, numerous literacy authorities and research studies contribute support for reading aloud to English learners.

- Children learn language by hearing it repeatedly in meaningful contexts (Trelease, 2006).
- Reading aloud leads to greater vocabulary learning (Elley, 1989; Morrow & Brittain, 2003).
- When listening to their teachers read aloud, children are exposed

to words they are unlikely to hear in spoken language (Sénéchal, Lefevre, Thomas, & Daley, 1996).

- Reading aloud nurtures listening skills, which is important since listening comprehension precedes reading comprehension (Trelease, 2006).
- Reading aloud introduces students to more and new syntactic and grammatical forms in English (Sénéchal et al., 1996).
- Reading aloud helps students become familiar with the reading process and how print on the page corresponds to spoken language.

In examining this list of reasons for reading aloud, it is apparent that the benefits of reading stories deal more with language development than literacy development. Typically, reviews of reading aloud include such benefits as improved reading comprehension and enhanced beginning reading. Yet, a review of research studies indicated that the approach "has more modest effect on the literacy development of non-mainstream children than is commonly believed" (Anderson, Anderson, Lynch, & Shapiro, 2003, p. 209). Some researchers suggest that too much emphasis on reading aloud can take away time better used for decoding, comprehension, fluency, or vocabulary instruction (i.e., Teale, 2003).

Researchers, however, note that it is the quality of engagement that occurs during reading that results in positive literacy and language effects (Morrow & Brittain, 2003). In short, "Most effective read-alouds are those in which children are actively involved asking and answering questions and making predictions rather than passively listening" (McGee & Schickedanz, 2007, p. 742). These read-alouds are called interactive or dialogic. Teale (2003, pp. 131–132) recommends teachers use the following strategies to maximize engagement and more fully benefit students:

- Encourage children to use their background knowledge in meaningful ways when approaching the book.
- Ask questions and invite reactions that keep students engaged in the book—especially generative questions that promote a variety of responses.
- Read in a lively, engaging way.
- Encourage children to make predictions about what will happen next or what a character will do.
- Keep discussions focused on important text ideas.
- Talk about a few of the words or phrases in the book in ways that build children's vocabulary knowledge.

Additional ideas for involving students during a read-aloud include

- Encouraging students to retell or dramatize stories (Cornell, Sénéchal, & Brodo, 1988; Pellegrini & Galda, 1982).
- Reading several books on a similar topic and having students manipulate objects related to the concepts or characters from the text (Rowe, 1998; Wasik & Bond, 2001).
- Reading a book repeatedly (Crago & Crago, 1976).
- Describing illustrations (Reese & Cox, 1999).

These strategies are especially important as English learners develop more and more competency in their new language.

Using Physical Activity

One popular instructional method that actively engages language learners is Total Physical Response (TPR). James Asher (1982) based his method on the premise that an effective way of learning another language is much like learning a first language. Somewhat like the children's game, Simon Says, children listen to commands and respond nonverbally. TPR lessons are active with the teacher using commands and modeling actions with the whole class, small groups, and individuals. Students do not speak until they have listened and observed the commands many times. For TPR lessons, Asher suggests that teachers begin with "survival" language or basic content and concepts first needed by language learners.

Supplementing traditional commands (e.g., point to your toe, your foot) of TPR with literature, teachers can read aloud poems or books and have students point to the various body parts noted. For instance, Shel Silverstein's poem, "Boa Constrictor" (*Where the Sidewalk Ends*, 2000, TL1–5, A, P) mentions parts of the body. Similarly, Byron Barton's *Bones, Bones, Dinosaur Bones* (1990, TL1–3, P, NF) and Bob Barner's *Dem Bones* (1996, TL1–3, A, NF) are good choices because of their simple and repetitive language. Other books that are natural links to physical activity include *Monkey and Me* (Gravett, 2008, TL1, P, F), *Dog Day* (Hayes, 2008, TL2–4, A, F), and *Pretend You're a Cat* (Marzollo, 1997, TL1–2, P, F) with their vivid descriptions of animal movements that prompt children to imitate the actions, and *Go, Go, Go! Kids on the Move* (Swinburne, 2002, TL1–2, P, NF) that depicts children's favorite ways to move ("I walk./ I skip./ I hop./ I run."). Lessons incorporating movement need not require standing up and moving about the classroom. Instead, students can match photos, sequence pictures or sentence strips at their desks, or

English learners can hold up a card with a word or phrase repeated during a read-aloud. Picture songbooks often have actions as well as words to involve students, as is the case with *If You're Happy and You Know It, Clap Your Hands!* (Carter, 1997, TL1–3, P, F) and *The Eensy-Weensy Spider* (Hoberman, 2004, TL1–3, P, F), and these songs can be sung and performed while seated. The idea is to incorporate movement alongside print, getting children involved in physically responding, not just passively listening.

Using Dramatic Play

Drama provides another active language learning approach. Among the many possibilities for implementing drama in the classroom are puppetry, storytelling, Readers' Theatre, and role play. Chris Raschka's *Yo! Yes* (1993, TL1–2, A, F) is a great book for a creative dramatics interpretation. This picture book illustrates an offer of friendship between two young boys. The interactions between the boys can be used as a nonverbal role play as the teacher reads the book aloud, or students can chant the words since each boy only uses one or two words per page of action. For an example of social language in the real world, teachers might use Rachel Isadora's *Yo, Jo!* (2007, TL1–3, A, F). This simple picture book depicts greetings among friends in the neighborhood with a focus on slang and colloquial terms, *yo, hey, whassup*. Again, this book is perfect for role play and a class discussion can address issues of informal and formal language since slang terms are particularly confusing for English learners in the early stages of language learning. Another basic book, *Say Hello* (Foreman & Foreman, 2008, TL1–2, P, F), focuses on being left out on the playground noting that "When someone's feeling left out, low, it doesn't take much to say … 'Hello!'" *Harriet Dancing* (Symes, 2008, TL2–4, A, F) has a repeated phrase several times in the book: "Twist and turn and skip and hop./ This way and that way./ That way and this way./ Spin around until you stop!" that is ideal for acting out to punctuate a read-aloud. Finally, predictable pattern books are also perfect for drama activities. *Stuck in the Mud* (Clarke, 2008, TL2–3, A, F) is a pattern story that has each of the animals getting stuck in the mud to help little chick: "Horse pushed/ and he pulled/ again and again …/ but then he was stuck/ with Sheep, Dog, Cat, and Hen." In a similar vein, *The Turnip* (Morgan, 1996, TL2–3, A, F) and *Out of the Egg* (Matthews, 2007, TL2–3, A, F) are two additional pattern stories with a sequence of events seemingly designed for dramatization. Figure 3.3 combines book suggestions for both physical activity and dramatic play.

TOTAL PHYSICAL RESPONSE METHOD

- *Where the Sidewalk Ends* by Shel Silverstein
- *Dog Day* by Sarah Hayes
- *Monkey and Me* by Emily Gravett
- *Go, Go, Go! Kids on the Move* by Stephen Swinburne
- *Bones, Bones, Dinosaur Bones* by Byron Barton
- *Dem Bones* by Bob Barner
- *Pretend You're a Cat* by Jean Marzollo
- *If You're Happy and You Know It, Clap Your Hands!* by David Carter
- *The Eensy-Weensy Spider* by Maryann Hoberman

DRAMA

- *Yo! Yes* by Chris Raschka
- *Say Hello* by Jack and Michael Foreman
- *Stuck in the Mud* by Jane Clarke
- *Out of the Egg* by Tina Matthews
- *Hattie and the Fox* by Mem Fox
- *Yo, Jo!* by Rachel Isadora
- *The First Music* by Dylan Pritchett

FIGURE 3.3. Using children's literature to encourage physical activity and dramatic play.

Academic Language

Children are generally quick to incorporate social language since it helps them get along with others and begin to make friends. All the while, some acquisition of more formal vocabulary should be occurring simultaneously. Academic language includes the subject area vocabulary for the English language arts, social studies, science, and math as well as health and physical education and the visual and performing arts. Moreover, English learners must interact in the classroom as they construct, process, and apply the language of the subject matter with the language of the learning activity. Whole-class discussion, group work, and paired interactions using literature and reinforcing the language through reader response, journal writing, and such offer a means to tap into the language of the assigned tasks and the process and application of learning (e.g., the writing process or prewriting through brainstorming).

Again drawing on their vocabulary research, Beck et al. (2002) refer to two other vocabulary tiers beyond the basic words of Tier I. These two tiers correlate to academic language. Tier III words are low-frequency technical vocabulary items related to the content of school subjects (e.g., photosynthesis, axis). Beck et al. argue that since these words are not of high utility to most learners, they should be taught only when needed—in the context of content classrooms when directly encountered in lessons or reading. In other words, teachers need to weigh carefully the time investment in Tier III terms and the ultimate payoff for English learners (e.g., transfer to other content areas). Tier II words, on the other hand, are frequently used words that occur in many domains, often academic in nature. These words add to an individual's language ability and have a tremendous impact on school achievement. They are the language of literature and more formal writing and speaking (e.g., *fortunate, absurd*). These words reflect more sophisticated word choice and descriptive language; for instance, the use of *elated* or *ecstatic* instead of the more common word, *happy*, and they add to individuals' language ability and influence school achievement. One example of more sophisticated word choice is Karma Wilson's *How to Bake an American Pie* (2007, TL3–5, I, F). Weaving together metaphors from cooking (*leaven, ladle, whisk,* and *garnish*) and illusions to America's history, Wilson offers images such as "Pat out/ a crust of/ fruited plains,/ then spread it/ as far as you dare./ Fold in some fields/ of amber grains,/ enough for/ all people/ to share." When students have a deep understanding of vocabulary with a developed network of word relationships, synonyms, and antonyms, the larger their literate vocabulary will be. Beck et al. propose that attention to Tier II vocabulary is the most productive use of instructional time.

Using the Curriculum and Instruction Planning Framework introduced in Chapter 1 and further developed in Chapter 2, Figure 3.4 highlights the escalating language demands that students encounter by moving from more contextualized language environments such as one-to-one text-to-visual children's books and face-to-face communication (upper Quadrants I and III) to communication without predictable routines and limited visuals for support (context-free language) (lower Quadrants II and IV) and from social/informal language (left Quadrants I and II) to academic language (right Quadrants III and IV). It also suggests helpful approaches a teacher can take to guide this learning. For instance, the plan begins with a read-aloud of *Ten Things I Can Do to Help My World* (Walsh, 2008, TL1–4, P, NF), which is ideal for Level 1 English learner participation, but the book also has some additional ideas with more elaborated language for students at Levels 2–4 to think about and discuss. The focus in Quadrants I and II is simply to explore in an informal way the general ideas about personal activities to help our world while in Quadrants III and IV, the emphasis moves to the academic language of

	Nonacademic or Lower-Cognitive-Load Activities	Academic or Higher-Cognitive-Load Activities	
CONTEXTUALIZED LANGUAGE	**Quadrant I** **Viewing/listening activity** **Follow a demonstration/directions.** Examples: • Teacher reads aloud *Ten Things I Can Do to Help My World* (Walsh, 2008). Only the main 10 activities are read aloud. • Teacher divides class in two groups and displays (LCD or overhead) a chart with two columns: (1) the beginning and (2) the ending of sentences for the 10 main activities and the students read their assigned part—start or finish. • Optional activity: While teacher reads the text aloud again, students use physical actions to perform the actions. • Beyond the 10 main activities in the book, there is an additional related tip on each page with more developed sentence structure and vocabulary. The teacher can share these tips for English learners at Levels 2–4.	**Quadrant III** **Participation activity** **Make a model, chart, graph.** Examples: • The last tip in *Ten Things I Can Do to Help My World* is about recycling. As a class, define the term. • In groups, compare *Ten Things I Can Do to Help My World* with the information in the following books: *We Are Extremely Very Good Recyclers* (Child, 2009), informational storybook; *Recycle: A Handbook for Kids* (Gibbons, 1996), nonfiction; *Where Does the Garbage Go?* (Showers, 1994), nonfiction. • Develop an individual illustrated chart and idea plan for personal/home recycling. • Develop an illustrated poster and idea plan for proposed classroom/school recycling plan.	**LOWER-LANGUAGE LOAD**
CONTEXT-FREE LANGUAGE	**Quadrant II** **Discussion activity** **Interaction is conducted in more informal language.** Examples: • Students are paired and discuss which of the activities from the read-aloud they do at home (Level 1 English learners) and suggest activities that are similar (Levels 2–4). • Class discusses the phrase, "fun and easy eco-tips" from the book cover and tries to come up with a definition for eco-tip and eco-friendly in their own words. • Compare the list of *Ten Things I Can Do to Help My World* with the list of ideas in the endpapers of *We Are Extremely Very Good Recyclers*. Note ideas that are similar or different (Levels 2–4).	**Quadrant IV** **Translation activity** **Transform the content from the previous activities into academic language to state the main idea of the lesson.** Examples: • Present class/school recycling proposal to the other classrooms and to school administrators. • Conduct research on the Internet related to other school and community efforts in recycling.	**HIGHER-LANGUAGE LOAD**

FIGURE 3.4. Curriculum and instruction planning framework moving from social/informal language to academic language. Based on Chamot and O'Malley (1987).

recycling and proposed action plans to accomplish personal, school, and/ or community recycling efforts. Along with the more basic *Ten Things I Can Do to Help My World*, English learners can also explore ideas presented in several other books focused only on recycling including the informational storybook, *We Are Extremely Very Good Recyclers* (Child, 2009, TL3–5, A, F) and two nonfiction books, *Recycle: A Handbook for Kids* (Gibbons, 1996, TL3–5, A, NF) and *Where Does the Garbage Go?* (Showers, 1994, TL2–4, A, NF).

Selecting Books and Instructional Strategies to Reinforce Academic Language

Teachers support the acquisition of academic language through (1) modeling academic language in their instruction and with the literature they use; (2) engaging students in challenging, theme-based curriculum to develop academic concepts; (3) activating and building students' prior knowledge; (4) contextualizing academic language with visuals, gestures, demonstrations, read-alouds, and read-alongs; (5) focusing on strategic thinking, problem solving, and comprehension techniques; (6) organizing collaborative activities with rich oral language opportunities; and (7) using hands-on learning activities that involve academic language (Thomas & Collier, 1995; Reed & Railback, 2003).

Linking trade books to instruction is a way to provide support and reinforcement to English learners. Fiction is an excellent resource to follow up on the lesson and to develop language and content connections. In addition, fiction and folklore offer a story "hook" that adds a personal quality to the study of content. Poetry can set the stage for a content lesson and provide a brief but powerful introduction of new content concepts as well as supplying rich language and visual images to assist with understanding vocabulary terms. For instance, J. Patrick Lewis offers "How Many Humps" in *Doodle Dandies: Poems That Take Shape* (2002, TL2–5, A, P), which helps readers to distinguish the two types of camels, by taking the first letters of their names and turning them on their sides to remember which camel has one hump (Dromedary) or two (Bactrian).

Pairing books or creating text sets is another excellent support technique. For instance, Angus suggests the idea of "perfect pairs" or "two related picture books, a picture book and an informational book, poetry and a book, or other books that go together in some way" (2007, p. 143). An example of a perfect pair might be two of the many books about a baby hippo who "finds" a new mother after a tsunami such as the fiction picture book, *A Mama for Owen* (2007, TL2–4, A, F) by Marion Bauer and the nonfiction book, *Owen & Mzee: The Language of Friendship* (Hatkoff, Hatkoff, & Kahumbu, 2007b, TL3–5, A, NF).

Similarly, Short, Harste, and Burke (1996) describe text sets as collections of books that are conceptually related in some way, such as a common theme or topic. The idea of perfect pairs or text sets is most often used for students to read multiple texts to extend their understanding and to gain multiple perspectives (Lehman & Crook, 1998). With English learners, perfect pairs or text sets may have books with different reading and content levels, which is ideal for the different language proficiencies of the students. Building on the previous perfect pair example of *Owen & Mzee: The Language of Friendship*, teachers might group the following books (listed from simple to more challenging):

- *Mama: A True Story, in Which a Baby Hippo Loses His Mama during a Tsunami but Finds a New Home, and a New Mama* by Jeanette Winter (2006, TL1–2, P, NF)
- *Owen & Mzee: Best Friends* by Isabella Hatkoff, Craig Hatkoff, and Paula Kahumbu (2007, board book, TL2–4, A, NF)
- *Owen & Mzee: A Day Together* by Craig Hatkoff and Isabella Hatkoff (2008, board book, TL2–4, A, NF)
- *A Mama for Owen* by Marion Dane Bauer (2007, TL2–4, A, F)
- *Owen & Mzee: The True Story of a Remarkable Friendship* by Isabella Hatkoff, Craig Hatkoff, and Paula Kahumbu (2006, TL3–5, A, NF)
- *Owen & Mzee: The Language of Friendship* by Isabella Hatkoff, Craig Hatkoff, and Paula Kahumbu (2007b, TL3–5, A, NF)

Some English learners with more developed language proficiency may be able to read all the selections within a set, but others may only be able to access one book or a part of the set. If students are not able to independently read the books chosen to reinforce concepts and academic language, teachers can select excerpts to read aloud and discuss as a class, drawing attention to important words to list on the class word wall. Such text collections are practical for the diverse conceptual and language backgrounds of English learners in a single classroom. Building text sets with nonfiction books is discussed further in Chapter 6.

Krashen and Terrell (1983) were perhaps the first to suggest narrow reading of books by the same author. Extending on that idea, narrow reading can be more broadly defined as reading in only one genre, one subject matter, or the work of one author. This may be the best technique for supporting English learners as it addresses some of the reading difficulties for English learners (Hadaway, 2009). For instance, textbooks such as basals, anthologies, or readers offer a variety of authors, topics, and themes. Such broad reading can be confusing with the presentation of much new vocabulary, repeated introductions to unfamiliar styles, and a lack of context, all resulting in deliberate decoding rather than comprehension. Research suggests it takes 12 encounters with a word in order to improve comprehension (Stahl & Nagy, 2006). So, teachers must plan on providing multiple opportunities and experiences using new vocabulary if they hope to make a difference in students' recognition and understanding of word meaning. Therefore, narrow reading/input may be more appropriate for English learners. "The case for narrow reading is based on the idea that the acquisition of both structure and vocabulary comes from many exposures in a comprehensible context, that is, we acquire new structures and words when we understand messages, many messages, that [we] encode" (Krashen, 2004, n.p.).

One reported benefit of narrow reading is the opportunity for readers to encounter key vocabulary multiple times. Since a topic has its own related vocabulary, narrow reading in that area should help English learners build a network of relationships linking new words and concepts. There are some caveats that teachers should bear in mind concerning the repetition of vocabulary and narrow reading by theme. Gardner (2008) found limited repetition of vocabulary in narrative (fiction) thematic collections. In thematic collections of expository material, there was more repetition of terms in tighter rather than looser themes; for example, predators (tight theme) versus animals (loose theme) or bees versus insects. Although the repetition of vocabulary is not the only benefit of narrow reading, teachers should consider this issue when choosing instructional themes.

In addition, narrow reading can help by the repetition of writing style and format. Each author, for instance, has an individual style—similar syntax patterns and vocabulary choice. Moreover, many authors write extensively in an area so that pairs of books or a thematic collection of books might be organized, thus linking the strength of repeated vocabulary in a theme with a consistent writing style. For instance, Seymour Simon has many books on the planets and the solar system, on weather, and on the human body, any of which could be the starting point for a thematic expository collection. Additionally, Gail Gibbons and Jim Arnosky have multiple titles about various animals. For each of these authors, their books have structural similarities. Both Gibbons and Arnosky make use of detailed and colorful illustrations with labeling of key vocabulary and captions, so that English learners can learn not only content and vocabulary but also important text features.

So, narrow reading provides more context and allows readers to increase their background knowledge, both of which facilitate comprehension. With themes and topics as the emphasis, teachers can maximize the opportunity for transfer of knowledge from one lesson to another. Thematic strands can connect lessons in one subject area or across multiple subjects. It is also possible to link a topic in science, math, or social studies to the language arts via the strategies and activities that are the instructional focus, as well as through fiction or poetry, to add a personal dimension to the content. Literature is easily interwoven into this approach. Whatever the focus, themes and topics offer English learners an immediate network of relationships linking new words and concepts as well as a motivating context for learning.

Genre or subgenre can also serve as a way to organize narrow reading. Nonfiction series books, for instance, such as those published by Franklin Watts (How Would You Survive series, TL4–5, I, NF), Kingfisher (Young Knowledge series, TL3–5, A, NF), and DK (Eyewitness series, TL4–5, I, NF) have a standard organization, and the predictable format helps English learners navigate through the content. Nonfiction subgenre, in particular, lend themselves to narrow reading that can lead to text tapping or write-like activities (Meeks & Austin, 2003). A collection of alphabet books, journals and diaries, question-and-answer books, life cycle books, or the story of . . . books can be used to not only build background knowledge but also to serve as mentor texts (Dorfman & Cappelli, 2007; Ehmann & Gayer, 2009) to support English learners' attempts at similar writing.

In short, narrow reading gives English learners support to continue past the "first few pages effect" (Yang, 2001, p. 452). And, students who read more in a content area acquire more background knowledge of that area and thus, find subsequent reading in that area easier. All the while, they are acquiring more language (Yang, 2001; Brozo & Flynt, 2008). Narrow reading provides for review, repetition, and reinforcement— critical factors in language acquisition.

What does narrow reading look like in the classroom? Figure 3.5 offers an overview of various narrow reading formats such as the use of books by the same author, series books with a similar focus, books with similar subject matter (including different approaches within this format such as stairstep, branching out, and wide angle to close up), and books with similar writing format. Once teachers have chosen a narrow reading

- Books by the same author
- Series books with similar focus
- Books with similar subject matter
- A collection of books with a stairstep approach/layering difficulty levels
- Branching out: Books that help students to explore different facets of a subject
- Wide angle to close up: Books that help students move from general to specific
- Books with a similar writing format (e.g., narrative/expository, journal, question–answer, alphabet, life cycle/timeline/process, the story of . . .)

FIGURE 3.5. Narrow reading formats.

format, the next step is selecting books. In addition to the recommendations that follow, there is an extensive list of example book pairs or text sets for each narrow reading format in Appendix D at the end of this book.

Teachers can use several different ways of organizing books within a thematic narrow reading experience. First, a thematic collection can be organized with a **stairstep** of books, a type of teacher-driven leveling with books that range in difficulty, based on content coverage, issues of length, print, layout, and illustrations, to meet the needs of English learners' different proficiency levels. For example, in a thematic unit on wolves, Jim Arnosky's *Wolves* (2001, TL1–3, A, NF) is a simple overview of one day with a wolf family as they explore, play, eat, rest, and protect each other. With only one sentence per two-page spread, this book is ideal for an initial introduction as a read-aloud to begin discussion or as independent reading once the topic for the lesson has been presented. Stepping up in difficulty is Sandra Markle's *Growing up Wild: Wolves* (2001, TL3–5, A, NF). Beginning with the wolves' birth, the text is divided into half-page color photos with accompanying paragraphs that describe their growth, play, and learning. Next, Seymour Simon's *Wolves* (2009, TL3–5, A, NF) provides even more information in alternating photographs and page-length text that details the family structure and behaviors of wolves. This is just a limited example of the many books that can form the basis of a collection about wolves for English learners to explore. Other outstanding nonfiction authors such as Gail Gibbons and Jean Craighead George have written books about wolves that could be added to this collection, and students can use the content textbook or online resources as well. The premise of this type of collection is to provide books of varying difficulty levels with both overlapping and different information so that English learners have multiple opportunities to encounter new content concepts and vocabulary and thus, to acquire both language and knowledge.

Another thematic format is **branching out** or exploring different facets of a subject. For this organizational format, teachers can start with a word web graphic organizer. Putting a theme, such as desert at the center, the class uses narrow reading to explore the many aspects of deserts including geography in *Desert Trek: An Eye-Opening Journey Through the World's Driest Places* (Le Rochais, 2001, TL2–5, A, NF), desert animals in *Who Lives Here? Desert Animals* (Hodge, 2008, TL2–4, A, NF) or *Dig, Wait, Listen: A Desert Toad's Tale* (Sayre, 2001, TL2–4, A, F), and desert plants in *Desert Giant: The World of the Saguaro Cactus* (Bash, 2002, TL3–5, A, NF). English learners can be grouped in a variety of ways for this exploration. Different groups can be assigned one aspect of the theme and after reading and research, share their findings with the class, or a group can be divided with each member focusing on one part of the theme so that the group explores all the facets of the subject. Throughout the process, the word web can be expanded by adding vocabulary and information that is discovered through reading and discussion.

The final thematic format presented here is **wide angle to close up** or general to specific. Sometimes students want to explore further and this organizational format allows students to do just that. As an example, collective biographies can lead to specialization. Starting with brief portraits of various people, a collective biography such as Bo Zaunders's *Feathers, Flaps, & Flops: Fabulous Early Fliers* (2001, TL3–5, A, NF) might spark a student's interest in one particular person to study in depth, for example, Bessie Coleman, the first African American to earn a pilot's license, spotlighted in *Fly High! The Story of Bessie Coleman* (Borden & Kroeger, 2001, TL3–5, A, NF). Or similar to a collective biography, Seymour Simon's *Animals Nobody Loves* (2002, TL3–5, I, NF) provides an overview of a variety of animals and then the student may choose one unlovable creature to focus on, perhaps through Sandra Markle's *Outside and Inside Rats and Mice* (2008, TL3–5, I, NF).

Conclusion

The gap between English learners' language ability in social and informal settings and their skills in the academically oriented and content-focused school setting poses a challenge. This chapter contrasts two types of language proficiencies needed by English learners in school—social and academic language. While both language types are important, English learners need to move quickly beyond social language only to the academic language needed for school achievement. English learners don't have an extended time frame to acclimate to their new language. They experience great cognitive demands when asked to quickly learn both language and content to participate fully in the school curriculum. In addition to encountering new content concepts in a new language, English learners often find the structure of textbooks confusing and the level of new vocabulary—especially academic terminology—very demanding. Placing meaningful materials in children's hands helps them develop and practice as readers and writers in a new language. As noted in this chapter, literature holds great promise for supporting English learners with their diverse language proficiencies and reading levels, assisting them in actively participating in class, and offering the flexibility to build both social and academic language.

The next chapter begins the second section of this book, one that focuses on three different genre of literature: fiction, poetry, and nonfiction. The first chapter in this section explores fiction and the ways that different types of fiction can meet the language development needs of English learners.

Creativity Begins at Home

PAT MORA

"Who's ready for a story?" the teacher or librarian asks. Don't we all, at any age, enjoy a story, sitting back and listening to someone read to us? I was born in El Paso, Texas, right on the U.S.–Mexico border, the setting for all my formal schooling and for my years as a teacher and university administrator. I've written often of my happy memory of hearing *B Is for Betsy* read to me in elementary school. Amazing what wonderful memories teachers and librarians give us.

I grew up in a bilingual home to bilingual parents and have always spoken two languages. Luckily, my maternal grandmother, who often lived with us, spoke only Spanish. Her first grandchild, I naturally spoke Spanish with her. "Naturally." Isn't it fascinating what the word "natural" means to each of us? Monolinguals tell me they can't imagine having two languages ever present in their brains, and I can't imagine the opposite, nor can I imagine the reality of my Swedish neighbor who spoke five languages. When she moved to New Mexico, she complained that she should have learned Spanish, of course.

Home languages are deeply tied to our sense of identity, a fact we quickly feel when we're surrounded by a language we don't understand, or when we attempt to express our selves in a foreign language, foreign to our tongue. In elementary school, I unconsciously realized that only one of my languages belonged at school. I was a good student but left a lot of myself at home. I didn't use any words in Spanish when I wrote, nor did I probably write about eating cheese enchiladas on Friday night, nor why we called my maternal grandmother "Mamande" and my maternal great-aunt "Lobo" which means "wolf."

Children are wisely self-protective. As I tell children when I visit schools, I didn't want anyone to laugh at my

81

relatives' names, a sad fact that can still happen when I talk about my life story at schools. I've always loved to read and didn't notice in my school years or when I began teaching that the textbooks and library books didn't reflect families like mine.

In my thirties, I was still living in El Paso but was a mom and teaching night courses at a community college. After a few years of occasionally submitting manuscripts for children's books, poetry and essays for publication, I decided to get serious about becoming a writer. I describe my writing journey and what I discovered when I began to make time for writing in my life in a book I recently completed on seven practices for nurturing creativity in ourselves and in our students. I discovered that being bilingual, from a Mexican American family and from the desert were key sources of inspiration. My first children's book, *A Birthday Basket for Tía*, is about the dear great-aunt mentioned above. It seemed fun and natural (that word again) to write about the desert that I suddenly began to really notice when I started writing and, since I consider both the languages I speak beautiful, it seemed natural to write some bilingual books such as *Listen to the Desert/Oye al desierto* and *The Desert Is My Mother/ El desierto es mi madre*. The latter ends with the words, "The desert is my strong mother."

Children do find strength from the positive relationships and experiences including strength in having their home languages and cultures honored in schools and libraries. Sadly, many more children's trade books that reflect our national diversity are needed. I firmly believe that teachers and librarians can be a powerful force for this necessary change.

By selecting evocative and authentic books that reflect the lives of our students, we not only help link them to text, to bookjoy, we also help them discover what I did: that at any age, our native languages and cultures are rich sources for our creative work. Whether we're writing, drawing, painting, or acting, our "roots" can boost us up to express ourselves imaginatively, to flourish.

PART II

SELECTING AND USING BOOKS
WITH ENGLISH LEARNERS

I Know the River Loves Me

MAYA CHRISTINA GONZALEZ

When we see ourselves reflected in our environment, something happens within us. We are calmed, soothed, validated in a way that has no thoughts or words. An osmotic communication that *we are, we belong.* So fundamental that it goes without saying, it is about *being,* being here now.

When I have gone into the classroom, I have had the privilege of working with what I call the "stressed out" kids. Many of whom not only don't see themselves in the white faces in the books at school or in the library, but sometimes not even in the few brown faces that exist. Their experiences are complicated and layered. Beyond their childhood awareness, their lives are rooted in the basic power dynamics of our culture that relate to race and economics and how those dynamics often affect communities and families. They are children, so they are brave and resilient and have taught me a great deal. And they have reminded me of many of my own lessons as a child and much of what my father taught me.

When I was asked to write and not just illustrate children's books I was immediately drawn to share what sustained me as a child. In my first book *My Colors, My World/Mis Colores, Mi Mundo* I began the conversation of finding one's self, one's reflection in nature. My father didn't have words for what he experienced in the United States as a child. When he was 5 years old he was placed in an all-English-speaking school when he spoke only Spanish. There were no bilingual books or teachers or parents. Only him. From his stories I sensed that although he didn't find himself reflected in the dominant culture around him, it was through his relationships with the desert and with animals that he knew his true self and kept himself solid. When I was a child he shared his engagement with nature with me so that I saw it as part of him *and* a part of me. He taught me on a deep level that we belong to the natural world and it is our ally and friend.

My relationship with nature has deepened into my adulthood and I consider the Yuba River one of my close friends. I don't know why it surprised me when she began telling me a story one summer while visiting. Because when I returned home I was asked to write and illustrate another book. I laughed out loud when I realized the river had just told me a tale to tell and I thought of my father and all the kids I could tell, "this is what the river told me."

In *I Know the River Loves Me/Yo Se Que el Rio Me Ama* I share that not only can we find ourselves in nature like in *My Colors, My World/Mis Colores, Mi Mundo*, but that we can have a relationship with her. We can love nature and she can love us back. I believe this is important because there are times when we will not easily fit into a new culture or the power dynamics that affect our lives, but through our awareness of and relationship with nature, we can know that we belong where we are and we are loved at all times. When we sense that we belong in the world we can learn and expand with greater ease and grace. Belonging and love always support our ability to learn, to be and to become empowered beings in a world we can trust is ours.

Nature travels with us. It is the greater reality of the world and is without language, a neutral place where we all live. Nature is beyond stress and beyond the dynamics of culture, community or family. Here in *the river, el rio ...* we are held and free to form new words, new understandings and connections that support our lives. My father did not teach me Spanish. He taught me nature. I dream that if we become aware that we are standing in the power and majesty of nature at all times, we can first see without words, without thoughts. Then open to the power of who we are and reach out for all that we can become. Like it did for my father, nature can hold us and reflect our truest sense of self when the world does not. From this strong place, we can learn with confidence all the languages our hearts and mouths can hold.

Even in urban settings nature is all around us. Like in *My Colors, My World/Mis Colores, Mi Mundo* we must open our eyes extra wide to see the colors around us. If we have never met a river or like many kids do not have the means to visit one, we can still draw our attention to the animals and growing beings around us. Birds and bugs, trees and what we call weeds. There are flowers that grow small and weedy in the most urban of environments. When we see ourselves in nature, love her and notice the ways that she loves us back, it gives us a way to engage with the world around us. The unspoken story about the little girl in *My Colors, My World/Mis Colores, Mi Mundo*, is that she does not see herself in school or library books, but she still needs to see herself. Her keen eye opens to the power and beauty of the brilliant sunset and there she is. Through this she is expanded and able to take flight. At the closing of *I Know the River Love Me/Yo Se Que el Rio Me Ama*, the little girl walks with joy and confidence knowing that her friend is always there waiting for her. The stable and constant love of the river transforms her so that she is part of it.

When we teach I believe we must always begin with ourselves. So in this moment I invite you to become aware of the sky. Are there clouds? Can you feel a breeze? Remember how your hair feels in a soft breeze, a strong wind? Is it raining? Foggy? Snowing? What color is the sky? What's your favorite time of sky? Do you know a river? An ocean? A mountain? A forest? A valley? A lake?

Can you see anything growing? How many colors of green can you see? What about brown or gold? Can you sense the roots below the dirt? How they reach and strive? What color is the earth? Is it moist and dark? Or dry and cracked? Do you have a favorite tree? Or flower? What do your feet feel like walking on the earth?

Do you hear birds? Can you see any? What must it feel like to fly? Do you have an animal friend? Do you love deer? Are you excited when you see a snake? Have you watched a spider web in the breeze? Or ants hard at work?

There is so much to be aware of, to hold us, to love and be loved by. We are a part of all this. And it is a reflection of us. Are you a tree? A sunset? A fish?

Know that you belong exactly where you are. See it all around you. Notice all the ways that nature is loving you right now. Even the air. Thank you for taking this moment.

CHAPTER FOUR

Selecting and Using Fiction with English Learners in Grades K–6

Nana even gave me a new
journal to write in for when I finish this one. She said,
"Never forget who you are and where you are from.
Keep your language and your culture alive in your diary
and in your heart."
—AMADA IRMA PÉREZ, *My Diary from Here to There/
Mi Diario de Aquí hasta Allá*
(Children's Book Press, 2002)

Fiction is a popular genre as children of all backgrounds enjoy escaping or identifying with a good story. And, reading aloud fictional stories is the usual way of introducing students to literature. Consequently, fiction dominates the textbooks published in reading and language arts. However, it is not necessarily the "easiest" genre for English learners to tackle. They may not be familiar with the usual story patterns (beginning, middle, end) or story language ("Once upon a time ...") that dominate American children's literature based on their cultural backgrounds or previous encounters with oral or written stories. It may take longer to engage English learners, if they need to focus on comprehending stories at both the word level and story schema level at the same time. Although it may seem counterintuitive, choosing fiction first for English learners is not necessarily easier reading; hence, this book's chapters on selecting poetry and nonfiction for English learners. However, with proper prior knowledge preparation, students can enjoy many wonderfully told and beautifully illustrated stories that entertain and enrich.

This chapter discusses the benefits of fiction for English learners and the potential of fiction to develop language and literacy. In addition, the chapter highlights issues in selecting fiction for English learners.

Literacy and Language Development of English Learners

Learning to read in another language appears to be influenced by the same set of skills used when learning to read in the first language (Lesaux, Koda, Siegel, & Shanahan, 2006). However, English learners may differ greatly from first-language readers in terms of the linguistic resources they have to bring to the process. Native English speakers arrive at school with quite a head start (Grabe, 2009). They already know 5,000 to 8,000 words orally, and they also have a large store of implicit knowledge about the morphology of their language, how sounds go together within words, most basic syntax structures, and the structure of stories and some other genres. In contrast, it will take English learners several years to develop these understandings, but at the same time, they must begin the process of learning to read while also learning a new language. Yet, English learners who arrive at school as readers in their home language do not have to start over and learn the process of reading again with English. They apply their knowledge of the reading process to their developing knowledge of English. Similarly, "children who arrive in the United States with strong first-language vocabularies have little difficulty acquiring English words. The mechanism widely suggested for this phenomenon is that knowledge of the known concepts need not be reacquired; all that is needed is new labels for those known concepts. In other words, conceptual knowledge is available in the first language and facilitates vocabulary acquisition in the second language" (Snow, 2008, p. 283). Snow further adds that "Use of reading strategies in the first language correlates with their use in the second language once second-language reading has developed sufficiently so such strategies can be used" (pp. 281–282). So, first-language knowledge and literacy development is an asset that some English learners can leverage in their journey to become English proficient.

The importance of creating an instructional environment and routines to foster literacy development is critical, though, since test results indicate that English learners generally underperform their monolingual peers (Lesaux & Geva, with Koda, Siegel, & Shanahan, 2008). Whereas English learners are likely to score in the adequate range on measures of word recognition and spelling, this is not the case on measures of reading vocabulary, comprehension, and writing (Snow, 2008). Yet, there are research-based results that can inform practice. For instance, reading aloud to students in English helps them develop English vocabulary and providing reading materials and time for students to read has also shown positive results on English reading outcomes (August et al., 2008). Grabe (2009) concurs noting that literacy development for English learners requires the development of linguistic knowledge about their new language as well as extensive exposure to texts and experiences and practice with reading in English.

According to Helman (2009, p. 122), a comprehensive emergent literacy curriculum for English learners should include opportunities to

- Experience focused, explicit, and short lessons that develop phonological awareness skills such as rhyming, hearing individual sounds in words, and blending.
- Learn the letters of the alphabet and begin to explore the sounds they represent.
- Develop oral language proficiency, including vocabulary knowledge in English.
- Practice connecting oral language to print.
- Learn to read a core group of important high-frequency words to use in their practice reading.

Since fiction selections are more numerous in core reading programs and because there are so many predictable fiction picture books with repetitive, rhyming language to develop oral language proficiency and phonemic awareness, fiction is a good genre to support the preceding literacy activities for not only emergent readers. Such activities will also assist beginning English learners at Levels 1 and 2 who are already readers in their home language but who need to become familiar with the English alphabet, sound system, and orthography.

Selecting Fiction for English Learners in Grades K–6

Although it may not always be popular to say so, the first criteria in choosing books to share with children should always be whether the book is well written and interesting. From a practical standpoint, students are generally uninterested in books that are didactic, sentimental, or boring. So the traditional literary tools of strong plot, interesting characters, integral setting, worthwhile theme, and captivating style are still useful measures of a book's worth. However, choosing books with our English learners in mind, with their possible cultural differences and with their developing language skills, can prove to be complex. What may be help-ful when choosing fiction for English learners is experimenting with the different types that are currently available and appropriate for English learners in the elementary grades as noted in Figure 4.1.

Picture books dominate the children's book publishing industry, with several thousand new books published each year. Good picture books are highly visual with clear images and plot flow depicted in the pictures. The language should also be clear, direct, and simple, without being contrived, and the topics and experiences depicted either universal or self-contained and self-explanatory within the text and illustrations.

Generally only 32 pages in length, picture books are usually intended for young audiences. Some, however, are so sophisticated and ground-breaking in their content or their art, they are really more appropriate for older readers. This makes them very useful for sharing with English learners who can rely on both visual and textual clues for gaining mean-ing from the story. Moreover, there are several interesting trends with picture books that benefit students learning English as well as reading skills. Advanced technology has now made it possible to reproduce full color art for book illustration leading to very colorful and visually excit-

---

Picture Books

- Wordless Picture Books
- Picture Storybooks
- Global Literature
- Folklore
- Predictable Books

  - Chain or circular story
  - Cumulative story
  - Familiar sequence (alphabet, counting, days of week, etc.)
  - Pattern stories
  - Question and answer
  - Repetition of phrase
  - Rhyme
  - Songbook

Transitional Books and Chapter Books

FIGURE 4.1. Different types of fiction books.

ing book art. There is also greater openness and experimentation in the content of the picture book, from the unusual to the controversial. This means picture books span a broader age and interest level. Thus, students whom we may have once believed too old for picture books, may find these more sophisticated picture books very appealing. Finally, more global literature is also being published—books depicting different cultural groups and perspectives in the United States as well as books originally published in other countries and other languages and then republished in the United States. These books offer topics and themes that may more closely reflect the lives and families of some English learners.

In terms of themes and topics, fiction picture books, just as chapter books or novels, run the gamut. They can deal with contemporary realism including humor, mysteries, sports and survival stories, adventure, animal stories, growing up, dealing with difficulties, and living in a diverse world. On the other hand, picture books can tell fictional stories while weaving in historical facts, people, and places. Historical fiction picture books may be intimidating for English learners if they present unfamiliar historical names, places, events, and terms. Then again, historical fiction may explore a familiar topic; for example, immigration in *Landed* (Lee, 2006, TL4–5, I, F). While English learners may not be familiar with the fact that many Chinese were held at Angel Island until they verified their "stories" of family already in the United States, many can relate to the affective side of immigration, if not through firsthand experience, then through family members. Two promising publishing trends include the increasing number of historical fiction picture books set in other parts of the world that may be home to immigrant students and more historical fiction that features the points of view and experiences of growing up on the "outside." Finally, there are fantasy picture books with imaginary creatures and stories set in different worlds. Similar to historical fiction, fantasy often presents challenges to English learners who may struggle with the imagined worlds, foreign or futuristic settings, animals that act like people, and characters that are imaginary beings or have special powers.

As to format, there are some picture books that have no (or very few) words, and the pictures *are* the book. **Wordless books** generally tell a story—but through illustrations alone. For instance, *Tuesday* (Weisner, 1991, TL2–5, A, F) is a Caldecott Award-Winning book with an imaginative story about flying frogs. The wordless format challenges students to create or narrate their own text. In doing so, English learners develop oral language as they tell the story in their own words and indirectly learn about narrative characteristics such as the beginning, middle, and end of a story. Most wordless books can be used across grade levels, and some have subtle nuances and mature themes that are especially suited for the intermediate grades and beyond as in Jeannie Baker's books (*Window*, 2002, TL2–5, A, F; *Home*, 2004, TL2–5, A, F) about environmental issues. Beyond developing storytelling and oral fluency, wordless books can also provide an excellent opportunity for writing captions and assessing visual literacy.

While illustrations can make stories comprehensible, repeated language patterns and predictable story structure are also support features. "Predictable and patterned stories with repeated refrains ... allow pupils to function quickly as readers of English text" (Savage, 1994, p. 372). In an analysis of **predictable books**, Bridge (1986) found various types of structures within text were used to accomplish the goal of predictability of text including refrain, cumulative, compare–contrast, and episodic or enumerative patterns. More importantly, as teachers examine books for aspects of predictability, they need to keep in mind some measures of predictability and the impact of these on the reader. Hiebert and Raphael (1997, p. 114) classify predictable units by the size of the unit (small = 3–5 words; sizable = 6–10 words; large = 11–15 or more words) and the proportion of the text devoted to the unit (low = less than one-fourth; moderate = one-fourth to one-third; high = one-half to two-thirds; very high = three-fourths or more). The larger the unit and the greater the proportion of the text devoted to the unit, the more the use of predictability will support readers and help them to comprehend the text. Accordingly, beginning English learners need books with large predictable units that account for a large portion of the whole text. As they develop language proficiency, the size and proportion of the predictable unit can decrease.

Although predictable books are designed for younger emerging readers, some lend themselves to use across the grades. Moreover, there are various formats of predictable books including chain or circular stories, cumulative stories, books with a familiar sequence, pattern stories, question-and-answer books, books with repetition of a phrase, rhyming books, and songbooks (Jett-Simpson, 1986). Examples of each format follow.

In the **chain or circular story**, the ending leads back to the beginning as exemplified by *Rabbit's Gift* (Shannon, 2007, TL2–4, A, F). As winter snow approaches, Rabbit goes in search of food and finds two turnips and decides to share one of his turnips. Donkey isn't home, so Rabbit leaves the turnip by the door. Thus begins a chain reaction as Donkey shares with Goat who in turn shares with Deer. Deer completes the circle of generosity by returning the turnip to Rabbit who divides the turnip and shares it with all of his friends to make a "cozy" meal.

In **cumulative stories**, "each time a new event occurs, all previous events in the story are repeated." Simms Taback offers a retelling of one of the most familiar cumulative tales in *This Is the House That Jack Built* (2002, TL2–4, A, F).

Some books are organized by a **familiar sequence**, the alphabet, counting, or days of the week. This sequence gives books a built-in structure as in *Counting Ovejas* (Weeks, 2006, TL1, P, F), a counting book appropriate for Level 1 English learners. When the young boy in this book is unable to sleep, he counts sheep. With each two-page spread, sheep of varying colors appear and then on the opposite page are bid farewell. "Una oveja blanca./ One white sheep./ Adios, oveja blanca!/ Goodbye, white sheep!" In simple rhyming text, *One Is a Drummer: A Book of Numbers* (Thong, 2008, TL2–4, A, F) spotlights Asian culture with text such as "One is a drummer/ One is a race/ One is a dragon boat/ that wins first place!" Multiple sentences on each page and less common vocabulary such as *mahjong, chirp,* and *egg tarts* make this a more appropriate book for Level 2 English learners at the primary and intermediate grades. However, the cultural focus accompanied by the author's notes about some of the items and events noted in the book extend the applicability of this counting book to Level 4 English learners. Days of the week are the familiar sequence featured in *Can You Hear the Sea?* (Cumberbatch, 2006, TL2–4, A, F), a story depicting the daily activities in a contemporary West African village and in *Mrs. Muffly's Monster* (Dyer, 2008, TL2–4, A, F), a humorous tale of an eccentric woman who goes shopping each day and buys large quantities of food leading the neighbors to guess that she has a huge monster at home when in fact, she is just baking an enormous cake for a contest.

Pattern stories have scenes or events that are repeated with some variation. In *The Fish Who Cried Wolf* (Donaldson, 2008, TL2–5, A, F), Tiddler is always late to school, but he always has an excuse that is a great story, which is then repeated to other ocean creatures: ("I *love* Tiddler's story," said Little Johnny Dory,/ and he told it to his granny, who told it to a plaice .../ who told it to a starfish, who told it to a seal,/ who told it to a lobster,/ who told it to an eel ...). One day, Tiddler gets swept up in a fishing net and then is thrown back in the ocean far from home. His stories that have been shared with other ocean creatures eventually help him find his way home. Another example, *If I Were You: A Daddy–Daughter*

Story (Hamilton, 2008, TL2–5, A, F), showcases the amusing back-and-forth exchange between Dad and daughter about what each would do if they were the other person. "Dad sat up and stroked his chin. 'If you were me—now let me see—while you washed up, I'd watch TV!/ Then I could play with Millie mouse, while you made beds and tidied the house!'"

Question-and-answer books have the same or similar question repeated throughout the book. In *Where's My Hug?* (Mayhew, 2008, TL2–5, A, F), Jake turns down a hug from his mother when she drops him off at school. Later, when Jake decides he wants that hug, he discovers that Mom has given it away to Dad, and so on, and he must track down the hug using the same question on each two-page spread: "Where's my hug?" as Jake learns how the hug was passed along from character to character.

Repetition of a phrase throughout a book can punctuate the text in an engaging and sometimes poetic manner. Such is the case in *Oye, Celia!: A Song for Celia Cruz* (Sciurba, 2007, TL2–5, I, F). As the young girl in the book celebrates the music of Cuban singer, Celia Cruz, the author emphasizes the connection of Cruz's music to Cuban and Latino culture using a repeated pattern: "When I hear you, I hear *la tristeza*—Your sadness, my sadness, Our sadness. When I hear you, I hear *la historia*—Your history, my history, Our history."

Stories in rhyme offer predictability and also teach English learners about the sounds of their new language. Two rhyming books by Roseanne Thong, *Red Is a Dragon: A Book of Colors* (2008, TL2–4, A, F) and *Round Is a Mooncake: A Book of Shapes* (2000, TL2–4, A, F), feature Chinese culture and also teach about the concepts of color ("Red is a dragon/ Red is a drum/ Red are the firecrackers—/ Here they come.") and shape ("Round is a mooncake/ Round is the moon/ Round are the lanterns/ outside my room.").

Picture songbooks for the primary grades generally have repetition and a predictable pattern. Moreover, some of them are participation songs with actions that involve students physically, a good language-building technique for English learners. Some good basic songbooks to have on hand in the classroom are *Old MacDonald Had a Farm* (Caberra, 2008, TL1–2, P, F), *If You're Happy and You Know It, Clap Your Hands!* (Carter, 1997, TL1–3, P, F), *Do Your Ears Hang Low?* (Church, 2003, TL1–3, P, F), *The Eensy-Weensy Spider* (Hoberman, 2004, TL1–3, P, F), *Twinkle, Twinkle Little Star* (Long, 2001, TL1–3, P, F), *There Was an Old Lady Who Swallowed a Fly* (Toback, 1997, TL2–4, P, F), *The Wheels on the Bus* (Zelinsky, 1990, TL1–3, P, F), and *Knick Knack Paddywhack* (Zelinsky, 2002, TL1–3, P, F).

Folklore refers to the stories, traditions, customs, and sayings of a group of people that have been passed down by word of mouth from generation to generation. All cultures participate in storytelling, children's chants, gestures, rhymes, riddles, and proverbs. So, all students have some background knowledge of this type of language and activity.

Traditional literature refers to the stories that were initially oral and later written down. As such, they are of such long duration that they cannot be traced to one single person. These stories have no known authors. Instead, they have story adapters or retellers. Many types of traditional literature have been published in trade-book format as highlighted in Figure 4.2. Students can read and listen to the entire range from riddles and rhymes to fables, fairytales, and folk tales, myths, and legends. Moreover, most published traditional literature is in picture-book format, with illustrations that may help cue the reader to important story elements, as well as provide visual cultural details for the story. However, due to the amount of text needed to tell the story, most traditional literature picture books are a better fit for Levels 3–5 proficiency levels.

Childhood folklore is featured in *Yum! Yum!: Delicious Nursery Rhymes* (Fitzgerald, 2008, TL2–4, A, F) with simple and classic rhymes from "Little Jack Horner" to "Peter Piper." These rhymes may work for oral language development and are accessible to Level 2 English learners, but they may make little sense to students. For instance, students may wonder why Jack Horner sticks his thumb in a pie to pull out a plum. Rachel Isadora gives a classic Hans Christian Andersen fairytale an African setting in *The Princess and the Pea* (2007, TL2–4, A, F). With a couple of simple sentences per page, this traditional tale is accessible to English learners at Level 2 and 3 language proficiency. The rest of the examples that follow are best for Level 3–5 English learners. Another well-known

Cumulative tales	Childhood Folklore
Pourquoi tales	• Riddles
Trickster tales	• Jokes
Fairytales	• Puns
	• Jingles
Tall tales	• Chants
Fables	• Jump rope rhymes
Myths	• Tongue twisters
	• Finger plays
	• Hand-clapping games

FIGURE 4.2. Different types of traditional literature and folklore.

folk tale is retold in *Glass Slipper, Gold Sandal: A Worldwide Cinder-ella* (Fleischman, 2007, TL3–5, A, F). Snippets of the many variants of the Cinderella tale are woven together in this book with notations about the origin of each piece of the story in the illustrations. The endpapers have a map with locations marked for each country's lore used in this retelling. Like the global settings of the variations of the Cinderella tale, traditional literature crosses many geographic boundaries from Ghana in *Pretty Salma: A Little Red Riding Hood Story from Africa* (Daly, 2006, TL3–5, A, F), to China in *The Pea Blossom* (Poole, 2005, TL3–5, A, F), a tale of the fate of five peas in a pod, and the Spice Islands in *Priceless Gifts* (Hamilton & Weiss, 2007, TL3–5, A, F), a story describing a trip that teaches two merchants what is valuable. Finally, *Twelve Dancing Princesses* (Isadora, 2007, TL3–5, A, F) is set in Africa and reveals the mystery of how 12 princesses wear out their shoes each evening, suppos-edly without leaving their bedroom.

Across the many different cultural origins and geographic settings of these tales, English learners will encounter similar themes in tradi-tional literature. In *Martina, the Beautiful Cockroach: A Cuban Folktale* (Deedy, 2007, TL3–5, A, F), Martina is ready to find a husband, but prior to beginning the search for a perfect match, Martina's grandmother shares some sage advice on testing the tempers of her suitors. Baba Diakite deliv-ers another tale about suitors in *Mee-An and the Magic Serpent* (2007, TL3–5, I, F). While Mee-An has many suitors, she is searching for a man with no flaws. Eventually, she finds love by overlooking imperfections. Likewise in the British tale, *The Great Smelly, Slobbery, Small-Tooth Dog: A Folktale from Great Britain* (MacDonald, 2007, TL3–5, A, F), a beautiful young woman must overlook the blemishes of the smelly, slob-bery dog that rescues her father from thieves. When she does so and calls him "sweet as honeycomb," the dog rips off his fur to become a handsome prince. Two of the basic functions of folklore are to entertain and to edu-cate as demonstrated in the following tales. For entertainment, *Conejito: A Folktale from Panama* (MacDonald, 2006, TL3–5, A, F) describes how Tia Monica helps Conejito make his way home, outwitting the animals that want to eat him. And for education, *Go to Sleep, Gecko!: A Balinese Folktale* (MacDonald, 2006, TL3–5, A, F) explores how Gecko learns about the connections among all things in nature, and with a serious mes-sage, *Feathers: A Jewish Tale from Eastern Europe* (Forest, 2005, TL3–5, I, F) points out the long-reaching effects of rumors and gossip and as such is a valuable book to share with the intermediate grades.

For primary- and intermediate-grade English learners, Lucy Cous-ins has a collection featuring some of the best-known fairytales in *Yummy:*

Eight Favorite Fairy Tales (2009, TL3–5, A, F). The basic language and bright, clear illustrations make this accessible for Level 3 English learners, but it could be used for read-aloud purposes with Level 1 and 2 students. For intermediate-grade English learners at Level 4 and 5 proficiency, there are several excellent collections of folk tales that teachers might use including *Tales Our Abuelitas Told: A Hispanic Folktale Collection* (Campoy & Ada, 2006, TL4–5, I, F), *The Great Snake: Stories from the Amazon* (Taylor, 2008, TL4–5, I, F), *The Land of the Dragon King and Other Korean Stories* (McClure, 2008, TL4–5, I, F), *Three Minute Tales: Stories from around the World to Read or Tell When Time Is Short* (Mac-Donald, 2004, TL4–5, I, F), and *Five Minute Tales: More Stories to Read and Tell When Time Is Short* (MacDonald, 2007, TL4–5, I, F). The first three collections are focused on stories from specific cultures, and they have some illustrations interspersed throughout the text although they are more general and aesthetic in nature rather than conveying direct meaning. The last two collections, both by Margaret MacDonald, are divided into sections such as participation tales, animal tales, riddle tales, and so forth, and the country or region of origin is noted.

While many picture books and easy readers/beginning-to-read books with their limited vocabulary and regulated sentence length are designed for beginning readers and therefore, useful for beginning English learners at Levels 1 and 2, the expectation is always that English learners will move on to more advanced reading. **Novels** can be effective with English learners once their language proficiency reaches Levels 4 and 5. Even with students still working toward that goal, chapter books and novels can be effective teacher read-alouds. To help move English learners toward the goal of independent novel reading, **transitional books** provide a bridge between picture books and chapter books or novels and thus, are ideal for students whose language and skills enable them to read beyond picture book easy readers, but are not yet ready for full-fledged novels. The reading level of transitional books is "similar to that in many picture books, but the stories are longer and text predominates" (Giorgis & Glazer, 2009, p. 19). Basically, they are beginning chapter books characterized by "short chapters, lively topics, and occasional illustrations" (Mitchell, 2003, pp. 85–86). Such books feature not only brief chapters (2 to 20 pages), but also shorter sentences—typically no longer than 20 words. Typically, the sentences are simple or compound with noun–verb–object structure. Mitchell (2003) notes other common features of these books. Illustrations are often interspersed throughout the text. These illustrations do not share in the meaning construction of the story as in picture books, but add to the interest of the story or help

- *If the Shoe Fits* (Bell, 2008)
- *Alice's Birthday Pig* (Kennemore, 2008)
- *Daisy Dawson Is on Her Way!* (Voake, 2008)
- *Daisy Dawson and the Secret Pond* (Voake, 2009)
- *The Silver Horse Switch* (Horse Crazy Series, Lester, 2009)
- *Horse Crazy* (Horse Crazy Series, Lester, 2009)
- *Martin Bridge: In High Gear* (Kerrin, 2008)
- *Martin Bridge Onwards and Upwards!* (Kerrin, 2009)
- *Clementine's Letter* (Pennypacker, 2008)
- *Ruby Lu, Brave and True* (Look, 2004)
- *Ruby Lu, Empress of Everything* (Look, 2006)
- *A Song for Harlem* (McKissack, 2007)
- *Dear Sylvia* (Cumyn, 2008)
- *The Last Cowboys* (Horse, 2008)
- *The Last Gold Diggers* (Horse, 2008)
- *Gran, You've Got Mail!* (Hoestlandt, 2008)
- *On the Road Again!: More Travels with My Family* (Gay, 2008)

FIGURE 4.3. Suggested transitional books and chapter books.

readers visualize the setting or characters. Authors of transitional books often employ themes that children find delightful or to which they can relate. Use of dialogue and animal characters with human characteristics often play prominent roles in these books. There are also many series books available in transitional and chapter book format. Characters such as Daisy Dawson, Martin Bridge, Clementine, and Ruby Lu can become student favorites. The consistent characters and settings help English learners become comfortable with the longer books and encourage them to engage in independent reading. Figure 4.3 offers a list of a few recent transitional and chapter books that are appropriate for Level 3–5 English learners.

Criteria for Selecting Fiction
for English Learners in Grades K–6

The rich diversity of fiction books offers many instructional choices to teachers, but it is important to take into account some of the special needs of students learning English, in order to choose fiction more selectively and with greater success. Fiction titles that spring from the students' cultures may be helpful in providing familiarity for ease of comprehension as well as for identifying with story characters. Thus, there is an impetus for seeking quality global literature reflecting the many home cultures of students. Students also enjoy other stories with direct, linear plot lines communicated in language that is clear and concrete. Stories full of flashbacks or colloquial expressions can be challenging for many English learners to understand. Finally, many themes in contemporary picture books and novels are appealing to English learners, especially those with themes about fitting in, being different, moving and adjusting, separating from family, seeking one's place in the world, and so forth.

The four basic criteria for matching books to English learners presented in Chapter 2 (level of content familiarity or background knowledge, level of language, level of textual support, and level of cultural fit) have been focused on the selection of fiction in Table 4.1. An in-depth discussion of these criteria and how they have been applied to examples of recently published fiction follows. Using these criteria and guiding questions, teachers can begin to carefully weigh the most appropriate works of fiction to meet English learners' varying language proficiency needs and backgrounds and to encourage language development.

Level of Topic/Theme Familiarity and Background Knowledge

This first criteria, level of topic/theme familiarity and background knowledge, deals with the accessibility and conceptual load of the topic or theme of the fiction text. The more unfamiliar and distant the text's topic or theme, the more difficult it will be for English learners. Again, learning new topics or understanding new themes along with learning them in a new language is a double load. Fiction texts that center around familiar topics, time and money, school, colors, days of the week, months of the year, signs and symbols, food, weather, clothing, family, homes, occupations, and animals furnish fundamental initial reading material that may be more comprehensible to English learners. These types of books provide engaging and "literary" texts for learning basic information and for coping with day-to-day routines in a new language. In addition to a familiar topic or theme, teachers should, of course, choose well-written and well-illustrated literature that will be enjoyable to English learners and lead to close examination and repeated readings so that students can practice their new language. As teachers consider how close a fit the text is to the learner's knowledge or background experiences, they might ask some of the following questions:

- What topics/themes are presented in the fiction text?
- Is this presentation an introduction to the topic/theme or is it continued conceptual development at a higher level?
- What is the English learner's level of familiarity or background knowledge related to the topic/theme? Is the topic or theme very familiar, familiar, unfamiliar, or not common?
- What background knowledge does the English learner have on the topic/theme of the fiction text?
- Has the topic/theme of the fiction text been previously covered in the curriculum? When? At what level? What was the level of success of English learners?
- Is the topic/theme of the fiction text likely to be part of the reader's background experience? How so? How can the teacher best link English learners' previous experiences/understandings to the fiction text?

Everyone has to adjust to different life events, so adjustment and change are familiar topics to most children including English learners. Some excellent books about the changes brought about by new siblings include *Babies Can't Eat Kimchee!* (Patz & Roth, 2007, TL2–3, P, F), suitable for Level 2 English learners, with its simple exploration of what the narrator's baby sister can and cannot do as well as *Rosie and Buttercup* (Uegaki, 2008, TL3–5, A, F), which would be more appropriate for Levels 3 to 5 due to longer text and the humorous plot twist of "giving away" her baby sister to the neighbor so life can return to "normal" with just Rosie, Mother, and Father. In *Martha in the Middle* (Fearnley, 2008, TL3–5, A, F), Martha doesn't have a new sibling, but she does have trouble adjusting to being the middle child. When she runs away, she meets some friends who point out that middle is best; for instance, ripples emerge from the middle, sunflower seeds, peas, and a flower's nectar are all in the middle, and finally, the juiciest part of the watermelon is in the middle.

Other adjustments concern personal adaptations such as overcoming fears. Emily Gravett highlights some potential phobias including fear of spiders and fear of water in *Little Mouse's Big Book of Fears* (2008, TL1–5, A, F) as well as teaching readers about the suffix *phobia*. The illustrations and captions in *Little Mouse's Big Book of Fears* are appropriate for Level 1 and 2 English learners but the focus on the suffix *phobia* and vocabulary study is better for Levels 3 to 5. Melanie Watt's series with *Scaredy Squirrel* (2006, TL3–5, A, F), *Scaredy Squirrel Makes a*

TABLE 4.1. Criteria and Guiding Questions for Selecting Fiction for English Learners in Grades K–6

Criteria	Guiding Questions
Level of topic/theme familiarity and background knowledge How close a fit is the fiction text to the English learner's knowledge or background experiences?	• What topic/theme is presented in the fiction text? • Is this presentation an introduction to the topic/theme or is it continued conceptual development at a higher level? • What is the English learner's level of familiarity or background knowledge related to the topic/theme? Is the topic or theme very familiar, familiar, unfamiliar, or not common? • What background knowledge does the English learner have on the topic/theme of the fiction text? • Has the topic/theme of the fiction text been previously covered in the curriculum? When? At what level? What was the level of success of English learners? • Is the topic/theme of the fiction text likely to be part of the reader's background experience? How so? How can the teacher best link English learners' previous experiences/understandings to the fiction text?
Level of language How close a fit is the fiction text to the English learner's vocabulary, syntactic knowledge, and overall proficiency level?	• What is the vocabulary load of the fiction text (e.g., basic and familiar, sophisticated/advanced and unfamiliar, concrete or abstract, general or technical/specialized, idiomatic, formal or informal, vocabulary with multiple meanings, figurative language)? • How many new vocabulary words are presented? • Does the fiction text present new vocabulary in meaningful contextual language? • How likely is the English learner to encounter the vocabulary in this fiction text in other reading? • What is the English learner's previous experience with the vocabulary of the fiction text (completely new, some exposure, should be part of active vocabulary)? Is the vocabulary currently or likely to be part of the English learner's speaking vocabulary? Listening vocabulary? Reading vocabulary? Writing vocabulary? • If the fiction text is predictable, what is the size of the predictable unit and what percent of the fiction text does the predictable unit account for? • What is the syntactic structure of the fiction text? Word level? Phrase level? Single simple sentences per page? Multiple simple sentences? Short paragraphs with simple sentences? Compound sentences? Complex sentences? Compound/complex sentences? Embedded clauses? • How familiar is the English learner with those syntax patterns? Does the English learner use that syntax pattern in speaking? Writing? • How familiar is the English learner with this genre?

(cont.)

TABLE 4.1. *(cont.)*

Criteria	Guiding Questions
Level of textual support What types of support does the fiction text provide and how familiar is the English learner with these types of text support?	• Are there visuals (photographs or illustrations)? • Are the visuals clear and direct? One-to-one correspondence of visuals to the fiction text? General connection? Primarily for aesthetic purposes? • What types of text features are used? Print style such as bold or italics? Headings and subheadings? Captions and labeling of visuals? Table of contents, index, glossary, author's note? • How familiar is the English learner with these types of text features?
Level of cultural fit How close a fit is the fiction text to the English learner's cultural or experiential background (ethnic, language, geographic, religious, socioeconomic, gender)?	• Is the fiction text culturally neutral (with general diversity portrayed but no focus on a specific group)? Culturally generic (with a group featured but less specific detail provided)? Culturally specific (with explicit details about a group portrayed)? • Does the fiction text reflect the background and/or experiences of recent immigrants? U.S.-born English learners? • Are the characters similar or different than English learners in the classroom? • Have English learners had an experience like one described in the fiction text? • Have English learners lived in or visited places like those in the fiction text? • How far removed is the fiction text from current times? • How close is the main character's age to English learners'? • Is the main character the same gender as the reader? • Do the characters talk like the English learners and their families? • Is this author/author style familiar to English learners?

Friend (2007, TL3–5, A, F), *Scaredy Squirrel at the Beach* (2008, TL3–5, A, F), and *Scaredy Squirrel at Night* (2009, TL3–5, A, F) also explores fears in a humorous way, but in the end, Scaredy Squirrel achieves some success with overcoming his fears. Similarly, *Cottonball Colin* (Willis, 2008, TL2–4, A, F) has a protective mother who worries about the little mouse because he is so small and as a consequence, refuses to allow him to go outside. Under pressure from the little mouse, she wraps him in cotton to protect him and allows him to venture out of the house. While he still ends up having some hazardous experiences, he manages to survive them and grows from the events. Finally, *Alligator Boy* (Rylant, 2008, TL2–4, A, F) is not about fear but boredom. A young boy is bored of being a boy and when he receives an alligator head and tail costume from his aunt, he decides to change. The story follows his daily activities in costume. Although the simple sentences are easy to follow for Level 2 English learners, the fantasy element ("He found his dear dad and told him the story of being a lizard, no longer a boy.") may be confusing.

English learners may identify most closely with the topic of change and adjustment as they adapt to a new language and perhaps, a new country. Immigration may be familiar to English learners, but all means of arriving to a new country may not be so well-known as in the case of *Ziba Came on a Boat* (Lofthouse, 2007, TL2–5, A, F). The simple language of the book explores the events leading up to leaving for a new home as well as the fears along the journey. Not all moves to a new home are as intense as the one portrayed in *Ziba Came on a Boat*, but they still result in change. In *Angelina's Island* (Winter, 2007, TL2–4, A, F), Angelina is homesick for her island home of Jamaica, but when she joins with other immigrants from the West Indies in the Carnival parade in Brooklyn, she begins to feel more connected. Adjusting to new school environments is the focus of *Sunday Chutney* (Blabey, 2009, TL2–4, A, F). Sunday has moved all over the world, which means she has been the "new kid" in school many times. While she is very adaptable, in the end, she wishes "to always have the same home." *Yoko Writes Her Name* (Wells, 2008, TL2–3, P, F) deals not only with adjusting to school but doing so in another language. Initially, her peers make fun of Yoko and her Japanese writing: "Olive whispered to Sylvia./ 'Books go left to right, not right to left!'/ 'Yoko is only pretending to read!' said Sylvia./ 'She'll never make it to first grade!' said Olive." The author also helps readers expand their understanding of the differences between English and Japanese through illustrations on the corners of opposing pages; underneath the left illustration is the English label and the Japanese label is on the right.

In *Children of Immigration*, Carola and Marcelo Suárez-Orozco (2001) suggest that recent immigrants develop identities, ethnic flight, transcultural identity, and adversarial identity based on their styles of adaptation to a new culture and language. Minor examples of ethnic flight might be represented by Unhei (*The Name Jar*, Choi, 2001, TL4–5, A, F), who at first considers adopting an Americanized name that would be easier for her peers at school to pronounce and by Na-Li (*Hannah Is My Name*, Yang, 2004, TL4–5, A, F), who has already changed her name to Hannah. Adversarial identity, in small doses, may come as a result of repeated teasing, name calling, and even fights at school as depicted in *La Mariposa* (Jiménez, 1998, TL3–5, P, F) and in *My Name is Jorge on Both Sides of the River* (Medina, 1999, TL3–5, A, P), where persistent teasing results in Jorge labeling himself "stupid." These examples demonstrate to teachers and to monolingual English peers how difficult transition experiences may cause children to withdraw and feel alienated. Finally, in *I Love Saturdays and Domingos* (Ada, 2002, TL2–4, P, F), a young girl embraces a transcultural identity, successfully navigating two language worlds—one with her paternal grandparents in English and the other with her maternal grandparents in Spanish. Other examples of transcultural identity, positively fusing two language and cultures, are visible in *Papá and Me* (Dorros, 2008, TL2–4, P, F) and *Tomás and the Library Lady* (Mora, 1997, TL4–5, A, F). Additional books that address the topics of immigration and English learners are provided in Appendix A at the end of this book.

Children often have some familiarity with animals and enjoy reading about them, and there are numerous fiction picture books that focus on animals. For instance, *The Zoo* (Lee, 2007, TL1–2, P, F), about a young girl and her parents who visit the zoo, is a very basic book suitable for Level 1 English learners while *Penguins* (Pinchon, 2008, TL2–4, P, F) is a humorous inside look at the zoo as penguins find a lost camera and experiment with taking pictures of each other. The latter book with several sentences per page is more suitable for Level 2 and 3 English learners, but some of the humor may be lost as when "The little penguin puts his flipper on the button and says, 'Everyone look at me and say FISH!'" Another consideration for these books might be whether the English learners have visited a zoo or have learned about zoos and the types of animals portrayed. Two predictable books by Katie Davis explore animal noise and movement using examples and nonexamples. In *Who Hoots?* (Davis, 2000, TL1–3, P, F), the focus is on animal noises. The author presents three options that are false followed by one that is correct: "Who hoots?/ Dogs don't hoot./ Pigs don't hoot./ Horses don't hoot./ Owls don't hoot./ Yes, they do!" The author uses a similar pattern in *Who Hops?* (Davis, 1998, TL1–3, P, F) only with three correct options and one incorrect: "Who hops?/ Frogs hop./ Rabbits hop./ Kangaroos hop./ Cows hop./ No, they don't." Both of these books would be appropriate for Level 1 and 2 English learners although there are some humorous side notes on pages that again may not register with students in the beginning language proficiency stages. In *Where's My Mom?* (Donaldson, 2008, TL3–5, A, F), a butterfly tries to help a little monkey find his mother. "Let's have a think. How big is she?"/ "She's big!" said the monkey. "Bigger than me."/ "Bigger than you? Then I've seen your mom./ Come, little monkey, come, come, come." Each time the monkey describes his mother, the butterfly jumps to a wrong conclusion until eventually monkey and mother are reunited. Through the patterned format, however, readers learn about the appearance and behaviors of many animals. *I Feel a Foot!* (Rinck, 2008, TL2–4, A, F) also features descriptions of animals, or at least part of the animal. Five animals hear a noise in the dark and go to explore. Each feels a part of the animal's body and makes guesses, albeit incorrect ones, about what the animal is. These last two books are a good match for Level 2 and 3 English learners.

Animal friendships are the focus of *Elephants Never Forget* (Ravishankar, 2008, TL2–4, A, F) when a young elephant is separated from his herd and joins a group of water buffaloes. In the end, the elephant must choose to stay with his friends, the water buffaloes, or go back to live among the elephants. While water buffaloes may not be a common animal to English learners, they can certainly relate to the ideas of being separated from those who are familiar and then bonding with new friends. Friendships between humans and animals are addressed in many books such as *My Cat Copies Me* (Kwon, 2007, TL1–3, P, F) that depicts the relationship of a young girl and her pet cat or *Dogfish* (Shields, 2008, TL2–4, A, F) about a boy who would like a dog but makes the most of his goldfish as he "trains" the goldfish to "catch sticks, or go for walks, or sit by your feet." Both the title and the humor may be difficult for beginning English learners, but the language is accessible to Level 2 English learners. In a similar humorous vein, *What Pet to Get?* (Dodd, 2008, TL2–4, A, F) shares a young boy's outlandish suggestions for housepets ("I think we should get an elephant," he announced. "I could ride it to school."). Through his ideas, readers learn what is and is not a good house pet: "An elephant would be nice, dear," said Mom, "but not very practical." English learners may wonder why someone would even suggest some of the animals as pets, however, if they are still in the very literal stage of language acquisition. Finally, in *I Completely Know about Guinea Pigs* (Child, 2008, TL3–5, A, F), Lola shares quite a few facts about guinea pigs when she brings home the class guinea pig for the weekend. Even though these books are fiction, they offer readers a hook to a familiar topic, animals, and then present additional information to build existing knowledge. Linking the many fiction books about animals with the scores of nonfiction books available, through perfect pairs or text sets as described in Chapter 3, is a good technique to provide even more background information developing both content and language.

Many picture books address the familiar topic of manners and social behaviors. A good book for a basic overview is Laurie Keller's *Do unto Otters: A Book about Manners* (2007, TL2–5, A, F), suitable for Level 2 and 3 English learners. Rather than multiple behaviors, authors may choose to focus on only one positive example as in *Rabbit's Gift* (Shannon, 2007, TL2–4, A, F), a wonderful folktale about sharing or *The Story Blanket* (Wolff, 2008, TL2–4, A, F) as Babba Zarrah shares all the wool from her prized blanket to knit socks, a scarf, and mittens for others in need. On the other hand, authors may compare positive and negative examples of behaviors as in *Please Don't Tease Tootsie* (Chamberlain, 2008, TL1–4, A, F), *Bad Kitty* (Bruel, 2005, TL2–5, A, F), and *Ping Pong Pig* (Church, 2008, TL2–4, A, F) when the pig fixes all the problems he created to make up for his thoughtless behavior while he played and his friends worked.

Winter weather is the focus of another pair of books. *The Snow Day* (Sakai, 2009, TL1–3, P, F) depicts the quiet day at home that bunny and Mother enjoy because school is closed and Father's flight is cancelled due to the inclement weather. The simple language and text make this accessible to Level 1 and 2 English learners. Because it has not snowed for several years, *Anna's Wish* (Hächler, 2008, TL3–5, A, F) is for snow. When snow finally falls, Anna is ready with a sled she has found in the basement. Indirectly related to a snow day is the book, *Holly's Red Boots* (Chessa, 2008, TL1–2, P, F), a basic book also appropriate for Level 1 and 2 English learners. Holly is ready to go out and play when it snows, but her mother tells her she must put on her red boots. The rest of the day is spent searching for the boots and discovering many other "red" things instead.

Clothing and food are universal topics, but their presentation in books may not always be that simple for English learners, or the terms used may not build basic vocabulary needed in the initial stages of language acquisition. *New Clothes for New Year's Day* (Bae, 2007, TL2–4, A, F) highlights traditional Korean clothing that a young girl puts on to celebrate New Year's Day. Terms such as *sash* or *embroidery* are not the most common and useful clothing vocabulary. Thus, this book may be better for cultural exposure than vocabulary development. And, in *No! That's Wrong!* (Ji & Xu, 2008, TL1–3, P, F), the rabbit has a new use for a pair of underpants that float off the clothesline. He thinks they are a hat. It makes sense to the rabbit, but may confuse English learners at the beginning level, which is the language level of this book. Finally, imaginary food items such as yak yogurt, warthog, and mashed monkey with fried rice are presented in *Bad Kitty* (Bruel, 2005, TL2–5, A, F) and *Fussy Freya* (Quarmby, 2008, TL3–5, A, F). The purpose and humor of these invented foods are best for Level 3–5 English learners who can understand that the author's intent is not to teach labels for food but to make a point about something else, fussy eating habits.

There are many fiction books that appear similar to nonfiction in that they present concepts and information but do so with fictional characters or events. Such books offer excellent opportunities to support academic concept and language development. *My Map Book* (Fanelli, 2007, TL1–3, P, F) is a simple collection of maps of a child's world; "my bedroom," "my family," "map of my day" (timeline), "map of my neighborhood," and thus, is an excellent introduction to maps for English learners. *I Am Latino: The Beauty in Me* (Pinkney & Pinkney, 2007, TL2–4, A, F) is a visual and simple presentation to the five senses, but each one is connected to what young Latino children might see, hear, smell, feel, and taste. For instance, the author tells readers: "feel my music explode" and offers as an example "hip-swinging salsa." To build on this musical form, teachers might share *Oye, Celia!: A Song for Celia Cruz* (Sciurba, 2007, TL2–5, I, F), a celebration of the Cuban singer's salsa music. Both books intersperse Spanish terms within the English text. In *Shadows* (Sayre, 2002, TL2–4, A, F), the author offers a simple story in rhyme about shadows: "We outline shadows with a piece of chalk./ But later they've moved on the hot sidewalk." Somewhat more challenging is Sayre's *Dig, Wait, Listen: A Desert Toad's Tale* (2001, TL2–4, A, F). With onomatopoeia, personification, and lyrical language, the author describes the life cycle of the desert toad. History is the focus of *Wind Flyers* (Johnson, 2007, TL3–5, I, F), which is about a fictional character whose love of flying takes him to new heights in World War II as a Tuskegee Airman. The historical setting and the text make this book more suitable for Level 3–5 English learners. Finally, environmental issues are the focus of *Winston of Churchill: One Bear's Battle against Global Warming* (Okimoto, 2007, TL2–5, A, F), which blends facts about global warming with a protest led by the polar bears.

In Chapter 6, several types of nonfiction literature are described including journals and diaries. While there are nonfiction journals and diaries published for young readers, there are also many that merge fact and fiction as with *Sir Reginald's Logbook* (Hammill, 2008, TL4–5, A, F) about an imaginary jungle expedition, *Sienna's Scrapbook: Our African American Heritage Trip* (Parker, 2005, TL4–5, I, F), *Rachel's Journal: The Story of a Pioneer Girl* (Moss, 2001, TL4–5, I, F), and *Archie's War: My Scrapbook of the First World War, 1914–1918* (Williams, 2007, TL4–5, I, F). The amount of text in each of the examples and the historical information in the last three books cited make all of these fictionalized journals more appropriate for Level 4 and 5 English learners in the intermediate grades.

Level of Language

The second criteria, level of language, deals with the language load or accessibility of text to English learners of varying proficiency levels. The more unfamiliar and advanced the vocabulary and syntactic structures in the text, the more difficult it will be for English learners. Teachers need to find a good fit of text to the English learner's current proficiency level, but to also find books that will build language abilities. For instance, predictable books with repetition, rhyme, and pattern formats are excellent for beginning English learners. Therefore, teachers must consider the following areas of language:

- What is the vocabulary load of the fiction text (e.g., basic and familiar, sophisticated/advanced and unfamiliar, concrete or abstract, general or technical/specialized, idiomatic, formal or informal, vocabulary with multiple meanings, figurative language)?
- How many new vocabulary words are presented?
- Does the fiction text present new vocabulary in meaningful contextual language?
- How likely is the English learner to encounter the vocabulary in this fiction text in other reading?
- What is the English learner's previous experience with the vocabulary of the fiction text (completely new, some exposure, should be part of active vocabulary)? Is the vocabulary currently or likely to be part of the English learner's speaking vocabulary? Listening vocabulary? Reading vocabulary? Writing vocabulary?
- If the fiction text is predictable, what is the size of the predictable unit and what percent of the fiction text does the predictable unit account for?
- What is the syntactic structure of the fiction text? Word level? Phrase level? Single simple sentences per page? Multiple simple sentences? Short paragraphs with simple sentences? Compound sentences? Complex sentences? Compound/complex sentences? Embedded clauses?
- How familiar is the English learner with those syntax patterns? Does the English learner use that syntax pattern in speaking? Writing?
- What is the genre of the fiction text?
- How familiar is the English learner with this genre?

Authors assist English learners in their comprehension of text in the initial stages of language acquisition by using familiar vocabulary and simple text at the word, phrase, or basic sentence level as in Suzy Lee's *The Zoo* (2007, TL1–2, P, F). All the while, teachers need to be searching for books that also encourage English learners to move from more basic to more sophisticated word use. Again, authors use supportive techniques to accomplish this goal. Some authors focus on one topic as with Emily Gravett's *Little Mouse's Big Book of Fears* (2008, TL1–5, A, F). This examination of different fears introduces the suffix *phobia*, and some sophisticated vocabulary including *hydrophobia* and *arachnophobia*. These words appear at the top of the page (*arachnophobia*) with a simple definition ("fear of spiders") followed by Little Mouse's personalized examples and illustrations underneath: "I'm scared of creepy crawlies (especially spiders!)." Likewise, in Laurie Keller's *Do unto Otters: A Book about Manners* (2007, TL2–5, A, F) different behaviors from cooperation to friendly are defined with examples and illustrations as in "I'd like otters to be FRIENDLY./ A cheerful hello,/ a nice smile,/ and good eye contact/ are all part of being friendly." And, descriptions of various facets of friendship are explored with simple text but mature insights in *A Friend* (Bley, 2009, FL2–5, A, F); for example, "Someone who is there .../ whenever I need help. But who doesn't try to help .../ when I want to do things on my own." The ideas about friendship are continued on the endpapers of the book. Authors may also use synonyms and antonyms to make their point as with *Please Don't Tease Tootsie* (Chamberlain, 2008, TL1–4, A, F). The author opens with some new, more sophisticated vocabulary cautioning the reader not to *tease, provoke, madden, disturb, bully,* and *wind up* pets. Then, antonyms or opposite behaviors are introduced such as *pamper* and *dote on*. The simple sentence structure of this text makes it appear a good match for Level 1 English learners, but the more sophisticated vocabulary may actually be a better fit for students at Level 2 or 3 proficiency. Finally, *My First Ramadan* (Katz, 2007, TL2–4, A, F) has many unfamiliar terms related to the celebration of this holiday but the author uses contextual support as in this clear definition of fasting: "For one month Muslims will fast from sunup to sundown. That means they will not eat or drink anything all day long."

Sometimes authors use unfamiliar terms, but they may not interfere with overall comprehension of the text. For instance, in *Angelina's Island* (Winter, 2007, TL2–4, A, F) Angelina is homesick for her island home of Jamaica causing her to "dream about mangos, guavas, papayas, green bananas, star apples, breadfruit, callaloo, chocho, johnnycake, sugarcane, ackee, and salt fish." Some of these foods may be unknown to English learners, but they do not need to have a full understanding of the items in order to understand the general point the author is making. The majority of these terms are not ones that English learners will be adding to their active vocabulary. However, *Buttercup's Lovely Day* (Beck, 2008, TL3–5, A, F) features the poetic musings of a cow. The language is sophisticated, and thus, challenging to English learners, particularly so because the illustrations are general. For instance, on one page, Buttercup shares "I love the fields/ we ramble and graze,/ lazy, languorous,/ lingery long days./ I follow the dips/ and jogs/ of the fence,/ the roll of the hills,/ and a thousand scents." This vocabulary is the type that is needed for English learners to move from the basic language of Levels 1 and 2 to proficiency Level 3 and beyond.

Some books use distinctive language such as dialect. When done well, it can really make a story "sing," and flavors the text with the voice of its people. Phyllis Root uses a down-home twang in *Big Momma Makes the World* (2002, TL2–5, A, F) with text such as the following: "Next day Big Momma looked around some more and she said, 'Got me some light, got me some dark, but I still can't tell what time of day it is. How am I gonna know when it's morning? Evening?' " Too, Black Vernacular English (BVE), or black dialect, is used in some African American literature as in Ann Grifalconi's *Ain't Nobody a Stranger to Me* (2007, TL4–5, I, F) when Gran'pa describes his flight to freedom. "We was coming close to the Ohio River, close to freedom! But bein' too tired an' hungry to go another step, we picked us out a barn nearby to hide inside." Dialect can be difficult for those outside the culture to follow, especially for English learners. Teachers may have to read a book aloud to help students follow the story. For English learners at Levels 3–5, teachers can discuss pronunciation variations and how an author uses language to create distinctive and authentic characters.

In terms of syntax, longer, more complex sentences can be challenging for beginning English learners, so authors sometimes divide text into manageable chunks such as phrases. This is especially helpful in a series of items to give each one emphasis. In *What Should I Make?* (Nayar, 2009, TL1–3, P, F), ideal for primary-grade Level 1 English learners, readers can follow the three simple steps: "Neeraj rolled the dough into a ball./ He patted it down, poked in two tiny eyes, and pulled out a nose./ At the other end came a long tail." The clothing may be unfamiliar to students in *New Clothes for New Year's Day* (Bae, 2007, TL2–4, A, F), but the instruction like text, divided into step-by-step phrases, explaining how to put on the clothing items, will help readers understand the process of dressing in these traditional Korean items: "Hold one side in each hand, then/ arms spread wide, wrap the crimson skirt around,/ take the sash and tie a knot." Finally, not all sentences in a book may be divided into smaller chunks, but occasional use of this technique can break up the text for the reader making it more comprehensible as in *Cottonball Colin* (Willis, 2008, TL2–4, A, F) when he explains to his mother: "I got wet. I got cold./ I got pecked./ I got chased./ But I swam,/ and I ran, and I jumped and .../ Mama, I'm ALIVE!" This listing of activities also serves as a summary of the previous few pages, and thus, is a nice review for comprehension purposes.

As noted earlier, predictable books with repetitive language are a strong support for English learners. The different formats for predictable books such as chain or circular stories, cumulative stories, books with a familiar sequence, pattern stories, question and answer books, books with repetition of a phrase, rhyming books, and songbooks help English learners in different ways. For instance, stories with rhyme can focus English learners on the sounds of their new language, stories with strong repetition help students master new vocabulary and sentence patterns, and stories with circular or pattern stories teach the reader about problems or events that move the plot forward within the story structure. Also, predictable books often serve as good mentor texts for writing models. *If I Were You: A Daddy–Daughter Story* (Hamilton, 2008, TL2–5, A, F) has a predictable back-and-forth dialogue between Dad and daughter as each share what they would do if they were the other person. After reading such books and discussing the patterns, the teacher can lead the class in a whole-class brainstorming for a class book or break the class into small groups for a guided writing exercise to write like the book.

Level of Textual Support

Next, teachers must consider the level of text support or accessibility. According to research by cognitive psychologists, the way texts are structured influences meaning-making (Beck et al., 1984; Stein & Glenn, 1979). For beginning English learners at Levels 1 and 2, in particular, books should have strong text support. Fiction has fewer text support features than nonfiction, but there are still some such features in fiction, and teachers can use these guiding questions for assistance:

- Are there visuals (photographs or illustrations)?
- Are the visuals clear and direct? One-to-one correspondence of visuals to the fiction text? General connection? Primarily for aesthetic purposes?

- What types of text features are used? Print style such as bold or italics? Headings and subheadings? Captions and labeling of visuals? Table of contents, index, glossary, author's note?
- How familiar is the English learner with these types of text features?

The illustrations and photographs in children's books serve as one source of text support, especially when there is one-to-one correspondence of visuals to the text as in *My Map Book* (Fanelli, 2007, TL1–3, P, F), a picture book of different maps with illustrations and labels only, or when they aid in conveying the storyline and relaying information as in the step-by-step dressing sequences of *New Clothes for New Year's Day* (Bae, 2007, TL2–4, A, F). Illustrations that are mainly decorative are not supportive and do not make a text more accessible. In fact, they may lead English learners astray in their attempts at "reading the illustrations" along with the text. And, even clear illustrations can be misconstrued. For example, in *Who Made This Cake?* (Chihiro, 2008, TL1–2, P, F), the simple text and illustrations, appropriate for Level 1 English learners, depict tiny people who make cakes with construction equipment. While the language and text are clear, the idea that dump trucks are adding flour and cranes with whisks are mixing dough may not register with English learners.

In addition to illustrations or photographs, the style of print, bold, italics, or all capital letters also provide support by drawing attention to important words. Beatrice Boutignon's *Not All Animals Are Blue: A Big Book of Little Differences* (2009, TL1–4, A, F) is a wonderful example of visual literacy and visual text support. The two-page spreads explore five illustrations of the same type of animal, but each is dressed or behaving differently. To the left of the illustrations, questions and statements ask readers to use key words to match the animals with the phrase. Key words are emphasized by larger font and color. For example, a page titled "Five Penguins on Parade" has these questions to the left: "Who is always eating?" referring to the penguin with a fish in its mouth and "Is there a King?" referring to the penguin wearing a crown. Likewise in *Do unto Otters: A Book about Manners* (Keller, 2007, TL2–5, A, F), the pages are somewhat busy but the important words are in all capital letters or large font. And, *Shadows* (Sayre, 2002, TL2–4, A, F), a simple story in rhyme about shadows, has some subtle meaning cues, for instance, the word *hot*, in red font.

In other stories, reading the illustrations is key to comprehending since the visuals carry as much information as the text. In *Millie in the*

Snow (Steffensmeier, 2008, TL2–4, A, F), Millie is a mail cow; she helps the mail carrier deliver packages. On Christmas Eve, the pair finish their route and the mail carrier sends Millie home with gifts for her and her friends on the farm. The reader initially sees the gifts as the mail carrier made them and intended them, but on the way home, Millie has an accident in the snow and all the presents are jumbled leading to some surprising variations in the gifts such as a coffeepot cover that becomes an udder warmer.

Wordless books offer the ultimate illustrated experience for students since the story is told entirely through the sequence of illustrations. Barbara Lehman has created several wordless books including *The Red Book* (2004, TL2–5, A, F) about a magical book with pages that characters enter and set out on an adventure, *Museum Trip* (2006, TL2–5, A, F), which depicts a young boy on a field trip who becomes separated from his class and subsequently enters the mazes in the pages of a drawing in the museum, and *Rainstorm* (2007, TL2–5, A, F) about a rainy day adventure with a mysterious key that leads to a magical journey to an island lighthouse. David Wiesner is another illustrator who has created numerous wordless books including *Tuesday* (1991, TL2–5, A, F), *Free Fall* (2008, TL2–5, A, F), and *Flotsam* (2006, TL2–5, A, F).

In addition to these wordless books that tell a story through illustrations only, there are some fiction books that have wordless sections interspersed with sections of text as in Suzy Lee's *The Zoo* (2007, TL1–2, P, F), which has wordless two-page color spreads that depict the "dream" zoo experience of the little girl who gets separated from her parents, *How to Heal a Broken Wing* (Graham, 2008, TL1–3, P, F) with its multiple boxed pictures and wordless pages that furnish most of the story about rescuing an injured pigeon, and *In the Town All Year 'Round* (Berner, 2008, TL1–5, P, F), which has one page of questions and events preceding a series of wordless pages for each season where those events unfold. *The Red Rock: A Graphic Fable* (Nitto, 2006, TL2–5, A, F) has a wordless, graphic section depicting Old Beaver convincing land developers to think about the environment and the consequences of a proposed construction project. This book could be linked to two wordless books by Jeannie Baker with environmental messages: *Window* (2002, TL2–5, A, F), which shows the 20-year change of a rural setting into urban sprawl and decay and *Home* (2004, TL2–5, A, F), which portrays the gradual reclamation of an urban neighborhood. Teachers can connect Maya Gonzalez's *I Know the River Loves Me/ Yo se que el rio me ama* (2009, TL1–3, P, F) for an additional message about nature.

When authors divide text into manageable chunks as discussed in the previous section on language, there are often illustrations that accompany each phrase and provide text support. Readers encounter this level of structured text support in *New Clothes for New Year's Day* (Bae, 2007, TL2–4, A, F) as the young girl adds each layer of clothing, page by page, and in *What Should I Make?* (Nayar, 2009, TL1–3, P, F) as Neeraj takes the dough and rolls it and pinches it to make the various shapes, and finally, in *Ping Pong Pig* (Church, 2008, TL2–4, A, F) as the pig repays his friends by fixing all of the disarray he created during the day: "He picked the apples …/ caught the bees …/ repainted the barn …/ and carefully stacked all the hay." In contrast to breaking up the text to simplify, Michael Foreman in *Mia's Story: A Sketchbook of Hopes and Dreams* (2006, TL2–5, A, F) adds additional information similar to the multiple layers of nonfiction text discussed in Chapter 6. The storyline is in regular font and then cursive writing is used for captions or labels for the illustrations. For instance, on a two-page spread, Foreman writes that "Mia's village is called Campamento San Francisco and is somewhere between the big city and the snowy mountains." Then, he adds four illustrations, similar to sketches as noted in the title, with captions or labels that provide "snapshots" of the village.

Graphic aids such as charts, graphs, and maps are associated more with nonfiction than fiction but some fiction books also use these features. The Scaredy Squirrel books have some interesting formatting that make these humorous books more accessible to readers such as numbered lists, "Scaredy Squirrel's Guide to Building a Safe Beach" with six items (paper and crayons, 1 inflatable pool, 1 plastic flamingo, etc.) and six activities ("1. Draw beach scenery." "2. Use stick to hold upright.") to create an imaginary beach in *Scaredy Squirrel at the Beach* (Watt, 2008, TL3–5, A, F) or a set of boxed examples, illustrations, and labels for the "Benefits of a Good Night's Sleep May Include: energy gain, sharper memory,…" in *Scaredy Squirrel at Night* (Watt, 2009, TL3–5, A, F). In many ways, this series of books is a compilation of graphics more than narrative text and thus, helps to develop English learners' comfort and skill level with graphic aids.

Other examples of graphics in fiction books occur in *Dig, Wait, Listen: A Desert Toad's Tale* (2001, TL2–4, A, F) as April Sayre offers support for the unfamiliar information on this animal's life cycle with boxed illustrations ascending the page showing the development from tadpole to frog. And, at the end of *New Clothes for New Year's Day* (Bae, 2007, TL2–4, A, F), there is a diagram of the traditional clothing with numbered items labeled and described with short phrases. Finally, text support can extend beyond the end of the book and onto the endpapers. In *Noko's Surprise Party* (Moodie, 2008, TL3–5, A, F), there is a map of the route that Takadu takes in the story. This can be used as a reference when reading the story independently or reading it aloud to the class.

Book format can also provide textual support for comprehension as in *Bad Kitty* (Bruel, 2005, TL2–5, A, F). Similar to four complete alphabet books, there are four sets of boxed illustrations depicting first the A–Z unacceptable food items, such as "asparagus" and "beets," when Kitty's owner runs out of cat food and next, the A–Z bad behaviors of Kitty ("Clawed the curtains/ Damaged the dishes") while the owner goes to the market. These are followed by an A–Z of foods that Kitty's owner brings home that result in a happy cat and then another set of ABCs of good feline behaviors. The format provides a strong structure for comprehension even though many of the food items are uncommon or imaginary ones that may not be familiar to students.

Level of Cultural Fit

The final criteria is the level of cultural fit or cultural accessibility. Teachers need to select books that are both culturally relevant, connected to the lives of English learners, and books that will be understandable to those outside the culture. The following guiding questions can help begin the process of examining the level of cultural fit:

- Is the fiction text culturally neutral (with general diversity portrayed but no focus on a specific group)? Culturally generic (with a group featured but less specific detail provided)? Culturally specific (with explicit details about a group portrayed)?
- Does the fiction text reflect the background and/or experiences of recent immigrants? U.S.-born English learners?
- Are the characters similar or different than English learners in the classroom?
- Have English learners had an experience like one described in the fiction text?
- Have English learners lived in or visited places like those in the fiction text?
- How far removed is the fiction text from current times?
- How close is the main character's age to English learners'?
- Is the main character the same gender as the reader?

- Do the characters talk like the English learners and their families?
- Is this author/author style familiar to English learners?

Even with the preceding guiding questions, considering cultural fit can be challenging for many reasons. First, teachers need a basic cross-cultural awareness in order to spot potential problems as in *Do unto Otters: A Book about Manners* (Keller, 2007, TL2–5, A, F), which presents characteristics of being friendly as "A cheerful hello,/ a nice smile,/ and good eye contact." Yet, good eye contact is more an American expectation than in some other cultures. Also, there is the issue of the "cultural conglomerate" (Yokota, 1993). There are significant differences between Chinese and Japanese cultures, for example, within the category of Asian American or between Cubans and Mexicans within the category of Latino. Too, there are students from bicultural backgrounds as with Alvina in *My Two Grannies* (Benjamin, 2008, TL3–5, A, F) who has a grandmother from the Caribbean and a grandmother from England. So, even those students within a culture/cultures may not find some books authentic representations of their lives. Finally, according to Bishop (1997), a literature collection that truly reflects our global village should include books that highlight the diversity that is part of all groups. Therefore, culturally relevant literature should not reflect only cultural and ethnic diversity but should also include the following (Beaty, 1997; Bishop, 1997):

- People of varying socioeconomic circumstances, occupations, lifestyles
- Differing perspectives on issues and events
- Nonfiction that provides factual information about a people and their way of life
- A balance of urban versus rural settings and of historical versus contemporary portrayal
- Detailed illustrations that avoid stereotypes
- Language or dialect that shows a respect for culture
- Characters from different cultures who interact with one another
- Recent immigrants as well as U.S.-born English learners

In the end, the point is to choose culturally relevant books, and to choose well. To do this, teachers must first become aware of the authors and titles available. To help with this task, teachers can explore the book awards that spotlight outstanding works by authors of color (Coretta Scott

King Award, John Steptoe Award, and Pura Belpré Award) or works that accurately portray the experiences of particular groups (Americas Award, Carter G. Woodson Award, National Jewish Book Award, Sydney Taylor Book Award, and Tomás Rivera Award) as well as more comprehensive booklists such as the Notable Books for a Global Society (NBGS). The NBGS recognizes a wide range of perspectives from both within and outside the United States with books that enhance understanding of people and cultures throughout the world. The Outstanding International Booklist (a project of the U.S. Board on Books for Young People, a division of the International Board on Books for Young People) spotlights the best children's literature from other countries that have been subsequently published in the United States.

Books with specific cultural detail about religious and cultural celebrations (*My First Ramadan*, Katz, 2007, TL2–4, A, F; *Sawdust Carpets*, Carling, 2005, TL4–5, I, F; and *The Best Eid Ever*, Mobin-Uddin, 2007, TL4–5, I, F), historical issues (Japanese internment camps in *A Place Where Sunflowers Grow*, Lee-Tai, 2006, TL3–5, I, F; and the bonfire signal system in *The Firekeeper's Son*, Park, 2004, TL2–5, A, F), art forms (wood carving in *Julio's Magic*, Dorros, 2005, TL4–5, I, F; floor art in *Romina's Rangoli*, Iyengar, 2007, TL4–5, I, F; and Japanese picture storytelling in *Kamichibai Man*, Say, 2005, TL3–5, I, F), and such may be more challenging to English learners, especially in the early stages of language acquisition, while books with universal themes and topics are more likely to provide a general cultural fit and be more accessible. For instance, themes of identity, family, acceptance, and cultural heritage are familiar across cultures and may have a natural relevance for English learners as well as for their native English-speaking peers. While specific elements of culture in some of these books, such as mask dancing and salsa music, may be unfamiliar to some students, the overall themes of family life, pride in one's background and heritage, or accepting others should be understandable to English learners. For instance, in *Behind the Mask* (Choi, 2006, TL3–5, A, F), a young Korean boy connects to his grandfather's past as a Korean mask dancer by wearing his grandfather's mask for Halloween, and in *Oye, Celia!: A Song for Celia Cruz* (Sciurba, 2007, TL2–5, I, F), a young girl celebrates the salsa music of Cuban singer Celia Cruz.

Many English learners maintain close connections with family members in their country of origin or that of their parents, and several books depict visits with relatives and communicating across language barriers. In *Sitti's Secrets* (Nye, 1997, TL3–5, A, F), a young girl visits her grandmother, Sitti, in Palestine and in *The Trip Back Home* (Wong, 2000, TL2–5, A, F), a young girl goes with her mother to visit family in Korea. In both of these books, the young girls speak only English, yet, they find ways to connect and communicate with their relatives. Visiting relatives in another country also means learning new customs as in *I Lost My Tooth in Africa* (Diakite, 2006, TL4–5, A, F). Amina visits her family in Mali, West Africa. While there, she loses her tooth and puts it under a gourd for the African tooth fairy who is supposed to exchange it for a chicken.

Cultural heritage is sometimes marked by special dress. *New Clothes for New Year's Day* (Bae, 2007, TL2–4, A, F) presents traditional Korean attire that a mother makes for her daughter, and endnotes provide information about the custom of dressing up for the lunar new year. In *My Dadima Wears a Sari* (Sheth, 2007, TL4–5, A, F) a granddaughter wonders if her grandmother would ever want to wear something different besides the traditional sari. But, the grandmother shows her granddaughter all the positive things she can do with a sari; for instance, using it as a fan, collecting seashells, or using it as an umbrella.

Language is a critical part of identity, and the importance of language is demonstrated by the growing number of bilingual books with complete text in two languages being published. Some criticisms, however, have been leveled against bilingual books (Multilingual Resources for Children Project, 1995; Walker, Edwards, & Blacksell, 1996). For instance, the presentation on the page may give one language precedence or higher status through the order of appearance as well as differences in font size, boldness, or spacing between lines, difference in type quality between the scripts such as a non-Roman versus Roman alphabet, and differences in directionality (e.g., English is read from left to right, Urdu is read from right to left). Finally, translations may be plagued by literal renditions that lack the flow of the native language as well as by incorrect lexical constructions, unclear phrases, awkward expressions, and grammatical, spelling, and/or typographical errors (Schon, 2004). An even greater number of books with the interlingual use of two languages, the main text in English with words from another language interspersed, are available. Just a few examples include the following: *I Am Latino: The Beauty in Me* (Pinkney & Pinkney, 2007, TL2–4, A, F) is a simple presentation of five senses, "listen/ to the melody of my language/ Buenos dias (Good morning)." *My Father's Shop* (Ichikawa, 2006, TL2–4, A, F) shows a rooster following a young boy into the marketplace in Morocco, which results in tourists from other countries sharing how a rooster crows in their languages. In *What Should I Make?* (Nayar, 2009 TL1–3, P, F), readers learn about Indian flatbread as they are introduced to a few words in another language. And, finally, readers learn several Japanese terms and some interesting characteristics of writing in Japanese in *Yoko Writes Her Name* (Wells, 2008, TL2–3, P, F).

Food is also a cultural marker, and one that varies tremendously across cultures. Instructions and recipes are included for Indian flatbread in *What Should I Make?* (Nayar, 2009, TL1–3, P, F) and for a popular Korean rice dish in *Bee-Bim Bop!* (Park, 2005, TL2–4, P, F). In *The Have a Good Day Café* (Park & Park, 2005, TL4–5, I, F), readers meet a Korean family that changes the strategy for their food cart business by selling Korean food items rather than typical American items. A glossary of the food items is at the end of the book. *Hiromi's Hands* (Barasch, 2007, TL3–5, I, F) features a young Japanese American girl who becomes a sushi chef in her family's New York restaurant. A two-page spread on different sushi is included. On the other hand, *The Wakame Gatherers* (Thompson, 2007, TL4–5, I, F) is an interesting story of a mixed ethnic girl, American and Japanese, but there is much specific detail about gathering wakame, a type of seaweed, which makes this book more challenging for students who have not lived near coastal areas and who are not familiar with the culinary uses of seaweed. This book could be paired with *Hiromi's Hands*, however, for English learners at Levels 4 and 5 who are interested in finding out more about the use of seaweed in cooking.

Education and schooling is a topic directly related to every student's life. However, access to education and schooling in the United States differs from other settings. The difficulties of getting to school are presented in *Running Shoes* (Lipp, 2008, TL3–5, A, F). Sophy wants to learn to read and write, but the school she would attend is 8 kilometers from her small Cambodian village. Eventually, she realizes her dream when she is given running shoes that enable her to run to school. The conflict of juggling family responsibilities and school attendance is portrayed in *Josias, Hold the Book* (Elvegren, 2006, TL3–5, A, F). Josias lives in rural Haiti and has difficulty attending school as he must tend his family's garden. Because the family garden is not faring well, however, Josias realizes that books might hold the key to the problems in the garden, and he convinces his family to allow him to attend school. Some schools are in very different settings as in *Armando and the Blue Tarp School* (Fine, 2007, TL4–5, I, F). The children in the colonia near the city dump in Tijuana, Mexico, attend a summer school held outside on a blue tarp. Historically, education was not been provided to all children as depicted in *Ruby's*

Wish (Yim, 2002, TL4–5, I, F), a story based on the author's grandmother who wants to attend school and go to the university, an atypical path for girls in China at that time. Going to school also means adjustments. In *Something for School* (Lee, 2008, TL2–3, P, F) for primary-grade English learners, Yoon goes to school and the children mistake her for a boy. Initially, she wears her sister's headband (a scarf with curls) to fit in, but eventually, she discovers she does not need the headband as she has become part of the class. Finally, cultural differences lead to difficulties at school in *My Name Is Bilal* (Mobin-Uddin, 2005, TL4–5, I, F). Bilal and his sister, Ayesha, must adjust to a new school where they are the only Muslim students in attendance. Ayesha is teased by boys who grab her headscarf, but Bilal ignores this and later tells the class that his name is Bill, not Bilal, to avoid more teasing. A teacher helps Bilal to ultimately stand up for his sister and his own beliefs.

Adjustments do not just happen at school. They can occur as a result of many different situations. The families of English learners are often separated due to family members working in another location. *Papi's Gift* (Stanton, 2007, TL3–5, A, F) depicts such a situation as Graciela's father has traveled to California to find work because of the drought in their village across the border. Some English learners have immigrated as a result of war or political turmoil in their countries. Some have even lived in refugee camps as the two girls in *Four Feet, Two Sandals* (Williams & Mohammad, 2007, TL3–5, A, F) who must share a pair of sandals, the last shoes available, brought by relief workers. And, finally, some English learners feel alone because they have lost family members, so they can identify with the young girl in *Home Now* (Beake, 2007, TL3–5, A, F) who has lost both parents to AIDS in Africa. Then she goes to live with her aunt, and there she meets an orphaned elephant at the elephant park, and this encounter helps her begin to adjust.

Holidays and family celebrations, even though they may be celebrated in very different ways, are universal and there are many stories about the festivities. Some are more culturally specific as in *This Next New Year* (Wong, 2000, TL2–5, A, F), which highlights the lunar new year. Simple language and text explain many of the folk customs associated with this celebration. *Uncle Peter's Amazing Chinese Wedding* (Look, 2006, TL3–5, A, F) also provides quite a bit of cultural detail about a traditional Chinese wedding amidst an amusing family story. Finally, *Happy Birthday, Jamela!* (Daly, 2007, TL3–5, A, F) is a general view of a young girl's birthday. There is no indication that the story takes place in South Africa except a reference to the grandmother as Gogo.

Conclusion

Fiction selections far outnumber other genre in core reading programs, and fiction children's books outnumber nonfiction books and poetry. Because fiction is such a dominant presence in any reading program or classroom, this chapter has explored the many types of fiction and how to best match those works to English learners. Selecting quality literature is only part of the process of helping English learners. In particular, the physical environment of the classroom contributes to literacy development. It is important that the environment allow for comfortable working areas for whole-class, small-group, paired, and individual working. Too, the classroom environment should clearly exhibit the importance and value of reading and language and celebrate the literacy accomplishments of the students. This emphasis on print includes prominent displays of students' written work for children to read and discuss, (multilingual) labels for classroom items and supplies, a word wall with sight words along with vocabulary drawn from current reading and student nomination, and bulletin boards with postings of the teacher's favorite fiction reads alongside student recommendations and reviews. Reading displays spotlighting a particular fiction author of the month and actual books as well as "real-world" print materials linked to current units of study serve to spark student interest and curiosity. Easily accessible and highly visible classroom libraries that showcase a variety of fiction texts, authors, reading levels, and topics/themes invite student browsing and encourage the reading habit with the ever-popular genre of fiction.

The next chapter in this section focuses on poetry, which is an excellent, but sometimes overlooked, genre for building oral language and reading fluency. Just as with the fiction highlighted in this chapter, there are many different types of poetry and even some overlap between fiction and poetry since so many predictable fiction books include rhyme and can therefore be discussed for their poetic features.

Fear and Joy
in Leaving Your Country

JORGE ARGUETA

When a young boy or a girl leaves his/her country, a great
number of fears come to the mind, heart, and spirit of
the young travelers. I can only think and speak of my
own experience as well as those of some members of my
family and close friends. I left El Salvador at a very young
age; the foundation of my life was not only fresh but also
shaky with different unresolved issues. Among them: The
uncertainty of my age, this was the least of my worries, I
wasn't sure if my family would have the money for me to
keep on going to school. Everything was uncertain. The
most frightening of all my worries was the cruel civil war.
I was confused. No young boy or a girl should have such
worries.

All of a sudden a decision was made, It was supposed
to be the "best" decision for my future. I was to leave
the country. Of course I had no opinion on this decision.
The excitement of leaving sounded like a fun idea, going
through Guatemala, Mexico, and finally the United
States. All of this sounded great, but when I sat with my
thoughts, I thought of my mother, my father, my brothers,
my grandmother. I felt fear, confusion, anger, sadness,
and complete loneliness. No fun games, no familiar voices,
no familiar trees, no friends, just plain loneliness. I was
terrified.... One early morning in 1981, I came to meet
my fear and loneliness. I found myself sitting in a bus
terminal going to Guatemala. I was fleeing the country
like a bandit. Hidden, I left my house in the wee hours
of the morning. I can still vividly see my mother crying
standing next to a bus window just before it took off. My

journey was long. It took a few months on the road and a great number of adventures, before I finally made it to the United States. I was just one of thousands of Salvadorans that were leaving the country because of the war....

Now after so many years I am capable of saying I've been able to heal some of those fears and scars. I had found healing in my spirituality and in the gentle power of words. In 2001, I published my first children's book, *A Movie in My Pillow/ Una Pelicula en Mi Almohada.*...

When We Left El Salvador

When we left El Salvador
To come to the United States
Papa and I left in a hurry
One early morning in December

We left without saying good bye
to relatives, friends, or neighbors
I didn't say good bye to Neto
My best friend

I didn't say good bye to Koki
My happy talking parakeet
I didn't say good bye to
Miss Sha-Sha-She-Sha
my very dear doggie

When we left El Salvador
in a bus I couldn't stop crying
because I left my mama
my little brothers
and my grandma behind

Although not every poem in the book deals with the sadness of war or leaving the country I've been fortunate

enough to learn from many children, countrymen and women how reading my book has helped them overcome their sadness, "just to know someone else has gone through the same struggle help me no to feel so lonely" a woman told me after one of my presentations. I am happy to know my poems have helped children from El Salvador, other countries in Central America, and elsewhere to heal their fear, wounds and to find joy and the beauty of words.

CHAPTER FIVE

Selecting and Using Poetry
with English Learners in Grades K–6

"I got an A on my poem!" I yell to everyone
in the front yard where Mama gives Papi a haircut.

I show Gabino my paper
as I fly through the kitchen to the backyard.

"Listen," I sing to the baby chicks,
with my hands up as if I am a famous conductor.

I sprinkle corn kernels and sing out my poem.
—JUAN FELIPE HERRERA, *The Upside Down Boy/*
El niño de cabeza
(Children's Book Press, 2000)

Listening to the spoken word is an important first step in learning any language. In fact, research shows that oral language development affords a foundation in phonological awareness and allows for subsequent learning about the structure of English that is important to later reading and writing efforts (Snow, Burns, & Griffin, 1998). Unfortunately, oral language activities with English learners often focus on basic communication skills or phonemic awareness drills, not exposure to authentic language. In contrast, poetry is a natural introduction to a new language. Its rhythm, repetition, and rhyme mirror the simple nonsense rhymes, songs, and finger plays that are a part of many folk cultures and are often shared with young children as part of early language experiences prior to school. Cunningham (2007) notes that "many children who come to school with well-developed phonemic awareness abilities have ... come from homes in which rhyming chants, jingles, and songs are part of their daily experience" (p. 163). Thus, she advocates that chants, jingles, and songs should be a part of daily instruction. Denise Fleming's *The Everything Book* (2000, TL1–2, P, F) is an excellent resource with an introduction to the alphabet and numbers, shapes, colors, rhymes, and finger games.

While poetry does so much for children developing language skills, it also has instructional applications across the curriculum, reinforcing concepts that students need to remember and providing sensory experiences—giving students the sense of touching, feeling, smelling, and seeing. Poems help to make a topic memorable through the use of vivid images.

This chapter discusses the particular language and literacy development needs of English learners and the appropriateness of poetry as a vehicle for providing practice and pleasure in the development of oral language and reading fluency as well as writing. In addition, the chapter highlights issues in selecting and using poetry for English learners.

The Benefits of Poetry for Language Learning

Many teachers assume that students learning English as a new language are not ready for poetry, which may be considered more abstract and indirect than narrative or expository text. Yet, poetry offers many benefits for English learners (Hadaway, Vardell, & Young, 2001). Rhyming poetry, for example, provides the sound qualities helpful for predicting words and phrases as with Bruce McMillan's two-word rhymes such as "sand hand" and "scoop group" in *One Sun: A Book of Terse Verse* (1992, TL1–3, A, P). Beginning readers more easily decipher the meaning of poetry because of the rhythm, repetition, and rhyme, and the fact that the accent falls on meaningful words (Christison & Bassano, 1995; Richard-Amato, 2003). Concrete or shape poems use the visual layout of the poem along with the words to describe an object or experience. Even free-verse poetry helps readers focus on the arrangement of words on the page and on the description and emotion that those words offer. Too, poetry can be a powerful vehicle for developing students' oral language capacity, which is key to functioning in a new language (Vardell, Hadaway & Young, 2002). Through hearing, reading, and rereading poetry, English learners can increase their exposure to language.

In addition to providing language support, poetry provides many instructional advantages. Brevity of form is one of the most obvious benefits, making poetry appear both manageable and not so intimidating. For teaching English learners, poetry has the advantage of coming "packaged" in very few words, relatively speaking (Cullinan, Scala, & Schroder,

1995). Poems can be read and reread in very little time. Each rereading can be approached in a slightly different way, too, through choral reading or poetry performance. The length is less daunting to English learners overwhelmed by longer prose and a barrage of new vocabulary. Although poetry may present new words and concepts, the shorter appearance is more approachable. Too, poetry can span grade levels and language proficiency levels because of its unique form and use of language helping English learners master concepts, stay motivated and interested, and even participate as equals.

Further, because of its brevity, poetry serves as a brief but powerful anticipatory set for longer texts and for the introduction of topics across the curriculum (Chatton, 2009; Cullinan et al., 1995). Teachers can quickly set the stage for a new topic or unit with a quick look at a poem, or they can weave poetry throughout a thematic or interdisciplinary study. In a thematic unit on weather, for instance, teachers can choose from numerous poetry collections or poem picture books including *Let's Count the Raindrops* (Kosaka, 2001, TL2–4, A, P), *Rainplay* (Cotton, 2008, TL2–4, A, P), *Voices on the Wind: Poems for All Seasons* (Booth, 1990, TL3–5, A, P), and *Snow, Snow: Winter Poems for Children* (Yolen, 2005, TL3–5, A, P). What is more, some poems can be a source of brief character sketches, scenes, and stories that serve as writing models (Vogel & Tilley, 1993). For example, *Gracie Graves and the Kids from Room 402* (Paraskevas, 1995, TL2–5, A, P) offers readers a series of brief character sketches of a variety of children in an elementary school, and *My Name Is Jorge on Both Sides of the River* (Medina, 2004, TL3–5, A, P) is a collection of poems describing Jorge's adjustment to school and life in the United States after moving from Mexico.

Another benefit of poems is that they tend to be about one topic. This crystallized focus can aid English learners as they use their word knowledge to make sense of a new topic. An example is the Thanksgiving poem "Leftovers" in *It's Thanksgiving!* (Prelutsky, 2008, TL2–4, A, P), which is very clearly about one subject. Moreover, *leftover* is also a word-study opportunity since it is a compound word (*left* + *over*) and can spark discussion about other compound words that English learners may encounter in their reading. Although words such as *bisque* and *fritters* from the poem may be unfamiliar, the poem's context provides clarification. Moreover, poems can help English learners learn new vocabulary. For instance, in *A Light in the Attic* (Silverstein, 2001, TL1–5, A, P), the poem "Ations" offers a list of words (e.g., *communication, negotiation, reconciliation*) that end in the sometimes troublesome -*tion*. In couplets, the poet playfully defines the words, providing a format that students can use to consider additional words with the same ending. Discussion of the ending -*tion* also invites a discussion of English–Spanish cognates since often, -*tion* endings in English can be replaced with -*cion* to translate words into Spanish. A mention of cognates is worth attention since cognates comprise approximately 30 to 50% of an educated person's active vocabulary (Nash, 1997). Further, English learners who are aware of cognates have higher levels of English reading comprehension than those not aware of these connections (Kamil & Hiebert, 2005). Silverstein has other poems that engage readers in word study such as "The Twistable Turnable Man" (A *Light in the Attic*, 2001, TL1–5, A, P) that focuses on morphology encouraging students to examine the use of the suffix *able*. Teachers should keep in mind that this kind of wordplay can be challenging for English learners who may interpret words and phrases literally. And, while poetry provides playful examples of the creative ways language can be used, teachers should not dissect poems too much for word-study lessons. However, when words and word features are central to poems, as in these examples, mini-lessons can be both natural and beneficial.

Finally, poetry formats such as list poems, biopoems, diamantes, and found poems help English learners talk about the concepts and ideas they are learning and lead them to beginning writing opportunities (Tompkins, 2007; Fagin, 1991). Too, collections of poems with similar form can help teachers provide multiple models of one kind of poem. *Splash Splash* (Graham, 2001, TL2–5, A, P), for example, a poetry book of only concrete (or shape) poems, allows English learners to look at several examples of the same form all in one place. Highlighting poems with a common format logically leads English learners to try writing poetry.

In summary, these benefits make matching poetry with English learners a natural. The next sections extend the discussion of two specific benefits of poetry, oral language development and reading fluency, and examine how poetry can be effectively used to address these areas of instruction.

Poetry and Oral Language

Although English learners initially spend some time in a silent period of language acquisition, they must move beyond this stage to learn English. Yet, recent research cites inadequate time for English language development as a major problem with current practice. A low level of student oral language use in class, only 21% of the time, was cited in a study by Arreaga-Mayer and Perdomo-Rivera (1996). Likewise, Ramírez (1992) noted "consistently, across grade levels within and between . . . . programs, students are limited in their opportunities to produce language" (p. 9). Using poetry in collaborative learning paired and small-group activities provides authentic listening and speaking opportunities (Scarcella & Oxford, 1992). For the greatest impact on language learning, English learners should be flexibly grouped according to their growing language proficiencies and provided with numerous occasions each day for interaction in large- and small-group activities (Mora, 2004).

Teachers help to develop English learners' oral language first through listening and nonverbal participation, ideal for the silent period of language development. Teachers can read aloud a poem, have students read along in unison, or engage students in pantomime actions for some poems or picture songbooks, similar to TPR discussed in Chapter 3. The class might, for instance, point to the parts of the body mentioned in Shel Silverstein's "Sick" or "Boa Constrictor," both from *Where the Sidewalk Ends* (2000, TL1–5, A, P). Read-alouds help English learners acquire correct word pronunciations and listening vocabulary and aid students' overall comprehension.

Using poetry for choral reading promotes oral fluency and lays a strong foundation for reading in a new language. As students participate in choral reading, they practice their word recognition and pronunciation and experience their new language in a supportive and engaging manner. When English learners read a poem, hear the poem, read it aloud, and participate in choral reading of the poem, they are given multiple modes of reinforcement for meaningful language learning. Following a teacher read-aloud of a poem, English learners can reread the poem with a partner and discuss it. To increase the amount of meaningful interaction once English learners have experienced different formats for choral reading, they can choose their own poem and work with a group to make decisions about how best to present the poem through a poetry performance; for instance, acting out a poem.

Linan-Thompson and Vaughn recommend the following process to scaffold English learners' choral reading experiences. "First, the teacher and the students preview the passage and make predictions about what the passage will be about. Second, the teacher reads the passage aloud. Third, the students and teacher read aloud together. Fourth, the teacher fades his or her voice and allows the students to take the lead in reading the passage aloud" (2007, p. 63). The first step helps keep the focus on meaning and the succeeding steps provide the support needed for the students to read with confidence.

There are various formats for choral reading or poetry performance including the following arranged from easy to implement to more challenging:

- Everyone reads the poem in unison.
- Students join in on a repeated line or refrain.
- Call and response with two student groups.
- Multiple groups, multiple stanzas.
- Individual solo lines or line-a-child format.
- Cumulative or crescendo/decrescendo.
- Two voices.

Some recent poems or poetry collections easily fit into these formats. For instance, Betsy Franco's "New Kid at School" and "Animal Reports" from her book *Messing Around on the Monkey Bars: And Other School Poems for Two Voices* (2009, TL1–5, A, P) are naturals for the "call and response" arrangement. A fragment of the poem "New Kid at School" follows:

Group 1:	Where did you come from?
Group 2:	Far away.
Group 1:	Miss your friends?
Group 2:	Every day.

Another example for this format is Aileen Fisher's "Caterpillars" found in Bobbi Katz's *More Pocket Poems* (2009, TL2–5, A, P). In part, the poem reads, "What do caterpillars do?/ Nothing much but chew and chew." And, Eloise Greenfield's poems in *The Friendly Four* (2006, TL1–4, A, P), a collection of poems about four children exploring the bonds of friendship, are already arranged into individual solo lines or line-a-child format. The following portion is from "Playground":

All:	We're running,
Dorene:	we're sliding,
Louis:	swinging,
Rae:	sweating.

Cumulative arrangement, adding voices and then having them fall out, takes more planning but the effect can be amazing. Here is an example of a cumulative arrangement for a portion of "Subways Are People" from *City I Love* by Lee Bennett Hopkins (2009, TL1–5, A, P):

Group 1:	Subways are people—
Groups 1 and 2:	People standing
Groups 1–3:	People sitting
Groups 1–4:	People swaying to and from

Finally, Avis Harley's "Legends," one of the many wonderful poems found in Lee Bennett Hopkins' *Sky Magic* (2009, TL2–5, A, P), works well for the poems for two voices arrangement. The first stanza of the poem is included here:

> In the Language of the stars
> > Lie stories of old
> > Brilliant legends
> Told;
> > Retold

As can be seen, poetry can be easily integrated into the classroom as a means of developing oral language. In the next section, the possibilities that poetry offers for building reading fluency are discussed.

Poetry and Reading Fluency

"When parents, caretakers, and ... teachers read aloud, they provide models of what fluent oral reading sounds like. The more models a child has, the better" (Allington, 2009a, p. 16). Some English learners may have parents who are literate in the home language and who read aloud to them in that language, which offers a model of fluent reading, just not in English. On the other hand, some English learners arrive at school with few read-aloud experiences in the home language or in English, and therefore, few models of fluent reading. The teacher then becomes critical in providing daily read-alouds to model fluent reading. Modeling fluent reading can be integrated as a brief mini-lesson or through a more focused lesson with one or more of the following methods (Allington, 2009a, p. 25):

- Reading aloud from children's literature.
- Reading aloud and tracking print with big books or an enlarged version of a poem displayed to the class.
- Rereading language experience charts that were developed with the children.

- Reading aloud in the Shared Book Experience, Oral Recitation Lesson, or Fluency Oriented Reading Instruction lesson models.
- Reading aloud the weekly story from the core reading program as children follow along.

Once teachers have modeled fluent reading through daily read-alouds, the next step is to reinforce this input by having students reread the text. Repeated reading has long been recommended as a strategy for improving students' oral-reading fluency, and recent research (Center for the Improvement of Early Reading Achievement, 2003) indicates that "repeated oral reading substantially improves word recognition, speed, and accuracy as well as fluency. To a lesser but still considerable extent, repeated oral reading also improves reading comprehension" (p. 24). Rasinski suggests that "Practicing short passages three to five times can help students develop greater automaticity and expression in their reading, especially if that practice is given with formative feedback" (2003, p. 17). Again, there are a variety of methods for having students reread text as follows (Allington, 2009a, p. 25):

- Rereading after the teacher has read a poem or story aloud.
- Rereading as a choral reading activity with some or all classmates and the teacher.
- Rereading as a partner reading activity.
- Rereading as independent seatwork activity.
- Rereading and practicing some segment of a poem or story for presentation to the class.

"One key to nurturing fluent reading is finding the appropriate text for the reader to read. Texts that are too difficult, overly dense with unfamiliar vocabulary and concepts, can make any otherwise fluent reader disfluent .... Thus, it is important that we find texts that are well within the reader's independent-instructional range in order to promote fluency" (Rasinski, 2000, p. 148). Raskinski further contends that the aim of the practice "should be meaningful and expressive oral interpretation or performance of text, not faster reading. To that end, certain texts lend themselves to oral interpretive reading" (2006, p. 706).

Poetry is meant to be read aloud. A poem's meaning is communicated more clearly when both read and heard. "Poetry ... contains elements of predictability such as rhyme, rhythm and repetition which make reading easier" (Gill, 1996, p. 28) and help English learners get a sense of the sound of English words and phrases. Too, poetry lends itself to expressive oral-interpretive reading with its brevity, lyrical word choice, repetition, abundance of white space, and rhythmic language. These characteristics help combat the monotony and boredom that can occur with repeated rereading of other types of text (Allington, 2009a) and make poetry an ideal entry point to expressive reading (Hadaway, Vardell, & Young, 2006). Moreover, poetry's potential impact on English learners is positive. "Reading and performing poetry provides numerous opportunities for children to practice—with pleasure—the essential skills of phonemic awareness, phonics, fluency, vocabulary and comprehension" (Stanley, 2004, p. 56).

Because the importance of multiple exposures to words is underscored in the research on comprehension improvement (Stahl & Nagy, 2006), teachers must plan on providing multiple opportunities and experiences using the words if they hope to make a difference in students' recognition and understanding of word meaning. Going further, Allington (2009a, p. 28) notes that "Perhaps the most critical skill in fluent reading is the ability to recognize a great many words 'at a glance.'" This is what has been called automaticity. Automatic word recognition is when you recognize the word with little conscious effort (thus, 'at-a-glance' recognition). Developing an at-a-glance store of words requires readers to encounter the word repeatedly and with each encounter read it accurately. Allington reports that such automaticity requires 10 to 25 successful pronunciations of a word. Once a word is in a reader's "at-a-glance" repertoire, then there is no lingering confusion over the word when it is encountered in reading. This helps readers move through text and attend to meaning at the text rather than the word level. This is important since many English learners use a halting word-by-word approach to reading text in their new language, and their slow progress down the page results in frustration and exhaustion, and eventually, they just quit.

Most research and instructional efforts aimed at English learners have focused on developing word-level skills and word reading so that these students can reach similar levels of attainment on word-level skills as their English-speaking peers (Solari, 2007). Unfortunately, as Solari reports, the 2006 National Literacy Panel on Language-Minority Children and Youth found that English learners did not reach the same text-level proficiency as their peers. Yet, this is the proficiency needed for long-term success in school. Fluency helps move readers past a focus on words and enables them to focus on text skills such as reading, comprehension, vocabulary, and writing. Poetry is certainly a strong tool to help English learners develop fluency. As Sharon Gill found in her classroom use of poetry, "Poetry is written to be read again and again.... Repeated readings allow children to gain fluency and build sight vocabulary while having successful reading experiences" (1996, p. 28).

Selecting Poetry
for English Learners in Grades K–6

Just as with fiction and nonfiction, poetry books are published in many different formats including some that do not look like poetry and are not classified as such, and each format has both positives and challenges in terms of its use with English learners. See Figure 5.1 for different poetry and poetic book formats. A recent positive change in publishing poetry books for young readers, especially English learners, is the development of more selective anthologies or collections. Lee Bennett Hopkins makes a distinction between collections and anthologies (Hopkins, 1993). Using his nomenclature, there are two types of collections: "single author" where all of the poems are by the same poet such as Monica Gunning's *America: My New Home* (2004, TL3–5, A, P), and "single-topic" collections where all of the poems address the same topic: for example, in Nikki Giovanni's *Hip Hop Speaks to Children: A Celebration of Poetry with a Beat* (2008, TL2–5, A, P) where all of the poems have strong rhythm—"poetry with a beat!" The contributors range from Maya Angelou, Queen Latifah, Nikki Grimes, Eloise Greenfield, Martin Luther King, Jr., and Langston Hughes. Another collection that is both single topic and single author is Pat Mora's *Yum! Mmmm! Que Rico! America's Sproutlings* (2007, TL3–5, A, P), a collection of haiku spotlighting foods native to the Americas. The fact that all of the poems are by Mora provides added consistency that may further support English learners.

In contrast, according to Hopkins, general collections or anthologies are "books put together by an anthologist to highlight a variety of topics with multiple poets" (1993, p. 202). The anthology was the traditional format for poetry in the past, and it has been around since publishing began. Anthologies were a practical way to collect a multitude of poems on a variety of subjects by many different poets. These collections, often oversized, may not be very inviting to today's English learners. Anthologies violate the basic idea of narrow reading—reading in only one genre, one subject matter, or the work of one author—recommended in Chapter 3 as an effective means of supporting English learners' language development. Narrow reading addresses both the issues of level of familiarity and background knowledge and the level of language, both criteria for selection of text for English learners. There are more selective anthologies,

General collections or anthologies

Single-author collections

Single-topic collections

Single-format collections

Culturally relevant poetry

Poem picture books

Song picture books (also discussed in Chapter 4)

And some types of rhyming books that may not look like "poetry"

- Rhyming picture books (*Sheep in a Jeep* by Nancy Shaw)
- Rhythmic picture books (*A Cool Drink of Water* and *A Little Peace* by Barbara Kerley)
- Predictable books (discussed in more detail in Chapter 4)
- Alphabet books (*N Is for Navidad* by Susan Elya and Merry Banks)
- Counting books (*We All Went on Safari: A Counting Journey through Tanzania* by Laurie Krebs)
- Folk songs in book form (*Arroz con Leche* collected by Lulu Delacre)
- Bible songs and spirituals (*Let It Shine: Three Favorite Spirituals* collected by Ashley Bryan)

Plus, childhood folklore

- Jump rope and ball-bouncing rhymes (*Anna Banana* by Joanna Cole)
- Clapping games, chants, and cheers (*Street Rhymes around the World* by Jane Yolen)
- Street songs and raps (*Night on Neighborhood Street* by Eloise Greenfield)
- Riddles, tongue twisters, counting games, and nonsense verse (*And the Green Grass Grew All Around* collected by Alvin Schwartz)

FIGURE 5.1. Types of poetry books.

however. For example, Hopkins's edited volume, *Small Talk: A Book of Short Poems* (1995, TL2–5, A, P), while it is an anthology or general collection of poems, seems suited for English learners because their brevity permits teachers to begin each day with a poem and thus, to practice oral language in just a few minutes.

Single-topic collections are easily connected to the content areas as is the case with works such as *Marvelous Math: A Book of Poems* (1997, TL3–5, A, P) and *Spectacular Science: A Book of Poems* (1999, TL3–5, A, P) both compiled by Lee Bennett Hopkins. English learners can find reinforcement of math and science concepts in both the illustrations and the descriptions. Although some vocabulary may need elaboration, the poems offer images, analogies, metaphors, and similes that help English learners visualize and remember the construct being described through poetry. Hopkins has compiled numerous single-topic collections that are visually appealing and inclusive without being overwhelming. The more narrow focus on a topic makes it simple for a teacher to conceive of how to link poetry with the current curriculum, and the focus on one topic can limit the vocabulary and conceptual load for English learners. These teacher- and reader-friendly thematic collections are effective for English learners and supported by research (Freeman & Freeman, 2006). Practically speaking, it makes it even easier to open a lesson with poetry when a book of poems on that topic is available. For English learners, this topic connection provides support for vocabulary development and comprehension when poems of related subject matter are shared (Krashen & Terrell, 1983). In addition to Hopkins's single-topic collections of poetry by a variety of authors, he has authored several single-topic collections of his own work and these are ideal for English learners with beginning-language proficiency. His books of poems such as *Blast Off! Poems about Space* (1996, TL2–5, A, P), *Dino-Roars* (1999, TL2–5, A, P), *Sports! Sports! Sports!: A Poetry Collection* (2000, TL2–5, A, P), and *Weather: Poems for All Seasons* (1995, TL2–5, A, P) all provide simple poems with strong rhyme and imagery perfect for language development.

Poetry also comes in single-author collections with the work of just one poet. Again, the consistent style of one author can be a benefit through a narrow reading instructional focus as discussed in Chapter 3. *Where the Sidewalk Ends* (Silverstein, 2000, TL1–5, A, P) is probably the most well-known example of a single-author collection. Such "standards" by Shel Silverstein and Jack Prelutsky are readily available, and these are the poets often voted by children as their favorites (Kutiper & Wilson, 1993). However, writers such as Kalli Dakos and Douglas Florian are gaining in popularity, so incorporating new voices into the classroom library is an ongoing endeavor. Florian's frequent use of the "list-poem" format in *Bing, Bang, Boing* (2007, TL1–5, A, P) and Dakos's focus on school topics have particular appeal to English learners. Moreover, Florian is an excellent example of a poet who has contributed many single-author/single-topic poetry collections including several collections of animal poems (*On the Wing*, 2000; *In the Swim*, 2001; *Insectlopedia*, 2002; *Mammalibilia*, 2004; *Lizards, Frogs, and Polliwogs*, 2005; *Zoo's Who*, 2005; and *Comets, Stars, the Moon, and Mars: Space Poems and Paintings*, 2007, TL2–5, A, P for all), and these can fit easily into the science curriculum of the intermediate grades for use with English learners at Level 2 and above.

In terms of choosing poets to spotlight in the classroom, one starting point might be Sylvia Vardell's *Poetry People: A Practical Guide to Chil-*

dren's Poets (2007), an excellent introduction to more than 60 contemporary young people's poets that showcases one entry for each poet along with biographical information, a list of his or her poetry books, and so on. In addition, the Internet offers an excellent resource for finding out more about individual poets; some even have their own webpage.

Another type of poetry collection beyond single author or single topic is a single-format collection with only poems of one type such as riddles, haikus, or list poems. The collection of haikus by Pat Mora, *Yum! Mmmm! Que Rico!: America's Sproutlings* (2007, TL3–5,A,P), cited earlier is one excellent example. Georgia Heard has also collected various list poems by well-known children's poets in *Falling down the Page: A Book of List Poems* (2009, TL2–5, A, P). The list-poem format offers straightforward language in a simple format that can help English learners to comprehend the text. Finally, there are numerous collections of concrete poetry (also referred to as shape or graphic poetry). With concrete poetry, the visual impact is important since the shape of the poem reflects its meaning, as with Joan Graham's collections *Splish Splash* (2001, TL2–5, A, P) and *Flicker Flash* (2003, TL2–5, A, P). These poems are designed to be seen more so than read aloud providing a visual literacy focus.

Poetry by authors of color and poetry addressing themes of diversity continues to grow in popularity. Whether organized into a single-author collection by such favorites as Janet Wong or Eloise Greenfield or into a themed (single-topic) poetry volume such as *Come to the Great World: Poems from around the Globe* (Cooling, 2004, TL2–5, A, P), culturally relevant poems and their authors address both universal themes and experiences as well as offer glimpses of life outside the mainstream. Related to this global emphasis, one of the most exciting trends in the recent publishing of poetry for young people is the emergence of bilingual poetry, poems offered in two languages within the same book such as the work of Francisco Alarcón (*Poems to Dream Together/ Poemas para sonar juntos*, 2005, TL3–5, A, P) and also, poetry that has been published first outside the United States and then subsequently published in this country as in Jorge Lujan's *Colors! Colores!* (2008, TL3–5, A, P).

One other innovative format for poetry book publishing that is particularly effective with English learners is the poem picture book or song picture book (also discussed in Chapter 4 on predictable books). These are picture books that include only the words to one single poem or song. For example, the poem picture books *America Is . . .* (Borden, 2005, TL2–5, A, P) and *My America* (Gilchrist, 2007, TL1–5, A, P) along with the anthem, *O Beautiful for Spacious Skies* ("America the Beautiful") by Katharine Bates (1994, TL3–5, A, P) help English learners begin to understand elements of American culture in both words and pictures.

Finally, there are poetic or rhythmic picture books; books that may not be classified as poetry but that are presented more in the format of poetry with lyrical language and descriptive phrases displayed across the page in a less linear manner than traditional text in sentences or paragraphs. Various nonfiction books could be described as having this presentation style including Barbara Kerley's *A Cool Drink of Water* (2006, TL1–4, A, NF), which spotlights water use around the world, and Kerley's *A Little Peace* (2007, TL1–4, A, NF) with a similar format, as well as Alice Schertle's *We* (2007, TL3–5, A, NF) with its focus on human evolution. Poetic picture books lend themselves to dramatic read-alouds in the classroom.

Just as there are different collections of poetry, there are also different kinds of poems, including narrative, free verse, haiku, limericks, ballads, concrete, and so on. Studies of children's preferences (Kutiper & Wilson, 1993) indicate that most children enjoy narrative storytelling poems that have a regular, distinctive rhythm, strong sound patterns, humor, and not too much abstract and figurative language. At least, that is what appeals to them at first. Experimenting with a varied menu of poetry adds richness to the classroom, and in this way, English learners have exposure to a variety of formats when they want to experiment with writing poetry. While studies have been conducted on children's poetry preferences, there is little research on the preferences of English learners. Yet, beginning-language learners (Level 1 or 2) enjoy the sound of poetry—the rhyme, the rhythm, and the music of the English language. This means two things. First, as teachers begin selecting poetry to share with English learners, they should start with poems that rhyme and have a strong rhythm. This enables students to use their developing language skills to guess how words and phrases should sound. Also, poetry should be read aloud and teachers can invite, not assign, children to read out loud with them. Poetry needs to be heard and spoken, especially when English is not the native language.

Criteria for Selecting Poetry
for English Learners in Grades K–6

The rich diversity of poems, poem picture books, poetry collections, and rhythmic/poetic text offers many instructional choices to teachers. The four basic criteria for matching books to English learners presented in

Chapter 2 (level of content familiarity or background knowledge, level of language, level of textual support, and level of cultural fit) have been focused on the selection of poetry in Table 5.1. An in-depth discussion of these criteria and how they have been applied to examples of recently published poetry follow. Using these criteria and guiding questions, teachers can begin to carefully weigh the most appropriate poetry to meet English learners' varying language proficiency needs and backgrounds and to help increase word knowledge, familiarity with English syntax patterns, and conceptual background knowledge.

Level of Topic/Theme Familiarity or Background Knowledge

Familiarity and background knowledge can be related to both the topic and theme of the poetry to be used in the classroom and also the genre of poetry in general. Following are some guiding questions for examining poetry for use with English learners:

- What topics/themes are presented in the poem/poetry collection?
- Is this presentation an introduction to the topic/theme or is it continued conceptual development at a higher level?
- What is the English learner's level of familiarity or background knowledge related to the topic/theme? Is the topic or theme very familiar, familiar, unfamiliar, or not common?
- What background knowledge does the English learner have on the topic/theme of the poem/poetry collection?
- Has the topic/theme of the poem/poetry collection been previously covered in the curriculum? When? At what level? What was the level of success of English learners?
- Is the topic/theme of the poem/poetry collection likely to be part of the readers' background experience? How so? How can the teacher best link English learners' previous experiences/understandings to the poem/poetry collection?

As noted, when teachers consider which poetry to use with English learners in their classrooms, they need to take into account whether the poetry deals with everyday or universal topics or it is a more academic topic. In the first case, does the English learner have personal background knowledge and experience on the topic and for the latter, has the topic been previously covered in the curriculum? Poetry, like all text material, can highlight topics and themes that are familiar to learners from

TABLE 5.1. Criteria and Guiding Questions for Selecting Poetry for English Learners in Grades K–6

Criteria	Guiding questions
Level of topic/theme familiarity or background knowledge How close a fit is the fiction text to the English learner's knowledge or background experiences? How close a fit is the poem/poetry collection to the English learner's knowledge or background experiences?	• What topics/themes are presented in the poem/poetry collection? • Is this presentation an introduction to the topic/theme or is it continued conceptual development at a higher level? • What is the English learner's level of familiarity or background knowledge related to the topic/theme? Is the topic or theme very familiar, familiar, unfamiliar, or not common? • What background knowledge does the English learner have on the topic/theme of the poem/poetry collection? • Has the topic/theme of the poem/poetry collection been previously covered in the curriculum? When? At what level? What was the level of success of English learners? • Is the topic/theme of the poem/poetry collection likely to be part of the readers' background experience? How so? How can the teacher best link English learners' previous experiences/understandings to the poem/poetry collection?
Level of language How close a fit is the fiction text to the English learner's knowledge or background experiences? How close a fit is the poem/poetry collection to the English learner's vocabulary, syntactic knowledge, and overall proficiency level?	• What is the vocabulary load of the poem/poetry collection (e.g., basic and familiar, sophisticated/advanced and unfamiliar, concrete or abstract, general or technical/specialized, idiomatic, formal or informal, vocabulary with multiple meanings, figurative language)? • How many new vocabulary words are presented in the poem? • Does the poem/poetry collection present new vocabulary in meaningful contextual ways? • How likely is the English learner to encounter the vocabulary in this poem/poetry collection in other reading? • What is the English learner's previous experience with the vocabulary of the poem/poetry collection (completely new, some exposure, should be part of active vocabulary)? Is the vocabulary currently or likely to be part of the English learner's speaking vocabulary? Listening vocabulary? Reading vocabulary? Writing vocabulary? • If there is predictable language, what is the size of the predictable unit and what percent of the total text of a poem does the predictable unit account for?

(cont.)

TABLE 5.1. *(cont.)*

Criteria	Guiding questions
Level of language (cont.)	• What is the syntactic structure of the poem/poetry collection? Word level? Phrase level? Simple sentences? Compound sentences? Complex sentences? Compound/complex sentences? Embedded clauses? • How familiar is the English learner with those syntax patterns? Does the English learner use that syntax pattern in speaking? Writing? • How familiar is the English learner with this genre?
Level of textual support How close a fit is the fiction text to the English learner's knowledge or background experiences? What types of support does the poem/poetry collection provide and how familiar is the English learner with these types of textual support?	• Are there visuals (photographs or illustrations)? • Are the visuals clear and direct? One-to-one correspondence of visuals to the poem/poetry collection? General connection? Primarily for aesthetic purposes? • Is the print style such as bold, italics, or punctuation used to provide clues to meaning? • Is the language/wording arranged on the page in such a way to give clues to meaning?
Level of cultural fit How close a fit is the fiction text to the English learner's knowledge or background experiences? How close a fit is the poem/poetry collection to the English learner's cultural or experiential background (ethnic, language, geographic, religious, socioeconomic, gender)?	• Is the poem/poetry collection culturally neutral (with general diversity portrayed but no focus on a specific group)? Culturally generic (with a group featured but less specific detail provided)? Culturally specific (with explicit details about a group portrayed)? • Does the poem/poetry collection reflect the background and/or experiences of recent immigrants? U.S.-born English learners? • Are the characters similar or different than English learners in the classroom? • Have English learners had experiences like those described in this poem/poetry collection? • Have English learners lived in or visited places like those in the poem/poetry collection? • How far removed is the poem/poetry collection from current times? • Are any characters the same gender as the reader? • Do the characters talk like the English learners and their families? • Is this author/author style familiar to English learners?

issues of self as in *Me I Am!* by Jack Prelutsky (2007, TL2–4, A, P) and real-world topics related to some readers' backgrounds such as themes of urban life depicted in *Mural on Second Avenue and Other City Poems* (Moore, 2005, TL2–5, A, P) to topics totally unrelated to their knowledge base. Lee Bennett Hopkins has even created an illustrated poetry book featuring the letters of the alphabet in *Alphathoughts: Alphabet Poems* (2003, TL1–5, A, P). The simple poems can help English learners with language and vocabulary development as shown by this brief sampling:

> Books
> Pages and pages of bound forevers
> C
> Custodian
> Keeper of clean

However, as a selection criteria, topic/theme familiarity and background knowledge may not factor into the decision making for poetry to the extent they do with nonfiction text where the content or conceptual load can quickly overwhelm the English learner. Yet, they are still important to consider.

As noted earlier, there are many single-topic poetry collections on content subjects such as math, science, and social studies. On the one hand, thematic collections can provide for a focus on one topic and the repetition of vocabulary that would assist English learners. On the other hand, the vocabulary in some of the poems could prove to be challenging to English learners, especially those at the beginning levels of proficiency. For Level 1 and 2 English learners, teachers need to select poems that address more universal topics and themes. Poetry that addresses basic or survival topics suggested in Chapter 3 to build social language and basic vocabulary is a good starting point. For example, *Big Is Big (and Little, Little): A Book of Contrasts* (Lewis, 2007, TL1–4, A, P) and *A Pig Is Big* (Florian, 2000, TL1–4, A, P) both explore the concept of size in humorous rhyming text, and most of the illustrations provide concrete clues to size differences. Either of these texts would be appropriate for Level 1 and 2 English learners and could be used with both primary and intermediate grades. So too, family, school, seasons, weather, and animals—all have some degree of familiarity—which can make a poem easier to understand. As a caution, some basic vocabulary and concepts such as numbers or days and months of the year are presented in rhyming poems, but just because the topic or the vocabulary is considered basic language needed for Level 1 English learners does not mean that the overall poem is easily understandable. For instance, *My Granny Went to Market: A Round-the-World Counting Rhyme* (Blackstone, 2005, TL2–4, A, P) is a counting book in rhyme but the text goes a bit beyond basic counting and numbers as objects are bought around the world, some of them not so familiar as in the lanterns bought in China and cowbells in Switzerland. Beginning English learners can, of course, enjoy the book and learn the numbers due to the illustrations and the summary table at the end of the book, but familiarity with the different countries and objects supposedly characteristic of that country may be limited. Another example is related to animals, always a favorite with children in the classroom, but the barnyard animals of the picture songbook *Old MacDonald Had a Farm* (Cabrera, 2008, TL1–2, P, F) may be more familiar than the animals and the geographic context of the South American rainforest in the bilingual poetry collection, *Animal Poems of the Iguazu/ Animalario del Iguazu* (Alarcón, 2009, TL3–5, I, P).

Teachers can maximize the connection of poetry to the curriculum by sharing poems related to classroom activities already going on—a lesson, a special event, or a shared experience. This provides for the needed repetition and reinforcement of vocabulary and concepts being taught. Again, teachers need to consider the learners, their proficiency levels, and their background knowledge. For instance, the poem picture book, *This Is the Dream* (Shore & Alexander, 2006, TL2–5, I, P), depicts the Civil Rights Movement and while the topic is presented in simple rhythmic text, the historical context may not be familiar to some English learners although the overarching theme of discrimination may be all too familiar. Thus, this book is best used with Levels 2–5 and with intermediate grades.

Topic and genre familiarity come into play with several recent poem biographies including *César: Sí se Puede/ Cesar, Yes We Can!* (Bernier-Grand, 2006, TL3–5, I, P) and *The Pot That Juan Built* (Andrews-Goebel, 2002, TL3–5, I, P), as well as the musical poem biography (sung to the tune of "The Old Grey Mare"), *Our Abe Lincoln* (Aylesworth, 2009, TL2–5, A, P). Some familiarity with the historical context and background knowledge about each of the featured historical figures, Cesar Chavez, Juan Quezada, and Abraham Lincoln, would be helpful. In addition, poem biographies are a blending of two genre, nonfiction/biography and poetry, and English learners may not expect to find biography via poetry. The repetition and basic vocabulary of *Our Abe Lincoln* make it an appropriate teacher read-aloud for Level 1 and 2 English learners, but the other two poem biographies are more appropriate for Levels 3–5 as well as for intermediate grades since some historical and fine arts context is needed.

Teachers can also invite students to search for and share poems that reflect their background knowledge and topics that are familiar to them. Sometimes, teachers gain valuable insights when learners bring their own ideas to the classroom. To encourage English learners in their search for poems to suggest, teachers should have an accessible classroom collection of poetry books or folders of poems. Because poems are brief, browsing can be accomplished throughout the day at the end of lessons or during center activity times.

Level of Language

As noted in the previous section, the topics or themes may not be as critical a factor in poetry selection for English learners, but the level of language is significant. Some guiding questions to help teachers consider the level of language in poetry include the following:

- What is the vocabulary load of the poem/poetry collection (e.g., basic and familiar, sophisticated/advanced and unfamiliar, concrete or abstract, general or technical/specialized, idiomatic, formal or informal, vocabulary with multiple meanings, figurative language)?
- How many new vocabulary words are presented in the poem?
- Does the poem/poetry collection present new vocabulary in meaningful contextual ways?
- How likely is the English learner to encounter the vocabulary in this poem/poetry collection in other reading?
- What is the English learner's previous experience with the vocabulary of the poem/poetry collection (completely new, some exposure, should be part of active vocabulary)? Is the vocabulary currently or likely to be part of the English learner's speaking vocabulary? Listening vocabulary? Reading vocabulary? Writing vocabulary?
- If there is predictable language, what is the size of the predictable unit and what percent of the total text of a poem does the predictable unit account for?
- What is the syntactic structure of the poem/poetry collection? Word level? Phrase level? Simple sentences? Compound sentences? Complex sentences? Compound/complex sentences? Embedded clauses?

- How familiar is the English learner with those syntax patterns? Does the English learner use that syntax pattern in speaking? Writing?
- How familiar is the English learner with this genre?

Rasinki (2000) emphasizes the importance of finding texts well within readers' independent-instructional range for fluent reading. Teachers should avoid texts with high levels of unfamiliar vocabulary and syntax, particularly for English learners. The language load of a poem or a poetry collection is related to a variety of factors including the number of new or sophisticated vocabulary terms, whether the language of the poem is abstract or has layers of meaning, the amount of figurative language, and so forth. In addition to vocabulary, the syntactic structure of poetry may be less familiar to English learners than traditional sentences and paragraphs. Often, poems lack conventional punctuation and complete sentences, and the language of the poem can be displayed on the page in different and unfamiliar formats. So, on the one hand, poetry appears simplistic because poems are often briefer than stories with shorter lines and fewer words. However, the compressed nature of poems is often related to their use of highly descriptive language, intensity of feeling, and frequent use of figurative language. If poets use fewer words, those words are frequently filled with symbolic or multiple meanings, which is one of the main reasons that teachers sometimes assume that poetry is not appropriate for English learners. Poetry that is deeply symbolic is too abstract for English learners at the beginning levels of proficiency, but "short, highly predictable selections that are meant to be read aloud and with expression, such as rhyming poetry, are ideal for reading fluency instruction" and thus, for Level 1–3 English learners (Rasinski, 2000, p. 148).

The format of poetry books complicates the selection process due to language-level variation. Poem picture books have a tighter level of language since they are essentially one poem by a single author in illustrated format. Multiple readings of the poem, especially with class or group discussion may yield deeper meanings or multiple interpretations, but in general, a poem picture book can target a specific proficiency level. Poetry collections and anthologies are different in that they offer teachers numerous poems to connect to the curriculum and to match a variety of English learners' interests and proficiency levels. Such collections and, in particular, anthologies include poems of varying lengths, some shorter and some longer, and they also include poems of varying language levels, some more concrete and some more abstract with more figurative language. However, single-author collections may not have as much language-level variation as single-topic collections with poems by a variety of poets, all with writing style differences. Therefore, collections can usually be matched to a range of TESOL proficiency levels but not all levels as noted in the following discussion.

In Jorge Lujan's *Colors! Colores!* (2008, TL3–5, A, P), the color poems look deceptively simple but the lyrical language is not direct, and the images of the colors are more abstract ("Burning spark/ lands on the elm./ Who's singing?/ Red.") Thus, this book may prove too challenging for Levels 1 and 2. A poet's emphasis on highly descriptive language also leads to sophisticated and less frequently used vocabulary, which can be a stumbling block to comprehension. While teachers need to encourage English learners to develop their word knowledge, Level 1 students will certainly find the description of the flying carpet ("it was trimmed with yellow tassels,/and made of knotted wool") in Stella Blackstone's *My Granny Went to Market: A Round-the-World Counting Rhyme* (2005, TL2–4, A, P) somewhat puzzling.

Slang and idiomatic expressions as well as figurative language make even simple text challenging for English learners. For instance, the counting book, *Cool Cats Counting* (Shahan, 2005, TL1–5, A, P), begins with a number and an animal in English and ends with the same number and animal in Spanish. In between are poetic riffs, slang phrases associated with rhythm and dance, as in "Nine chickens/ struttin' stuff/ shakin' it up./ Lickety-split!/ Nueve gallinas." Similarly, the color concept book, *Spicy Hot Colors/ Colores Picantes* (Shahan, 2007, TL2–5, A, P), blends metaphors about dance into the mix with examples such as "Green as Mexican iguanas/ Slither/ Slide/ Samba!" or "Yellow as gourds/spitter-sputter seeds/ Yellow as cobs of corn/ hip-hoppin' treat."

In the area of syntax, the cumulative rhyme pattern of *The Pot That Juan Built* (Andrews-Goebel, 2002, TL3–5, I, P) with multiple embedded clauses ("These are the cows all white and brown/ That left manure all over the ground/ That fueled the flames so sizzling hot/ That flickered and flared and fired the pot/ The beautiful pot that Juan built") makes for a wonderful read-aloud, but it could prove exhausting and unclear to a beginning English learner who needs simple and direct sentence patterns. On the other hand, the cumulative text in *Tweedle-Dee-Dee* (Voake, 2008, TL2–5, A, P) is more direct and the vocabulary clear-cut. In this picture poem/songbook based on a traditional folk song, the reader encounters simple sentences, joined by commas ("The eggs were in the nest, the nest was on the branch, the branch was on the tree, the tree was in the wood, and the green leaves grew around, around, ..."), but the meaning is straightforward and very visual even for the beginning English learner.

Level of Textual Support

In the world of nonfiction literature and expository textbooks, there are numerous forms of textual support as in photographs and captioned illustrations, bold and italicized print, graphic aids (e.g., charts, graphs, maps) and text features such as the index, glossary, and table of contents. These features support the conceptual load of nonfiction text helping the reader construct meaning and perhaps, making the text more interesting. There is far less textual support in poetry where the emphasis is more on the language itself as discussed in the previous section. However, there are a few guiding questions to help teachers pinpoint any text support features in poetry including the following:

- Are there visuals (photographs or illustrations)?
- Are the visuals clear and direct? One-to-one correspondence of visuals to the poem/poetry collection? General connection? Primarily for aesthetic purposes?
- Is the print style such as bold, italics, or punctuation used to provide clues to meaning?
- Is the language/wording arranged on the page in such a way to give clues to meaning?

Poets use vivid description to create visual images or rhythm and rhyme to create a musical quality to the text. In children's poetry, textual support may be provided in illustrations that accompany one poem (although these may be more aesthetic and less an example of the specific meaning of the poem) to the illustrations throughout a poem picture book, which generally provide more direct support about the overall meaning of the poem. Occasionally, there may be clues to meaning through print style or punctuation or in the case of concrete poetry, the shape of the words on the page is the shape of the object highlighted in the poem. In addition, textual support can be provided by compilations of poems with a similar form/format. Single-format collections can serve as textual support by helping the teacher provide repetition, particularly if the emphasis is on understanding the format and replicating it as in composing list poems, haikus, or limericks.

In Rebecca Kai Dotlich's *When Riddles Come Rumbling: Poems to Ponder* (2001, TL2–5, A, P), there are visual and print clues along with the language clues in the poem pointing readers to the answer to the riddle. For instance, a partial view of a kite is hidden behind the riddle describing one. Around each riddle are also letters that spell the answer to the riddle. Thus, for this book, there is a close connection of visual support to the poem's meaning. *Once around the Sun* (Katz, 2006, TL2–5, A, P) offers poems that describe the changing of the seasons. The illustrations complement the poem by providing a connection to the poem. For "April," daffodils are referred to in the poem and the reader sees those flowers in the family's yard, and for "September," there is a back-to-school illustration that accompanies the poem. These general illustrations can be used for discussion to help focus English learners on the visual and word descriptions. Just as with *Once around the Sun*, in the single-authored collection, *America: My New Home* (Gunning, 2004, TL3–5, A, P), some illustrations have a link to the poem's meaning as in the poem, "Cathedral," with an illustration of the interior view of the church. However, the illustrations that accompany "The Queen's English" or "Why Such a Hurry?" are more generic and provide limited clues to specific meaning. In fact, the term *queen's English* will need some explanation to English learners not familiar with the British-influenced history of the author's home, Jamaica.

As noted previously, poem picture books are illustrated versions of a single poem as the text and as such, are an innovation with instructional potential for English learners. The single-poem focus with accompanying illustrations support English learners' comprehension. For example, Jan Gilchrist's *My America* (2007, TL1–5, A, P) offers stunning illustrations with simple questions directed to the reader: "Have you seen my country?/ Seen my magic skies?/ Seen my mighty waters?/ Have you seen my land?" While some of the words such as *beasts, fowl,* and *water creatures* would be less familiar to beginning English learners, the simple syntax pattern and related illustrations would support Level 1 students. The full text of the poem is at the end of the book. Another poem picture book that is appropriate for beginners is Pamela Porter's *Yellow Moon, Apple Moon* (2008, TL1–5, A, P), a bedtime rhyme depicting a child saying goodnight to the moon: "Yellow Moon, Apple Moon,/ Time to sleep. See you soon." Also, for Level 2 English learners, Jack Prelutsky's *Me I Am!* (2007, TL2–4, A, P) offers ideas about our individuality and uniqueness: "There is no other ME I AM/ who thinks the thoughts I do."

As with poem picture books, song picture books usually combine illustrations and text to support English learners in meaning-making, but *not* always. Several recent books feature spirituals including Ashley Bryan's, *Let It Shine: Three Favorite Spirituals* (2007, TL1–5, A, P), a collection of three songs: "This Little Light of Mine," "Oh, When the Saints Go Marching In," and "He's Got the Whole World in His Hands." Two other works feature individual versions of songs including E. B. Lewis's *This Little Light of Mine* (2005, TL1–5, A, P) and Kadir Nelson's *He's Got the Whole World in His Hands* (2005, TL1–5, A, P). Bryan includes a brief background on spiritual tunes that may provide some historical and cultural context for English learners. Also, the informal language usage of *gonna* and *little bitty* may require clarification, particularly for Level 1 students. The more basic and straightforward lyrics of "This Little Light of Mine," and "He's Got the Whole World in His Hands" may be easiest for Level 1 or 2 English learners to understand, but the figurative image of God holding people, and so on in His hands may need some discussion. "Oh, When the Saints Go Marching In" is probably best saved for Level 3 students as the meaning is less direct given issues of vocabulary, imagery, and some dialect ("the sun refuse to shine"). In *Dem Bones*, Bob Barner (1996, TL1–3, A, NF) offers a straightforward presentation of the spiritual tune coupled with clear illustrations that can easily be used for a TPR lesson on the skeleton. See Chapter 3 for more discussion of children's books for TPR or physical activity lessons.

Painting a portrait of the diverse landscape of the United States, Diane Siebert has authored numerous poem picture books that spotlight different geographic areas. Vivid language and repeating phrases that serve as a type of refrain are accompanied by illustrations of the areas described as in *Cave* (2000, TL3–5, I, P); "I am the cave,/ So cool and dark,/ Where time, unending, leaves its mark/ As natural forces build and hone/ A crystal world from weeping stone." Similar works by Siebert include *Sierra* (1996, TL3–5, I, P), *Mojave* (1992, TL3–5, I, P), and *Mississippi* (2001, TL3–5, I, P). These are excellent resources to connect to the curriculum, but even with the visual support of illustrations, the topic focus means that these poem picture books are more suited for Level 3–5 English learners at the intermediate-grade level.

Perhaps the most evident text support in poetry comes with concrete, or shape poems, which provide visual accessibility as the poem reflects the shape of what is being described. In addition, there are numerous collections of concrete poems from J. Patrick Lewis's *Doodle Dandies: Poems That Take Shape* (2002, TL2–5, A, P) to Paul Janeczko's *A Poke in the I: A Collection of Concrete Poems* (2001, TL2–5, A, P) and others, so that in reading the poems, English learners become aware that the shape of the words equals the meaning. Among the many collections of shape poems, some depend on accompanying illustrations to help the words reflect the shape and the meaning as with Joan Graham's *Flicker Flash*

(1999, TL2–5, A, P) and *Splish Splash* (1994, TL2–5, A, P) and thus, the poems may not be as clear to Level 1 students. Other collections such as *Come to My Party* (Roemer, 2004, TL1–5, A, P) simply reinforce very "concrete" word structures with illustrations to provide clear meaning for beginning English learners in simple poems such as "It's Raining" in the outline of an umbrella or "Jump Rope Jingle" in the shape of the rope. In general, concrete poetry collections work well for English learners at Levels 2–5 with some of the poems appropriate for Level 1.

Level of Cultural Fit

The diversity of our schools, in particular, the many English learners in classrooms, means that teachers need to take into account the level of cultural fit of the poetry used for instruction. It is important to select poetry that connects with English learners, poems that have more relevance in their lives and experiences. So, teachers need to consider how close a fit the poetry may be to the learner's cultural or experiential background, be it ethnic, geographic, linguistic, religious, socioeconomic, or gender background. As teachers browse through poetry collections or individual poems, they should ask a few questions including the following:

- Is the poem/poetry collection culturally neutral (with general diversity portrayed but no focus on a specific group)? Culturally generic (with a group featured but less specific detail provided)? Culturally specific (with explicit details about a group portrayed)?
- Does the poem/poetry collection reflect the background and/or experiences of recent immigrants? U.S.-born English learners?
- Are the characters similar or different than English learners in the classroom?
- Have English learners had experiences like those described in this poem/poetry collection?
- Have English learners lived in or visited places like those in the poem/poetry collection?
- How far removed is the poem/poetry collection from current times?
- Are any characters the same gender as the reader?
- Do the characters talk like the English learners and their families?
- Is this author/author style familiar to English learners?

Poetry books or collections that exemplify the distinctions among culturally specific, generic, and neutral include the following: *N Is for Navidad* (Elya & Banks, 2007, TL2–5, A, F) provides a rhyming alphabet book that targets the many sights, smells, and activities of a traditional Latino Christmas celebration. The many vocabulary words and longer sentences make this book appropriate for Level 2 and above, although Level 1 students can enjoy the illustrations and terms in Spanish and would benefit from a read-aloud of the book. Even more culturally specific is *Talking with Mother Earth/ Hablando con Madre Tierra* from Salvadoran poet, Jorge Argueta (2006, TL3–5, I, P) with poetry about a Pipil Nahua Indian, his encounters with racism, and the power of nature to heal. Some of the shorter, simpler poems in this collection will work for Level 2 English learners, but in general, this book is more appropriate for Level 3 and above. *Sopa de Frijoles/ Bean Soup* (Argueta, 2009, TL2–5, A, P) can be labeled culturally generic. It has few culturally specific markers, only the Spanish–English text and what appears to be a Latino family enjoying bean soup (black beans are mentioned) with tortillas. The book is a delightful recipe in poem that can reinforce the sequence of events in cooking, and so on. Finally, *When the Horses Ride by: Childen in the Times of War* (Greenfield, 2006, TL2–5, A, P) would be classified as a culturally neutral book. There is great diversity within the illustrations and the various poems that feature war in different historical and geographic contexts, but the poems are not targeted toward any culture. Thus, the poet offers a powerful message about how war transcends all ethnic, geographic, and socioeconomic boundaries. This poetry collection can be used with Level 2 and above as the poems vary in length and complexity. Couple this book with Alice Walker's *Why War Is Never a Good Idea* (2007, TL3–5, I, P), another culturally diverse yet neutral portrait of the devastation of war that is more appropriate for intermediate-grade English learners at Levels 3–5.

In recent years, there has been an increasing focus on literature that reflects the diversity of the schools, hence the publication of culturally relevant poetry often first published in themed collections. Culturally diverse authors are making their voices heard, and their works may speak to English learners, in particular, with their themes of biculturalism, cultural identity, and cultural heritage. Poets such as Janet Wong, Francisco Alarcón, and Monica Gunning give voice to these and many other experiences. However, teachers should not assume, for instance, that such poetry will automatically resonate with an English learner from a similar background. The variation within a cultural group is just as diverse as the range of experiences for individuals outside a cultural group. For instance, some children's literature focuses on the Latino migrant farm work experience as in Carmen Bernier-Grand's poem biography, *Cesar: Yes, We Can!/ César, Sí se Puede* (2006, TL3–5, I, P), but the majority of Latinos are actually urban dwellers. This makes the issue of cultural fit very complex.

Teachers must also be careful of pigeonholing authors as addressing diversity issues only because each writer has many facets and continues to grow as an artist and as an individual. In fact, this can be a helpful demonstration for English learners as is the case in Janet Wong's early work in *Good Luck Gold* (2007, TL3–5, I, P) or *A Suitcase of Seaweed and Other Poems* (2008, TL3–5, I, P). There her focus is clearly on her family roots and relationships as an American of both Chinese and Korean descent. Her next works, *Night Garden: Poems from the World of Dreams* (2007, TL3–5, I, P) and *The Rainbow Hand* (2008, TL3–5, I, P), on the other hand, are beautiful collections that explore other experiences, not exclusively cultural in nature. Either way, her writing is fresh and clear, and intermediate-grade English learners at Levels 3–5 will respond to her simple and direct style.

Part of the push for more culturally relevant literature includes bilingual collections of poetry that are more readily available as well. Bilingual poetry books can have several different formats (Ernst-Slavit & Mulhern, 2003): those with the complete poem in two languages as in any of Francisco Alarcón's (2005, TL3–5, A, P; 2008, TL3–5, A, P) collections as well as *Laughing Out Loud, I Fly/A Carcajadas Yo Vuelo* by Juan Herrera (1998, TL4–5, I, P) and *My Mexico/ México Mío* by Tony Johnston (1999, TL3–5, I, P); those published in different versions, one collection all in English and one completely in another language; and interlingual poetry in English interspersed with words and phrases from another language such as *Confetti: Poems for Children* by Pat Mora (1999). English–Spanish poetry dominates this category of poetry collections with fewer examples of bilingual poetry in other languages. Because of the greater number of English–Spanish bilingual poetry collections, there is a greater range of poems from more simple and easy to read to more complex poems aimed at English learners more proficient in both English and Spanish. Other bilingual collections include Michio Mado's Japanese–English anthologies, *The Animals* (1992, TL3–5, I, P) and *The Magic Pocket: Selected Poems* (1998, TL1–5, A, P).

Finally, the cultural fit arises not only from ethnic characters, geographic settings, and mention of religious, socioeconomic, or gender diversity. Culture is an integral part of the language itself, in the words and the meanings behind the words, especially when it comes to humor. Unlike previous research findings on children's poetry preferences, English learners may not enjoy the same humorous poems that native speakers do. Why? Humor is culturally specific, and English learners may not have experienced humor in that way before. Puns, parodies, irony, and sarcasm are communicated differently in different languages. Teachers should not be surprised when sharing a funny poem, if some English learners don't laugh. Beginning English learners will likely not understand the humor even with an explanation. It might be best to share poetry for the words, sounds, rhythm, and meaning first.

Conclusion

Teachers often neglect poetry in their classrooms and across the curriculum. In part, they may feel intimidated by this genre and feel that poetry is too difficult for students learning a new language. Yet, poetry has many benefits for all students and English learners, in particular. Poetry is an ideal entry point to language and literacy development. Its repetition, rhythm, and rhyme make it an ideal choice for oral language activities and for repeated reading to build fluency as discussed in this chapter. Plus, poetry comes in a variety of styles and addresses topics and themes that speak to English learners, and so, it is a wonderful tool for use across the curriculum. And, poetry offers students many possibilities for writing. English learners can try one of the many poetry formats as a model for writing including acrostic poem, biopoem, color poem, concrete/picture poetry, how-to poem, letter/note/diary poem, list poem, question poem, rap, recipe poem, or riddle poem. Finally, teachers create an inviting, poetry-friendly environment through selecting an inviting classroom poetry collection and creating a listening center where students not only listen to poetry but can also record their own classroom anthologies.

The final chapter in this section focuses on nonfiction literature. While all genre offer possibilities in terms of language and literacy development, the emphasis on developing academic language with English learners makes nonfiction literature a genre that needs more attention.

Books as Mirrors

LULU DELACRE

I first became aware of the tremendous need for books that reflected a Latino child's heritage, traditions, and customs in 1986. My awareness arrived in the most mundane of ways. At the time, I was living in El Paso, Texas, and relished sharing gentle games and lullabies from the Latino oral tradition with my 1-year-old daughter. One day, it occurred to me to search for a picture book that collected these rhymes and songs. I not only wanted to recall complete lyrics, but also for my daughter to see herself in the pictures of a book, and for us to sit together and sing through the pages in joyful unison. So I went to the public library convinced that if there were dozens of illustrated versions of Mother Goose rhymes, there had to be one or two titles like the one I had in mind. My quest proved fruitless. I couldn't borrow the book I was seeking. I couldn't even buy it, since it didn't exist. This search prompted me to imagine that if I needed this book, so did other Spanish-speaking parents—parents eager to preserve their heritage as they raised their children in an English-speaking country. At that moment, *Arroz con Leche: Popular Songs and Rhymes from Latin America* was born.

Since then, I have dedicated myself to creating books that feature Latino children and their heritage, both in pictures and words. I believe that pride in one's roots fosters inner strength. I have witnessed countless times how the Latino students in a school assembly brighten when I address them in Spanish at the beginning of a program. The pride they show as I acknowledge their language and heritage when I ask what Spanish-speaking country their family hails from is unmistakable. The peer acceptance some feel as I read aloud a chapter from *Salsa*

159

Stories that mirrors their life situation or that of their parents is palpable.

In *Salsa Stories* the adults in an extended family recount their experiences growing up in different countries of Latin America. I have conducted creative writing workshops with fourth and fifth graders and showcased the book as an example of using one's heritage as inspiration for fiction. First, I introduce the idea that gave birth to the book: foods inspire warm memories of childhood or a special occasion when that food is always served. Then, I talk about the main elements of a good story and let the children brainstorm ideas. In my latest workshop I witnessed how freeing it was for Latino children to be able to tell about experiences that related to foods like pupusas, tamales, or sancocho. One young girl was so taken by the idea of telling about a picnic at the beach in El Salvador that she wrote the whole story in Spanish. Who is to say that if you can tell the story in one language you cannot transfer it to English once the proper skills are learned? Giving Latino children and their parents books that mirror their customs fosters confidence in them. As they feel accepted and included they will be more confident in embracing the multifaceted culture of the United States of America.

In 2004, *Arrorró mi Niño: Latino Lullabies and Gentle Games* was published. Four years later, an Argentinean librarian—an early literacy coordinator and mother from Washington state—e-mailed me to express her gratitude for the countless hours of happiness the book had provided her and her son. She explained how she cuddled with her 3-year-old, sang through the pages of the book, and expanded on the pictures by creating stories about the characters. In 2008, this young mother was able to do with her little one exactly what I had yearned to do with mine 22 years before.

CHAPTER SIX

Selecting and Using
Nonfiction Literature
with English Learners
in Grades K–6

Just in front of the caterpillar . . . , was a picture book of
caterpillars and butterflies. Francisco liked to look through it
page by page, studying all the pictures. . . . He knew caterpillars
turned into butterflies because Roberto had told him. But just
how did they do it? How long did it take? The words written
underneath each picture in big black letters could tell him, he
knew. So he tried to figure them out by looking at the pictures.
He did this so many times he could close his eyes and see the
words. But he still could not understand what they meant.
—FRANCISCO JIMENEZ, *La Mariposa* (Houghton Mifflin, 1998)

Literature-rich classrooms offer students a wealth of language and visual
appeal along with current, relevant, and interesting information (Duke,
2000; Duke & Bennett-Armistead, 2003; Guthrie, 2002; Kletzien &
Dreher, 2004; McGill-Franzen, Allington, Yokoi, & Brooks, 1999; Morrow, 2003; Young, 2006; Young & Moss, 2006). And, teachers have more
good books on more diverse topics than ever before making it possible
for them to integrate literature across the curriculum (Cullinan, 1993).
Among the many literature choices, nonfiction is preferred by many children. Nonfiction literature, with its emphasis on academic language, can
help English learners, in particular, unlock the content areas as highlighted in the quote from *La Mariposa* at the beginning of this chapter.

The intent behind nonfiction literature is to provide readers with
information about the world around them. Thus, nonfiction is an excel-

lent literacy tool for English language development, presenting new vocabulary and concepts needed for school achievement. Nonfiction literature offers an opportunity for English learners to see literature as a vehicle for understanding their surroundings and for finding answers to their questions. Too, nonfiction literature can help to bridge the gap between the two types of language proficiency highlighted in Chapter 3, English learners' social language or their ability to interact in everyday settings and their academic language and literacy skills in the content areas. Through nonfiction literature English learners gain access to models of many organizational structures, language styles, and techniques used by writers to describe, instruct, persuade, generalize, demonstrate solutions, and trace events (Moss, 1992). In particular, nonfiction books can supplement and substitute for content addressed in textbooks that are not always user-friendly. By connecting nonfiction literature to content study, an impressive variety of topics is available, and a collection of nonfiction books offers a better range of reading levels to meet the variation in English learners' proficiency levels than a single textbook could. English learners respond to the highly visual look and factual content of nonfiction literature. With nonfiction, the focus is less on interpretation, as with fiction, and more on information gathering. Plus, nonfiction reading does not have to progress in a linear, page-by-page fashion as with much fiction.

This chapter explores the powerful genre of nonfiction literature, discovering how it is a natural complement to the expository material from textbooks and reference materials of the content-area classroom. In addition, the chapter highlights the critical issues in selecting nonfiction for English learners. The recommended titles throughout the chapter provide teachers with a wealth of resources for teaching the curriculum to English learners.

Nonfiction Literature and Content Learning

Chapter 3 highlighted the focus of the TESOL Pre-K–12 English Language Proficiency Standards (2006) with four of the five standards devoted to academic language in the content areas. A similar focus can be seen in the research-based recommendations for the effective instruction of English learners from the National Council of Teachers of English in their *English Language Learners: A Policy Research Brief* (2008, pp. 5–6).

- Present English learners with challenging curricular content, organized around "big questions," and involving authentic reading and writing experiences and meaningful content.
- Teach English learners the basics of academic literacy, focusing on content-specific and academic vocabulary.
- Help English learners make connections between academic content and their own knowledge about home and community literacies.
- Teach English learners to simultaneously develop their skill with academic English and learn content in a variety of disciplines.

To address these research-based recommendations, a variety of curriculum and instruction approaches have been designed with a focus on content and academic language including content-based language instruction, sheltered subject matter teaching, theme-based instruction, sheltered instruction, and the Cognitive Academic Language Learning Approach (CALLA; Center for Applied Linguistics, 1987).

Despite this apparent emphasis on academic language and content, Duke (2000) reports little classroom time devoted to informational text in the primary grades. Her study of first-grade classrooms found only 3.6 minutes per day spent with informational texts and in low socioeconomic districts, the amount of time was even less, only 1.4 minutes. Particularly in primary grades, the use of informational text or nonfiction literature is limited. Duke (2003) cites two reasons typically given for this situation. First, the feeling that primary-age children are not able to handle informational text, and second, they do not have an interest in this type of text. Similar reasons are cited for the limited use of informational literature with English learners. In contrast, Duke (2003, pp. 3–5) offers six research-based reasons that teachers should include informational or nonfiction literature in the curriculum:

- Informational text is key to success in later schooling.
- Informational text is ubiquitous in the larger society.
- Informational text is preferred reading for some children.
- Informational text often addresses children's interests and questions.
- Informational text builds knowledge of the natural and social world.
- Informational text has many important text features.

Nonetheless, fiction selections far outnumber nonfiction choices in core reading programs used in the schools. Yet, as Duke and many others have noted, one has only to look at standardized test passages used to measure student academic achievement to see that nonfiction passages far outnumber fiction passages. This focus on fiction may actually work to the students' disadvantage, particularly English learners, who need the academic and technical language that nonfiction literature selections could provide.

Nonfiction books provide the most current information, on a wide variety of subject matter, in many innovative formats, using appealing illustrations and language. Moreover, they provide excellent support for content textbooks and instruction. Nonfiction literature offers meaningful texts that approach English learners' zone of proximal development or their varied levels of optimal input. A growing body of nonfiction picture books provides the supportive structure, in-depth coverage of new concepts, and visual cues to assist with comprehension for the student learning English (Buhrow & Garcia, 2006; Hadaway, Vardell, & Young, 2002a, 2002b, 2002c; Ranker, 2009). A wide range of nonfiction has emerged in recent years, and the publishing world continues to deliver a variety of nonfiction for children as reflected in the growing list of outstanding recipients of the Orbis Pictus Award for Outstanding Nonfiction for Children and the Sibert Award (see *www.ncte.org/elem/pictus* for the Orbis Pictus Award and *www.ala.org/ala/mgrps/divs/alsc/awardsgrants/book-media/sibertmedal/index.cfm* for the Sibert Award).

Utilizing nonfiction literature to lay a foundation for the textbook and to later extend the content presented in textbooks seems ideally suited to students learning English and provides extra opportunities for language exposure. Besides, Crafton (1983) found that reading two selections on the same topic had a positive impact on students' comprehension of the second reading. As vocabulary along with grammatical and discourse structures are repeated, English learners have additional chances to comprehend the meanings of the text they read. This repetition is essential considering "the amount of input required to learn English has probably been grossly underestimated" (Scarcella, 1990, p. 78).

The fascination of facts found in the best nonfiction literature appeals to readers of all ages and language proficiency levels. In fact, nonfiction is a genre ideally suited to sharing across the grade levels since the content of the books offers new information not necessarily linked to particular grade levels. Too, nonfiction books, with their emphasis on information and not characters, often have a more generic appearance increasing their applicability to a wider range of age groups.

Selecting Nonfiction Literature
for English Learners in Grades K–6

Teachers can choose from several different kinds of factual books within the general category of nonfiction as they begin to link the literacy focus of their classroom with the content curriculum. As students and teachers explore the many fine nonfiction works available today, they will readily recognize the numerous ways these works support the content areas providing a repetition and extension of key concepts and ideas. To further strengthen the connection between language and content concepts, teachers can scan content textbooks to familiarize themselves with the important topics and themes and to help plan interdisciplinary units. Figure 6.1 lists some of the types of nonfiction books available today. Teachers should keep in mind, however, that some books cross over formats including characteristics of more than one type of nonfiction book. For instance, Anne Rockwell's *Becoming Butterflies* (2002, TL3–5, A, NF) is both an informational storybook and a life cycle book. The list of nonfiction book types is sequenced from simple to more challenging for English learners. To choose which types of nonfiction books to use, teachers can consider how the books fit the lesson as well as how they facilitate English learners' content and academic language development. A discussion of each of the formats follows with specific points about the use of each with English learners at different proficiency levels.

Alphabet books are one of the oldest types of children's books. Once used as a way to acquaint young children with the letters of the alphabet, today, the letters of the alphabet generally form a structure to introduce a variety of objects, images, or terms. For teachers of English learners, alphabet books offer a broad range of instructional possibilities because of the variation of language, from simple to complex, and the variety of topics addressed. This means that alphabet books can extend over grade

Most accessible	More challenging	Most challenging
• Alphabet books • Counting books • Concept books • Life cycle books • Survey books	• Picture book biographies • How-to and activity books • Informational storybooks	• Complete, partial, and collective biographies • Journals and diaries • Photo essays

FIGURE 6.1. Types of nonfiction books.

levels, K–6, and across English learners' diverse proficiency levels. Alphabet books vary in complexity from single words with photographs or illustrations as in *A Gardener's Alphabet* (Azarian, 2000, TL1–5, A, NF) to phrases and sentences in *Zoo Flakes* (Howell, 2002, TL1–3, A, NF) and *America: A Patriotic Primer* (Cheney, 2002, TL2–5, A, NF) to paragraphs and full-page text in *Children from Australia to Zimbabwe: A Photographic Journey around the World* (Ajmera & Versola, 1997, TL3–5, A, NF). There are alphabet books that address almost every topic in the curriculum—food, art, and music, celebrations, science and nature, sports, history, and mathematics—to name just a few (Evers, Lang, & Smith, 2009). For instance, Jerry Pallotta has numerous alphabet books about animals. Cultural diversity has also been the focus of many recent alphabet books, and some of these may interest English learners, in particular. Specific countries have been highlighted as in *K Is for Korea* (Cheung & Das, 2008, TL3–5, A, NF) or *M Is for Mexico* (Cordero, 2008, TL3–5, A, NF) as well as different regions of the world with *A Is for Asia* (Chin-Lee, 1997, TL3–5, A, NF) or *A Is for the Americas* (Chin-Lee & de la Peña, 1999, TL3–5, A, NF) and various cultural events such as the lunar new year in *D Is for Dragon Dance* (Compestine, 2006, TL2–5, A, NF). Yet, despite the incredible scope of alphabet books, "they generally follow a consistent and predictable organization pattern rendering them user-friendly and effective" for language development of English learners of different ages and proficiency levels (Evers et al., 2009, p. 462).

Counting books, like alphabet books, also have a built-in structure. Often this is simply counting from 1 to 10 as in *Ten Seeds* (Brown, 2001, TL1–3, P, NF), but sometimes counting books incorporate 0, sets, and multiples. For example, *One Watermelon Seed* (Lottridge, 2008, TL2–4, A, NF) includes 1 to 10 and then counting by 10s with mention of hundreds and thousands. *One Is a Snail, Ten Is a Crab: A Counting by Feet Book* (Sayre & Sayre, 2003, TL1–4, A, NF) also includes multiples ("30 is three crabs .../ or ten people and a crab."). A little more complexity is added in *The Coin Counting Book* (Williams, 2001, TL1–3, A, NF) as simple math with coins is presented. This is a helpful book for recent immigrants who are beginning to learn English as it helps to acquaint them with the different U.S. coins and their values.

Counting books, like alphabet books, often focus on different cultures as in *One Child, One Seed: A South African Counting Book* (Cave, 2003, TL2–5, A, NF), and there are many bilingual counting books, some with complete text in two languages and others with interlingual words and phrases as in *Cool Cats Counting* with some Spanish words used (Shahan, 2005, TL1–5, A, NF) and *We All Went on Safari: A Counting*

Journey through Tanzania (Krebs, 2003, TL2–5, A, NF) with the numbers 1–10 in English and Swahili. Just as with alphabet books, counting books may have limited text per page or there may be more information. Barbara McGrath's *Soccer Counts!* (2003, TL2–5, A, NF) offers two rhyming sentences with a number and term related to soccer followed by a paragraph with more in-depth information. While counting books sometimes have more elaborated text, they usually don't have the reach of grade levels or language proficiency levels that alphabet books display. In general, counting books are most appropriate for Levels 1–3, with some occasional use with Level 4 and 5 students when there is extended text information. As to grade-level application, counting books will be most useful in the primary grades, but they can be used at the intermediate grades with newly arrived English learners who have limited language proficiency and who need to learn basic concepts.

Concept books present basic information about a single topic simply, in an interesting manner. The purpose of a concept book is to teach, to present information, not to tell a story. The best ones are very simple and highly visual and thus, they are ideal for Level 1 and 2 English learners. They usually deal with challenging concepts such as color, direction, time, proportion, and so on. While these books are often thought of as books for young children, teachers working with Level 1 English learners will find them a source of wonderful language support. For primary-grade English learners, concept books may be needed to target both a new concept to learn as well as the new language for that concept. For intermediate-grade English learners, concept books may be a convenient way to address the new language or labels for a concept that they already know in their home language. However, it is possible that limited formal schooling English learners who are just entering the classroom on a consistent basis may need both the conceptual as well as the language support of concept books.

Tana Hoban is an acknowledged expert in creating distinctive and useful concept books through the effective use of photographs. For instance, she uses photographs illustrating groupings of objects in larger and smaller numbers to help readers understand quantity concepts in *More, Fewer, Less* (1998, TL1–3, A, NF). Some of Hoban's books are wordless, and thus, offer room for rich discussion and an excellent means of tapping into the background knowledge of English learners. In addition, there are numerous concept books for colors including Stephen Swinburne's *What Color Is Nature?* (2002, TL1–2, P, NF), which has a brief introduction about colors and then photographs with a simple question and answer format: "What color is this apple?/Red." For a more lively and poetic color concept book, teachers can use Sherry Shahan's bilingual *Spicy Hot Colors/ Colores Picantes* (2004, TL1–5, A, P): "Green as cilantro and cactus/ Wiggle/ waggle/ Rumba! Green Verde." More elaborated information is presented in the two concept books by Maya Ajmera and John Ivanko, *To Be an Artist* (2004b, TL2–5, A, NF) and *Be My Neighbor* (2004a, TL2–5, A, NF), which define art and neighborhoods, respectively, with a global emphasis.

Cycle/life cycle books, such as Lois Ehlert's *Waiting for Wings* (Harcourt, 2001, TL1–3, A, NF) about butterflies, extend information from the science textbook to present the life of an animal in more detail and with more appeal than is possible in the textbook format. Another snapshot of the life cycle of butterflies is presented in Anne Rockwell's informational storybook, *Becoming Butterflies* (2002, TL3–5, A, NF), as an elementary class observes three caterpillars undergoing the process of metamorphosis over the course of a month. *Little Green Frogs* (Barry, 2008, TL1–2, P, NF) uses repetitive, rhyming language to examine the life cycle of the frog while Nicola Davies in *One Tiny Turtle* (2001, TL3–5, A, NF) also uses poetic language to describe the life cycle of the Loggerhead turtle: "Just beneath the surface/ is a tangle of weed and driftwood/ where tiny creatures cling./ This is the nursery of a sea turtle." In *Ten Seeds* (Brown, 2001, TL1–3, P, NF), 10 sunflower seeds are planted, but only one survives ("Ten seeds,/ one ant./ Nine seeds,/ one pigeon.") to bloom and drop 10 seeds so that the cycle can begin anew. Not all cycle books focus on a life cycle. For instance, the water cycle unfolds over the course of a year in Neil Waldman's *The Snowflake: A Water Cycle Story* (2003, TL3–5, A, NF) with each month highlighting a part of the process (e.g., a snowflake in January, a frozen water droplet in February, a melted water droplet in March). In the informational storybook, *A Taste of Honey* (Wallace, 2005, TL2–4, P, NF), Lili Bear asks where honey comes from. In an attempt to answer her questions, the steps in the production of honey are described, but in reverse order from the supermarket shelf to the bee. Finally, Susan Steggall offers readers simple steps in *The Life of a Car* (2008, TL1–2, P, NF) from beginning, "Build the car," through an accident, to "Recycle the car," and start the process over again.

Photo essays, much like a documentary film or an issue of *National Geographic*, document and validate the text with photographs on nearly every page. Whatever their language proficiency level, students can simply browse through the many splendid photos, or they can read captions or pay closer attention to the text. Photo essays are ideal to gain an overview of a topic without focusing on every single idea presented. However, due to the elaborated description of the photographs with paragraph- or page-length text, photo essay books are most appropriate for the intermediate grades and for Levels 3–5 with limited instructional use with Level 2 English learners for short read-alouds or browsing opportunities.

English learners will enjoy encountering relevant and at times controversial issues through this format. Moreover, many recent photo essays have a culturally relevant focus, ideal for today's diverse classrooms. Two authors, in particular, Diane Hoyt-Goldsmith and George Ancona, have numerous photo essays that are excellent for connecting to the curriculum and for building language with English learners in the intermediate grades. Hoyt-Goldsmith has focused many of her books on religious holidays and cultural events including *Celebrating a Quinceanera: A Latina's 15th Birthday Celebration* (2002, TL3–5, I, NF), *Las Posadas: An Hispanic Christmas Celebration* (1999, TL3–5, I, NF), *Cinco de Mayo: Celebrating the Traditions of Mexico* (2008, TL3–5, I, NF), *Celebrating Chinese New Year* (1998, TL3–5, I, NF), *Three Kings Day: A Celebration at Christmastime* (2004, TL3–5, I, NF), *Celebrating Passover* (2000, TL3–5, I, NF), and *Celebrating Ramadan* (2001, TL3–5, I, NF) as well as having a photo essay of the game of lacrosse, its origins, and both historical and contemporary connections to the Iroquois in *Lacrosse: The National Game of the Iroquois* (1998, TL3–5, I, NF). George Ancona's work spans many topics but most of his books reflect his Latino heritage including *Mayeros: A Yucatec Maya Family* (1997, TL3–5, I, NF), *Murals: Walls That Sing* (2003, TL3–5, I, NF), *The Piñata Maker/ El Piñatero* (1994, TL3–5, I, NF), *Barrio: El Barrio de José* (1998, TL3–5, I, NF), *Harvest* (2001, TL3–5, I, NF), about migrant farm work, and *Fiesta Fireworks* (1998, TL3–5, I, NF), which documents how the people of Tultepec, Mexico, honor their patron saint, San Juan de Dios, with a fiesta complete with extraordinary fireworks.

How-to and activity books invite readers to engage in actions beyond reading. The hands-on approach of books, such as Seymour Simon and Nicole Fauteux's *Let's Try It Out in the Water: Hands-On Early-Learning Science Activities* (2003, TL3–5, A, NF), *Let's Try It Out in the Air: Hands-On Early-Learning Science Activities* (2003, TL3–5, A, NF), and *Let's Try It Out with Towers and Bridges: Hands-On Early-Learning Science Activities* (2003, TL3–5, A, NF), or Vicki Cobb's *I Get Wet* (2002, TL3–5, A, NF) directly involve English learners, a technique supported by methods such as TPR. Another example of an activity book for the area of social studies is Scot Ritchie's *Follow That Map! A First Look at Mapping Skills* (2009, TL3–5, A, NF), which has readers join several friends as they search for their missing dog and cat by reading information on maps. While the hands-on potential of these books is motivating, the authors of these books must use more vocabulary and sentences per page because authors need to provide enough elaboration to enable readers to follow the instructions. Therefore, these books are more appropriate for Levels 3–5. For Level 2 English learners, teachers can use the books as sources of activities for class demonstrations and for reading aloud the instructions and leading students through the steps.

Journals and diaries provide the basis for either the content or organizational structure of many recent information books, and these books supply an excellent framework or model for writing activities. The format may already be familiar to learners, which helps in their comprehension of the specific examples shared in the classroom. However, journals and diaries are all about writing and therefore, have more complex text with at least a paragraph per page and few, if any, visuals for textual support. Journals sometimes have illustrations as in two works about the Antarctic, *Antarctic Journal: Four Months at the Bottom of the World* (Dewey, 2001, TL4–5, I, NF) and *My Season with Penguins: An Antarctic Journal* (Webb, 2000, TL4–5, I, NF), as they reflect a log of scientific observations. Yet, both of these journals have longer, more complex text and so, require more developed language proficiency. Therefore, journals and diaries are more appropriate for Levels 3–5, and in general, more applicable for the intermediate grades and beyond. One of the more simple journals recently published is *My Tour of Europe by Teddy Roosevelt, Age 10* (Jackson, 2003, TL3–5, A, NF). With illustrations on each page, this book could be used with Level 2 English learners with support. In addition, *How We Crossed the West: The Adventures of Lewis and Clark* (Schanzer, 1998, TL3–5, I, NF) combines illustrations and text with entries, some shorter, some longer, making parts accessible to Level 3 intermediate grade students.

Survey books acquaint readers with a topic. Either as a prereading tool to introduce a topic or a postreading follow-up for extension, these books furnish a scaffold to English learners as they encounter text or reference material on the same topics. Survey books come in a wide range of topics and language from very simple books ideal for Level 1 English learners as in the series by Cathryn Sill including *About Birds* (1991, TL2–4, A, NF), *About Mammals* (1997, TL2–4, A, NF), *About Reptiles* (1999, TL2–4, A, NF), *About Insects* (2000, TL2–4, A, NF), *About Amphibians: A Guide for Children* (2001, TL2–4, A, NF), *About Rodents* (2008, TL2–4, A, NF), and *About Penguins* (2009, TL2–4, A, NF) to more complex books by Gail Gibbons or Seymour Simon and others. As a result, teachers can easily address English learners' language proficiency levels in grades K–6.

Using survey books can also be excellent preparation for tackling content textbooks because they use many of the same access features as the longer, more challenging textbooks. For example, biologist Nicola Davies acquaints young readers with the world's largest mammal in the *Big Blue Whale* (2000, TL3–5, A, NF). Bold illustrations attract children to Martin Jenkins's *Chameleons Are Cool!* (2001, TL3–5, A, NF) where they will learn amazing facts about these reptiles, their features, their behaviors, and their ability to change colors. The prolific nonfiction author Gail Gibbons offers basic survey books with colorful cartoon-style illustrations, helpful captions, and exposition on over 200 different subjects that are suitable for English learners at Levels 3–5. *Polar Bears* (2001, TL3–5, A, NF), *Owls* (2005, TL3–5, A, NF), *The Vegetables We Eat* (2007, TL3–5, A, NF), and *Hurricanes* (2009, TL3–5, A, NF) are just four examples by Gibbons.

Informational storybooks contain facts embedded in a story form. This hybrid subgenre utilizes a storyline to carry the information in a lively fashion as in *George Washington's Teeth* (Chandra & Comora, 2003, TL2–4, A, NF). In simple narrative with only two to four simple sentences on most pages, readers discover information about this leader's problems with his teeth. There is a timeline and list of sources at the end. *Ice Cream Cones for Sale* (Greenstein, 2003, TL3–5, A, NF) is another example that explores the story of who really invented the ice cream cone. Author's notes and tips for eating an ice cream cone are at the end of the book. While the previous examples appear more like traditional narrative picture books with the information directly integrated into the storyline, *Vote!* (Christelow, 2008, TL3–5, A, NF) has more of a blended format with expository information about the voting process at the top of the page and below, cartoon illustrations with the "story" about a city mayoral election. This format is similar to the Magic School Bus series. In these books, Joanna Cole deftly weaves three strands, the narration, the dialogue bubbles, and the children's reports, to make these books appealing to children. The innovative writing style allows these books to function as both fantasy and information and can be used to help English learners differentiate between the two. The *Magic School Bus Explores the Senses* (1999, TL3–5, A, NF) and *The Magic School Bus and the Electric Field Trip* (1997, TL3–5, A, NF) are two examples of the exciting field trips Ms. Frizzle and her students undertake on their school bus. Because blended-format books are so "busy" with text, they generally take multiple readings to make sense of all the layers.

Biographies today are varied, and a recent trend is the availability of biographies on all kinds of people—women, people of color, and ordinary citizens. Authors can write biographies in a variety of approaches, formats, and types including picture book biographies, complete or partial biographies, collective biographies, and autobiographies and memoirs.

Picture book biographies make it possible for young children to experience biography. However, this is not to say that picture book biographies are only for young children. They are shorter books, which may make them less intimidating to English learners. They are also more focused in their presentation of information, with illustrations that often convey as much detail as the text and that help the English learner begin to visualize the subjects and their times. These books provide English learners with extra support so they can read biographies as they acquire English. David Adler is one nonfiction author who has numerous picture book biographies to his credit including ones spotlighting Jesse Owens (1992, TL3–5, A, NF), Anne Frank (1994, TL3–5, A, NF), Rosa Parks (1995, TL3–5, A, NF), and Sacagawea (2000, TL3–5, A, NF), to name just a few. Some individuals have been the subject of multiple biographies by different authors who use a variety of presentation and writing styles. While Adler generally uses a traditional style of writing in his picture book biograhies, Carole Boston-Weatherford adopts the second person in *Jesse Owens, Fastest Man Alive* (2007, TL3–5, A, NF) to poetically narrate the athlete's triumphant performance at the 1936 Olympics in Berlin, Germany, against the backdrop of Hilter's prejudice: "Taste the bratwurst; enjoy the bands and fireworks./ But know that Nazi flags/ on storefronts do not fly for you./ Hitler does not want your kind here,/ does not believe you belong./ Prove him wrong." The repetition of information in different authorial voices offers an excellent opportunity for English learners to engage in multiple readings across different biographies to develop their language proficiency and to build their understanding of an individual.

Complete biographies span the subject's entire life and are perhaps the most ambitious to read or write. To assist students in getting started with these more lengthy and complicated works, a visual such as a timeline might be used as a prereading organizer. To focus on the information provided in complete biographies, students may continue to use the same timeline as a summary or note-taking organizer. **Partial biographies**, on the other hand, deal with only a portion of an individual's life, often a pivotal event as in *The Bus Ride That Changed History: The Story of Rosa Parks* (Edwards, 2009, TL3–5, A, NF) or *Stealing Home: Jackie Robinson against the Odds* (Burleigh, 2007, TL2–5, A, NF). In the last example, Robert Burleigh's main text describes Robinson's attempt to steal home in a 1955 World Series game although he also includes boxed insets with additional information about this baseball great. **Collective biographies** contain paragraph-, page-, or even chapter-length sketches of a number of figures. These biographies lend themselves to interdisciplinary or thematic units in that the subjects have a common connection. Collective biographies may appeal to English learners since they can read about a number of people's lives in a relatively small amount of text. Moreover, collective biographies may inspire students to read other longer biographies about subjects of particular interest. Two recent collective biographies, both by Cynthia Chin-Lee, are also alphabet books: *Akira to Zoltan: Twenty-Six Men Who Changed the World* (2006, TL3–5, I, NF) and *Amelia to Zora: Twenty-Six Women Who Changed the World* (2005, TL3–5, I, NF). **Autobiographies and memoirs** are biographies written by the subjects themselves. Thus, these books can be biased or more subjective than those written by impartial authors but can also provide interesting personal insights into character and personality.

Of all the biography types, picture book biographies may be the most flexible for English learners. They can be used with Levels 2–5 at both primary- and intermediate-grade levels. Complete biographies, autobiographies, and memoirs, due to their length and the complexity of text, are more appropriate for Level 4 and 5 English learners who have more developed language proficiency. Collective biographies with several sentences or a simple paragraph for each individual might be used with Level 2 English learners as in Lynne Cheney's *A Is for Abigail: An Almanac of Amazing American Women* (2003, TL2–5, A, NF).

In summary, each of the types of nonfiction books discussed in this section has both positives and challenges for use with English learners. In terms of ranking the difficulty levels, alphabet and counting books, concept books, life cycle, and survey books have the broadest language and instructional range as they can reach across all proficiency levels from Level 1 through Level 5 and all grade levels K–6. This does not mean that all books in these categories of nonfiction can be used at each proficiency level. There will be some very basic books that could be used effectively with Level 1 English learners and with primary grades and others that are better suited for students with more developed language proficiency levels and at the intermediate-grade levels, depending on the content addressed and its connection to the curriculum. In general, these books have photographs and illustrations on every page, and most of the time there is a one-to-one correspondence of visual to text or at least a close connection. In addition, alphabet and counting books and concept books have text ranging from the single-word or phrase level, appropriate for Level 1, to sentences and paragraphs for English learners with more developed proficiency. The text in life cycle and survey books varies from simple to complex sentences, but they may have labeled illustrations, short captions, and graphics for clarification and support of comprehension and language development.

In the middle range of difficulty for English learners among nonfiction book types are how-to or activity books, informational storybooks, and picture book biographies. These nonfiction books can be used with Levels 2 or 3 through Level 5 and grades K–6 depending on content and textual complexity. Use of these types of nonfiction books with Level 2 English learners, however, may require support from the teacher through read-alouds or hands-on activities. Most how-to or activity books, informational storybooks, and picture book biographies have photographs or illustrations on every page. The visuals may not correspond directly to the text although with how-to books, there should be a close connection of visual to text in order for readers to follow the step-by-step sequence. The text of these books ranges from simple sentences and paragraphs to more complex ones.

Finally, the most challenging among the nonfiction book types mentioned in this section are photo essays, journals and diaries, complete and collective biographies, and autobiographies and memoirs. While photo essays have photographs and illustrations on each page, there is generally a paragraph or more of text on each page, and the complexity of the sentence structure varies from simple to more complex. Journals and diaries as well as complete and collective biographies, and autobiographies and memoirs tend to have limited visuals but the same level of text complexity, so they are slightly more difficult. Therefore, photo essays, journals and diaries, complete and collective biographies, and autobiographies and memoirs are most appropriate for Level 3–5 English learners in the intermediate grades. Photo essays might have limited instructional application with Level 2 students in the primary grades. Students might be interested in looking through such books when they are related to a unit of study or to their own interests or backgrounds, so primary-grade teachers should include photo essays in classroom libraries and learning centers.

The many types of nonfiction texts described in this section are sure to engage English learners and meet the needs of different proficiency levels. The diverse formats both complicate the process of targeting a book to a single proficiency level and broaden the applicability of many nonfiction books to various proficiency levels. Just one example is Irene Kelly's *It's a Hummingbird's Life* (2003, TL3–5, A, NF). The facts in the book are in script print and placed in different places on the page with different orientations, both vertical and horizontal, to mimic the tiny bird's flight. Taken as single sentences, the book could be used with Level 2 and 3 English learners, but the content and language of the whole text make it more appropriate for Level 3–5 students. These types of considerations are discussed in more detail in the next section.

Criteria for Selecting Nonfiction Literature for English Learners in Grades K–6

The varied formats of nonfiction books offer many instructional choices to teachers, but the literacy criteria often used for evaluating and selecting fiction (character, plot, setting, theme) do not apply when choosing quality nonfiction. The most important criteria is accuracy. Other features such as organization and style are also important, particularly when working with English learners. The four basic criteria for matching books to English learners presented in Chapter 2 (level of content familiarity or background knowledge, level of language, level of textual support, and level of cultural fit) have been focused on the selection of nonfiction in Table 6.1. The issues of accuracy, organization, style, and so on have been integrated within these four criteria. An in-depth discussion of the selection criteria and how they have been applied to examples of recently published nonfiction literature follow. There are areas where the criteria may seem to overlap. For instance, content coverage influences the level of language used and language can be a type of text support. However, using these criteria and guiding questions, teachers can begin to carefully weigh the most appropriate nonfiction books to meet English learners' varying language proficiency needs and backgrounds and to help increase their academic language and conceptual background knowledge.

Level of Content Familiarity or Background Knowledge

The content load in nonfiction coupled with attempting to master those concepts and facts in a new language can be overwhelming for English learners, so it is important to consider how close a fit a text is to students' existing content knowledge or background experiences. Is the text laying a conceptual foundation or adding to an existing knowledge base from the curriculum or from the learner's own experience? To weigh these issues, teachers should consider the following questions:

- What content and concepts are presented in the nonfiction text? What is the content/conceptual load of the nonfiction text? Basic and familiar? New but general? New and specialized?
- Is this presentation an introduction to the content and concepts or is it continued conceptual development at a higher level?
- What is the English learner's level of content familiarity or background knowledge related to the content and concepts? Is the concept very familiar, familiar, unfamiliar, or not common?
- What content background knowledge does the English learner have on the topic/focus of the nonfiction text?
- Has the topic/focus of the nonfiction text been previously covered in the curriculum? When? At what level? What was the level of success of English learners?
- Is the topic/focus of the nonfiction text likely to be part of the readers' background experiences? How so?
- How can the teacher best link English learners' previous experiences/understandings to the nonfiction text?

For an introduction to new content-area concepts and when the teacher is laying a foundation, the selected book should have only a few concepts and facts presented in clear language. If the concepts have been previously presented, then more elaboration of information is possible. For Level 1 English learners, in particular, teachers need to select nonfiction books that address more universal content and topics. Books that address basic and concrete topics suggested in Chapter 3 to build conceptual background are a good starting point. For instance, movement is a universal concept and two excellent books with basic content that support Level 1 and 2 English learners are Stephen Swinburne's *Go, Go, Go! Kids on the Move* (2002, TL1–2, P, F) and *Move!* by Steve Jenkins and Robin Page (2006, TL1–4, A, F) about the ways that animals move. Food is another basic concept, and George Levenson's *Bread Comes to Life: A Garden of Wheat and a Loaf to Eat* (2004, TL2–5, A, NF) offers a view of this ancient staple that is still a part of diets today around the world: "Bread is the food we eat every day./ So many kinds. So many ways./ White bread/ black bread/ small bread/ tall bread." The author extends the overview of bread including simple information on the process of growing wheat and making bread with thumbnails, reduced-size versions of the illustrations or photographs in the book, and additional facts at the end. This book is similar to Ann Morris's *Bread, Bread, Bread* (1993, TL1–4, A, NF), which highlights the shapes, sizes, textures, and colors of bread around the world. In fact, the Morris book is part of a

TABLE 6.1. Criteria and Guiding Questions for Selecting Nonfiction Literature for English Learners in Grades K–6

Criteria	Guiding questions
Level of content familiarity or background knowledge How close a fit is the fiction text to the English learner's knowledge or background experiences? How close a fit is the poem/poetry collection to the English learner's knowledge or background experiences? How close a fit is the nonfiction text to the English learner's content knowledge or background experiences?	• What content and concepts are presented in the nonfiction text? What is the content/conceptual load of the nonfiction text? Basic and familiar? New but general? New and specialized? • Is this presentation an introduction to the content and concepts or is it continued conceptual development at a higher level? • What is the English learner's level of content familiarity or background knowledge related to the content and concepts? Is the concept very familiar, familiar, unfamiliar, or not common? • What content background knowledge does the English learner have on the topic/focus of the nonfiction text? • Has the topic/focus of the nonfiction text been previously covered in the curriculum? When? At what level? What was the level of success of English learners? • Is the topic/focus of the nonfiction text likely to be part of the readers' background experiences? How so? • How can the teacher best link English learners' previous experiences/understandings to the nonfiction text?
Level of language How close a fit is the nonfiction text to the English learner's vocabulary, syntactic knowledge, and overall proficiency level?	• What is the vocabulary load of the nonfiction text (e.g., basic and familiar, sophisticated/advanced and unfamiliar, concrete or abstract, general or technical/specialized, idiomatic, formal or informal, vocabulary with multiple meanings, figurative language)? • How many new vocabulary words are presented? • Does the nonfiction text present new vocabulary in meaningful contextual language? • How likely is the English learner to encounter the vocabulary in this nonfiction text in other reading? • What is the English learner's previous experience with the vocabulary of the nonfiction text (completely new, some exposure, should be part of active vocabulary)? Is the vocabulary currently or likely to be part of the English learner's speaking vocabulary? Listening vocabulary? Reading vocabulary? Writing vocabulary? • If the nonfiction text is predictable, what is the size of the predictable unit and what percent of nonfiction text does the predictable unit account for? • What is the syntactic structure of the nonfiction text? Word level? Phrase level? Single simple sentences per page?

(cont.)

TABLE 6.1. *(cont.)*

Criteria	Guiding questions
Level of language (cont.)	Multiple simple sentences? Short paragraphs with simple sentences? Compound sentences? Complex sentences? Compound/complex sentences? Embedded clauses? How familiar is the English learner with those syntax patterns? Does the English learner use that syntax pattern in speaking? Writing?
	• What types of text structure does the nonfiction text use? Chronological? Sequential? Description? Listing? Cause–effect? Problem–solution?
	• How familiar is the English learner with this text structure pattern? Has the English learner encountered this pattern previously?
	• What type of nonfiction text is this (alphabet or counting book, biography, etc.) and how familiar is the English learner with the type?
	• How familiar is the English learner with this genre?
Level of textual support What types of support does the nonfiction text provide and how familiar is the English learner with these types of text support?	• Is the nonfiction text well organized? • Are there visuals (photographs or illustrations)? • Are the visuals clear and direct? One-to-one correspondence of visuals to text? General connection to text? Primarily for aesthetic purposes? • Are there graphic aids in the nonfiction text (charts, maps, tables, graphs)? • How much does the English learner know about these types of graphic aids? Has the English learner successfully used these types of aids in previous reading? Is the general format of the aid new or familiar (e.g., different types of graphs, picture, bar, line, circle)? • What types of text features are used? Print style such as bold or italics? Headings and subheadings? Captions and labeling of visuals/graphics? Table of contents, index, glossary? • How familiar is the English learner with these types of text features?
Level of cultural fit How close a fit is the nonfiction text to the English learner's cultural or experiential background (ethnic, language, geographic, religious, socioeconomic, gender)?	• Is the nonfiction text culturally neutral (with general diversity portrayed but no focus on a specific group)? Culturally generic (with a group featured but less specific detail provided)? Culturally specific (with explicit details about a group portrayed)? • Does the nonfiction text reflect the background and/or experiences of recent immigrants? U.S.-born English learners? • Are the characters similar or different than English learners in the classroom?

(cont.)

TABLE 6.1. *(cont.)*

Criteria	Guiding questions
Level of cultural fit (cont.)	• Have English learners had an experience like one described in the nonfiction text? • Have English learners lived in or visited places like those in the nonfiction text? • How far removed is the nonfiction text from current times? • Do the characters talk like the English learners and their families? • Is this author/author style familiar to English learners?

series of concept books with a global emphasis featuring clothing (*Shoes, Shoes, Shoes,* 1998, TL1–4, A, NF; *Hats, Hats, Hats,* 1993, TL1–4, A, NF), transportation (*On the Go,* 1994, TL1–4, A, NF), work (*Tools,* 1998, TL1–4, A, NF), and so on. The minimal text and simple details in each book are extended through thumbnails at the end offering at least two levels of content in a single book.

As mentioned earlier, basic counting and alphabet books and concept books are excellent initial nonfiction texts for English learners at Levels 1 and 2, and they can be used with both primary and intermediate grades. As a caution, some alphabet books and counting books are not as simple as they appear; they go beyond numbers or letters. The most basic counting books present the numbers 1 to 10 with phrases or simple sentences as in *One Is a Snail: Ten Is a Crab* (Sayre & Sayre, 2003, TL1–4, A, NF), so the focus is on the numbers and the concept of counting and multiples of numbers even though there is an indirect lesson about differences in number of feet among creatures. Some counting or alphabet books require more background knowledge as in *Smoke Jumpers One to Ten* (Demarest, 2002, TL2–4, A, NF), a book that counts forward from 1 to 10 and then in reverse, to describe the job of smoke jumpers. A need for some initial context for smoke jumpers and what their job entails along with a diagram of their equipment with the technical terms and a lengthy author's note make this book a better choice for Level 2 and 3 English learners.

As a means of helping with the content load, some authors use analogies or comparisons of the new information to knowledge that readers may already possess. For instance, in *Like People* (2008, TL2–4, A, NF), Ingrid Schubert explains that "Many animals in the world have babies— just like people." And further, "Animal parents teach their babies how to take care of themselves." Thus, the author connects what the reader already knows about human parenting behavior to animals. This type of support is especially helpful to English learners. In addition, *Are Trees Alive?* (Miller, 2003, TL2–5, A, NF) was inspired by a question from the author's daughter. In response to the child's question, "Are trees alive?" the author explains that there are features of trees that are similar to those of humans. For example, "Bark protects the inside of a tree from harsh weather and insects, like your skin protects you." In *Sparrows*, Hans Post and Kees Heij (2008, TL2–5, A, NF) offer some concrete comparisons: "It can weigh as much as seven sugar cubes" and "The heart of a sparrow beats eight hundred times in a minute. The heart of a person beats only seventy times in a minute." Finally, the question and answer book, *Have You Ever Seen a Duck in a Raincoat?* (Kaner, 2009, TL1–3, P, NF) uses concrete comparisons of human clothing to animal adaptations (e.g., a parka for humans and blubber for a whale). These books serve to remind teachers that all students bring background knowledge that can be helpful in understanding some of the academic requirements of school.

All classrooms have students, including English learners, at different levels in terms of content knowledge. Some nonfiction authors actually use a format that addresses differences in content background as they provide layers of information, a type of spiral curriculum that revisits the information with increasing complexity at each level. Steve Jenkins's books *Biggest, Strongest, Fastest* (1995, TL1–5, A, NF), *Hottest, Coldest, Highest, Deepest* (1998, TL2–5, A, NF), and *Animals in Flight* (2001, TL2–5, A, NF) are excellent examples of this content-layering technique. He uses a simple sentence that serves as a basic overview of the information for that page or two-page spread, a type of entry level or foundational knowledge. Then, on the same page, additional facts and illustrations are provided with more information, a second layer of content knowledge. Finally, Jenkins sometimes provides thumbnails at the end accompanied by paragraphs with further elaboration for another level of content information. Through small group or paired sharing, English learners can move through the layers with multiple readings. Due to the different levels of content information, Jenkins's books can be used by English learners at Levels 2–5 and in both the primary and intermediate grades.

Many other nonfiction authors use dual levels of text to provide different levels of content. While the dual levels of text address different reading levels, the technique also tackles the idea of drilling deeper into more complex and sophisticated types of content knowledge. Other examples of multiple levels of content include *Stick Out Your Tongue! Fantastic Facts, Features, and Functions of Human and Animal Tongues* (Bonsignore, 2001, TL3–5, A, NF) along with Sneed Collard's survey books, *Leaving Home* (2002, TL1–5, A, NF), about the many ways that animals leave home, and *Beaks* (2002, TL2–5, A, NF), which examines the types of beaks that birds have and how they use them. The simple line of text at the top of the page can be read aloud to the class and would be appropriate for Level 1 and 2 English learners. Reading aloud the simple text from *Leaving Home*, for instance, readers are reminded of some real-world background knowledge: "Sooner or later, we all leave home./ Some of us walk./ Some of us crawl." The paragraphs below are suitable for students at Levels 3–5 although Level 3 students may need support due to the technical information related to these science topics. *To Be an Artist* (2004b) and *Be My Neighbor* (2004a), both written by Maya Ajmera and John Ivanko (TL2–5, A, NF), are concept books that focus on universal, and thus, more accessible, content using the layers of information format. Each of these books adds a global focus with photographs from around the world and a map at the end that notes where each photograph discussed in the book was taken.

Whether or not different levels of content are presented within the same book, teachers can build collections of books, or text sets, that target different language proficiency levels and different depths of content, a practice discussed in Chapter 3 with narrow reading. Such collections may also feature different writing styles. On the topic of sharks, there are many nonfiction books to choose. Three with different styles are *All about Sharks* (2008, TL3–5, A, NF), part of the All About Series by Jim Arnosky, *Sharks* (2006, TL4–5, I, NF) by Seymour Simon, and *Surprising Sharks* (Davies, 2003, TL3–5, A, NF). Nicola Davies's book is more conversational in tone, with some humor thrown in: "You see, MOST sharks are not at all what you might expect. After all, who would expect a shark to … have built-in fairy lights … or blow up like a party balloon … or lie on the sea floor like a scrap of old carpet …" (pp. 10–11). Davies's main text is sentence length and accessible to Level 3 English learners with illustrations and additional facts that can be revisited by Level 4 and 5 students. *All about Sharks* has paragraph-length descriptions of sharks, what they eat and how they give birth, and so on. Illustrations with labels and some additional facts in simple sentences surround the main text. This book can be used with Level 3–5 English learners. Finally, Simon's books have a distinctive style with full-page text (several paragraphs) about the topic opposite stunning full page photographs. The photographs are connected to the text, but Simon uses few diagrams and little labeling in his books. Therefore, the *Sharks* book would be suitable for Level 4 and 5 English learners in the intermediate grades. As an extension to the shark text set, teachers might add books about the habitat of the shark. Two possibilities include *Oceans: The Vast, Mysterious Deep* (Harrison, 2003, TL3–5, I, NF) and *Exploring the Deep, Dark Sea* (Gibbons, 1999, TL3–5, A, NF). Gibbons's books always include diagrams and illustrations with labels to clarify the text and this book on underwater exploration is no exception. Harrison's book, on the other hand, has illustrations connected to the text descriptions but there is little labeling to focus attention on specifics.

In another text set, the topic of evolution is explored. Alice Schertle uses a poetic writing style in *We* (2007, TL3–5, A, NF). With limited punctuation and spacing that resembles a poem's layout on a page, she offers a simple and rhythmic recounting of evolution that is accessible to Level 3 English learners in the intermediate grades. Another first-person narrative version of evolution is Lisa Peters's *Our Family Tree: An Evolution Story* (2003, TL3–5, I, NF) as she begins with "All of us are part of an old, old family./ The roots of our family tree/ reach way back/ to the beginning of life on earth./ We've changed a lot since then." Peters includes thumbnails and a timeline at the end with more detailed information that extends the content level. Finally, Steve Jenkins's *Life on Earth: The Story of Evolution* (2002, TL4–5, I, NF) reads more like a traditional informational text but there are multiple layers including (1) the main text (designated by a larger font size) in simple paragraphs with more specific facts in smaller font; (2) a narrated timeline with paragraphs related to each time entry; (3) a summary timeline at the end of the book that compares the time periods in evolution to a single day, 24 hours, as a means of simplifying earth's 4.5 billion-year history; (4) a brief history of Darwin, in the middle of the book, with details of his expedition and the development of his ideas about evolution; and (5) highlights of Darwin's ideas explained in simple paragraphs (e.g., variation and mutation, with illustrated examples and additional explanation). This last book could be divided into multiple readings for several purposes just as the entire text set could provide opportunities for English learners at different proficiency levels to discover more about evolution.

Again, as teachers examine nonfiction books for the level of content knowledge needed by the reader, they always need to keep in mind the importance of accurate and up-to-date information. Readers go to nonfiction literature for facts. Once the accuracy of the content has been verified, then teachers can consider whether the nonfiction book is a good fit for the English learners in the classroom. As teachers examine the content and consider their English learners, they need to distinguish between concepts and vocabulary, too. Considering the conceptual load of a nonfiction book is a content issue as highlighted in this section. If English learners understand the concept, then they may only need to learn the new English vocabulary labels for that content. That is a language issue and will be discussed in the upcoming section.

Level of Language

The content load of informational writing directly correlates with the level of language. Nonfiction is challenging not only because of the content and concepts presented but also because of the academic language and technical and specialized vocabulary required to present the content. Depending on the topic and grade level, the number of new terms can rapidly escalate, thereby increasing the language load of the text. Also, authors may or may not present new vocabulary in meaningful context. More complex syntactic structure also increases with topic and grade level. While basic concept books may have word- and phrase-level text, many nonfiction books have more elaborated text with compound and complex sentences and paragraphs. To determine the match of text to learner, the teacher should consider the following language issues:

- What is the vocabulary load of the nonfiction text (e.g., basic and familiar, sophisticated/advanced and unfamiliar, concrete or abstract, general or technical/specialized, idiomatic, formal or informal, vocabulary with multiple meanings, figurative language)?
- How many new vocabulary words are presented?
- Does the nonfiction text present new vocabulary in meaningful contextual language?
- How likely is the English learner to encounter the vocabulary in this nonfiction text in other reading?
- What is the English learner's previous experience with the vocabulary of the nonfiction text (completely new, some exposure, should be part of active vocabulary)? Is the vocabulary currently or likely to be part of the English learner's speaking vocabulary? Listening vocabulary? Reading vocabulary? Writing vocabulary?
- If the nonfiction text is predictable, what is the size of the predictable unit and what percent of nonfiction text does the predictable unit account for?
- What is the syntactic structure of the nonfiction text? Word level? Phrase level? Single simple sentences per page? Multiple simple sentences? Short paragraphs with simple sentences? Compound sentences? Complex sentences? Compound/complex sentences? Embedded clauses?

- How familiar is the English learner with those syntax patterns? Does the English learner use that syntax pattern in speaking? Writing?
- What types of text structure does the nonfiction text use? Chronological? Sequential? Description? Listing? Cause–effect? Problem–solution?
- How familiar is the English learner with this text structure pattern? Has the English learner encountered this pattern previously?
- What type of nonfiction text is this (alphabet or counting book, biography, etc.) and how familiar is the English learner with the type?
- How familiar is the English learner with this genre?

To select appropriate nonfiction books for English learners, the teacher must consider how close a fit the text is to students' vocabulary and syntactic knowledge and their overall language proficiency level. Beyond judging if the language of the text is accessible to the reader or the listener, teachers should also take into account the potential of the text to develop language such as moving English learners from basic to more sophisticated vocabulary or introducing them to different sentence patterns. While basic vocabulary and syntax contribute to beginning English learners' comprehension of text, ultimately they need to have frequent encounters with text that is slightly beyond their proficiency level, so that their language ability is constantly developing. Literature can encourage vocabulary growth by exposing English learners to the idea of word analysis, a useful strategy for independent learning. For instance, some terms have clues to meaning. In the case of the polar bear, white shark, or rat snake, the name provides helpful descriptive information. Using simple language in *They Call Me Woolly: What Animal Names Can Tell Us* (DuQuette, 2002, TL2–4, A, NF), the author highlights these name clues and key words along with thumbnails containing more elaborate text. This is a useful text for vocabulary building that almost seems designed for English learners.

Just as with content complexity, authors have techniques that they use to support all readers with the language level of the text. For instance, English learners often view all new words as equally challenging and important. So, authors need to emphasize key vocabulary. One way they accomplish this is by using basic vocabulary and focusing on the words that convey the meaning for beginning readers and Level 1 English learners. The simple phrases in *The Life of a Car* (Steggall, 2008, TL1–2,

P, NF) are a good example of this technique. Strong, concrete verbs begin the phrases emphasizing the key term and putting the meaning at the front ("Fill the car./ Wash the car./ Fix the car."). Only the verb changes with each page, thereby lessening the language load. Similarly, Steve Jenkins and Robin Page spotlight action verbs in *Move!* (2006, TL1–4, A, F) by presenting the key term on its own at the top of the page with a sentence underneath that incorporates the term: "Swing/ A gibbon swings through jungle trees/ Walk/ or walks on two back legs."

While basic vocabulary assists in comprehension, English learners need to move beyond simple vocabulary and to encounter more sophisticated and advanced words to expand their vocabulary. As an example, Lois Ehlert in *Waiting for Wings* (2000, TL1–3, A, NF) uses simple sentences and chronological text structure to support the reader, but she integrates descriptive verbs as butterflies *pump their wings, catch a whiff, dip and sip,* and *circle*. Similarly, Melissa Stewart in *When Rain Falls* (2008, TL3–5, A, NF) emphasizes description with words such as *nestles, dangle,* and *crouches* and with the following sentence: "When rain falls in a desert … a rattlesnake squeezes into a rocky crevice. It curls up tight and falls asleep."

As authors employ more colorful language, they sometimes use slang, colloquialisms, and figurative language that are excellent to build informal "insider" language for English learners at Levels 3–5 but that can cause difficulties for beginning English learners at Level 1 or 2 proficiency level. For instance, Pat Mora (2008, TL2–4, P, NF) in *Join Hands: The Ways We Celebrate Life* uses the terms *hoopla* and *ballyhoo*. Vocabulary of different eras also presents a problem for English learners. In *Colonial Voices, Hear Them Speak* (Winters, 2008, TL4–5, I, NF), a book of poems about different professions in Colonial times, both the text style and the terms for jobs from the time period (*errand boy, milliner, tavern keeper, journeyman*) make this a challenging text and so more appropriate for Level 4 or 5 English learners. In another example, readers are introduced to a jazz great in *Before John Was a Jazz Giant: A Song of John Coltrane* (2008, TL3–5, I, NF). The language is simple with short, basic sentences, but Carole Boston-Weatherford references a different era and a specific style of music with phrases such as "a saxophone's soulful solo, blue notes crooning his name" and vocabulary such as *hambones, phonograph,* and *jitterbuggers*. This type of specialized language adds another layer of complexity for English learners.

Just as English learners have problems deciding what words are important, they also have difficulties determining what facts are significant. To emphasize the key facts, Cathryn Sill uses simple sentence structure, one sentence per page ("Most amphibians spend part of their lives in water ..." or "Wetlands are places covered with shallow water." or "The water may be fresh or salty."), in her series of basic survey/concept books on animals: *About Reptiles* (1999, TL2–4, A, NF), *About Amphibians* (2000, TL2–4, A, NF), *About Fish* (2002, TL2–4, A, NF), and *About Arachnids* (2003, TL2–4, A, NF); and about habitats: *About Wetlands* (2008, TL2–4, A, NF) and *About Deserts* (2008, TL2–4, A, NF). Multilevel or dual-level text is one means of supporting English learners in their transition from simple sentences to more complex sentences and paragraphs. The use of dual-level text, as discussed in the previous section, is common in many nonfiction books. A sentence at the top of the page, a type of summary statement, provides more simple language for readers. This is complemented by more complex sentences or paragraphs below the summary. In this way, readers are exposed to increasingly complex text with more elaboration. Again, Steven Jenkins often uses this technique in his books.

Repetition is another way that authors support readers with the language load. Steve Jenkins and Robin Page use repetition in their concept book, *What Do You Do with a Tail Like This?* (2003, TL2–5, A, NF). This book concentrates on the ways animals use their nose, ears, tail, eyes, mouth, and feet. The authors begin each exploration with a similar question: "What do you do with a ... like this?" With each response, that part of the body is repeated in a sentence with the same beginning phrase; for example, "If you're a bat, you 'see' with your ears./ If you're a jackrabbit, you use your ears to keep cool." This repetition supports comprehension and language development in several ways. First, there is less new language for the English learner to decipher, and so, hopefully, comprehension is easier. Second, the repetition helps build fluency and automaticity in silent and oral reading. Third, the repetition signals that certain words are key terms to take away from the reading and that cumulatively, in this case, those terms or concepts are the overall focus of the text. *One Watermelon Seed* (Lottridge, 2008, TL2–4, A, NF) uses repetition as a means of dividing the counting book in two sections, first for numbers 1–10, the verbs *planted* and *grew* are repeated ("They planted two pumpkin seeds ... and they grew."). Next, for multiples of 10, the verb changes to *picked* ("They picked ten watermelons, big and green, and twenty pumpkins, glowing orange.") to signal the change from ones to tens.

Different levels of language and repetition are combined in *We're Sailing to the Galapagos: A Week in the Pacific* (Krebs, 2005, TL2–5, A, NF). The book appears to be a simple reinforcement of the days of the week and an introduction to island life in the Galapagos. Each day a different animal is highlighted in one sentence of rhyming text ("On Monday, giant tortoises, with weathered shells of green,"), and each page closes with a repeated refrain: "We're sailing to the Galapagos, Galapagos, Galapagos,/ We're sailing to the Galapagos./ I wonder who we'll see." At the end of the week, there is a summary page listing all seven animals with the associated descriptive adjective ("swimming sea lions"). Then, the language shifts to more advanced text including two pages of background on the Galapagos Islands, six pages on "The Creatures of the Galapagos" with a paragraph each on the many animals found in the islands, and a final page on Charles Darwin and his explorations in the Galapagos. The first part of the book can be used as a participatory read-aloud with Level 1 and 2 English learners, but the additional pages have a content and language load that would be more suitable for proficiency Levels 3–5.

When authors present new vocabulary in meaningful context, this supports English learners and helps them to comprehend the text. Nagy (1988) notes some problems with the idea of learning vocabulary in context. First, contexts in most normal texts are not that helpful as they seldom give complete information about the new word. Additionally, helpful context information is only useful to a reader who already has some idea about the new term. It is not adequate for the reader who has no other knowledge about the meaning of the word. Still, teachers can draw student attention to instances of common types of context clues (e.g., synonyms, compare–contrast, summary or examples, definition or example, and punctuation) when they are encountered in reading. In *How Animal Babies Stay Safe* (2002, TL2–5, A, NF), Mary Ann Fraser uses an example to help readers grasp the meaning of instinct, noting "There are babies who don't need their parents./ When turtles, snails, snakes, and saltwater crabs hatch, they already know how to find food and escape from their enemies./ This kind of knowledge is called instinct." And, Gail Gibbons in *Snakes* (2007, TL3–5, A, NF) features constrictor snakes using a definition: "Other kinds of snakes squeeze their prey to death. This kind of snake is called a constrictor because the word *constrict* means 'to squeeze.'"

Writing style influences the language level and readability of all texts. While teachers may associate nonfiction with a series of facts presented in the third person, authors sometimes choose a conversational tone or voice to convey information. Alice Schertle's poetic writing style and use of the first person in *We* (2007, TL3–5, A, NF) and Lisa Peters's first-person narrative in *Our Family Tree: An Evolution Story* (2003, TL3–5, I, NF) bring a personal touch to this controversial topic. Some English learners may understand better with an informational story as opposed to traditional exposition.

A characteristic of nonfiction and expository writing is the use of certain semantic and syntactic organizational patterns or text structures such as chronological, sequential, description, listing, cause–effect, comparison–contrast, and problem–solution. These text structures are signaled by certain key terms that authors use to point out the organization. In comparison–contrast, for instance, signal terms include *similar to* and *different from* and for chronological text, words such as *after, now, when, first, second,* and so on help readers follow the sequence. *Building Manhattan* (Vila, 2008, TL3–5, A, NF) is a chronological text about the history of Manhattan with examples of signal words that teachers can point out to assist English learners as in "**Long ago**, before maps or words were used, a little island formed." or "The **first** people came and built homes using sticks and bark." Another chronological nonfiction book is *Little Panda: The World Welcomes Hua Mei at the San Diego Zoo* (Ryder, 2001, TL2–5, A, NF), which chronicles the birth and first year of Hua Mei, the first giant panda cub to survive in captivity in the Western Hemisphere. The cub's progress is observable in these written signals: "**At first** she can't hold up her head. **Then** .../ Look at her! She is sitting and standing **now**, and eager to take her **first** steps." Text structure is also emphasized in nonfiction books and textbooks with graphic aids such as timelines or Venn diagrams. Such visuals are part of the text support discussed in the next section.

Level of Text Support

"Interesting texts are well organized, illustrated, and aligned with the child's conceptual knowledge base. The features of such texts include a table of contents, an index, headings, bold print for new words, captioned illustrations, a clear macro structure, and strong topic sentences. Vivid details are included, but do not detract from the conceptual theme of the content" (Guthrie, 2003, p. 124). Elements such as the table of contents, index, author notes, glossary, visuals and graphic aids, and print features provide tools that enable readers to drop in and out of nonfiction texts. These features are distinctive in nonfiction literature as they provide accessibility to the challenges of the increased content and language load of informational texts. As teachers examine different nonfiction texts, they should consider the following questions about the types of support the text provides to the English learner:

- Is the nonfiction text well organized?
- Are there visuals (photographs or illustrations)?
- Are the visuals clear and direct? One-to-one correspondence of visuals to text? General connection to text? Primarily for aesthetic purposes?
- Are there graphic aids in the nonfiction text (charts, maps, tables, graphs)?
- How much does the English learner know about these types of graphic aids? Has the English learner successfully used these types of aids in previous reading? Is the general format of the aid new or familiar (e.g., different types of graphs, picture, bar, line, circle)?
- What types of text features are used? Print style such as bold or italics? Headings and subheadings? Captions and labeling of visuals/graphics? Table of contents, index, glossary?
- How familiar is the English learner with these types of text features?

For English learners, it is essential that a book have a clear and well-organized layout as the content and language load of nonfiction reading are enough of a challenge. Visual layout is one organizational issue. As an example, a simple concept book, *Oh, Canada!* (Gurth, 2009, TL1–2, P, NF), provides a consistent layout to introduce readers to each province in the country. On the two-page spreads, the name of the province is provided on the left page and below that four squares show illustrations of the province flag, tree, flower, and bird with the last three labeled. The opposite page offers an illustration with one sentence about a location in the province. As English learners turn from page to page, they know what to expect. Likewise, alphabet, counting, and question and answer books as well have consistent and predictable organizational patterns that make them user-friendly. *Hello, Bumblebee Bat* (Lunde, 2007, TL2–5, A, NF), for instance, uses a simple question and answer format. For every two pages, the left side features a question and the right, the answer ("Bumblebee, what do you look like?/ My fur is reddish brown...."). Steve Jenkins also uses this format in *What Do You Do with a Tail Like This?* (2003, TL2–5, A, NF) as he explores how animals use their ears, eyes, tail, nose, mouth, and feet. The question is asked on one page and then readers turn the page to see different animals featured with responses related to each. Nonfiction books with a chronological or sequence text structure offer support through organization as well.

Neil Waldman traces a single drop of water throughout 1 year in *The Snowflake: A Water Cycle Story* (2003, TL3–5, A, NF). Each month is a two-page spread with a paragraph about the changes and movement of the water droplet on one page and an illustration on the other.

Visuals are critical elements to help English learners access the difficult conceptual and vocabulary load of nonfiction writing. For Level 1 English learners, in particular, there should be a direct correlation of the content, terminology, and the visual within the text. Concept books, in general, have photographs that clearly depict spatial relationships, shapes, and antonyms as in *Hot Cold Bold Shy* (Harris, 1996, TL1–3, P, NF) and *What's Opposite?* (Swinburne, 2000, TL1–3, P, NF). As the content depth and language difficulty increases, the correlation of visual to text sometimes becomes harder to accomplish. Still, more concrete ideas are easier to convey with visuals. Some successful text to visual examples in *Fabulous Fishes* (Stockdale, 2008, TL2–4, A, NF) include the distinction between fish that have spikes or are striped and fish that "swim in numbers" or "alone," but the difference between fish that leap and those that glide is not as strong. Too, Cathryn Sill's books have clear connections for many of the simple statements of fact that appear opposite full-page illustrations. In *About Fish* (2002, TL2–4, A, NF), she begins, "Fish live in water./ They may be found in nearly freezing water .../ or in warm tropical water." By separating the last sentence in two parts with two different illustrations, Sill is able to clearly illustrate the fish that live in cold conditions by showing the layer of ice at the top of the water and the fish below. Readers rely on the strong visual support of this example to understand the second half of the sentence since it is more difficult to visually demonstrate warm water. Later in the book, Sill notes, "They can breathe underwater because they have gills." While it may be easy for those with background knowledge to "see" the gills in the illustration, there is no label or arrow to direct the English learner who is just beginning to learn about this concept and thus, help with comprehension.

One way that some authors clarify illustrations is to include labels or arrows to focus the reader or to use insets for a close up. Jim Arnosky and Gail Gibbons are masters of these techniques in their many nonfiction books. For instance, teachers might compare the illustration and statement in Cathryn Sill's *About Fish* (2002, TL2–4, A, NF) "Most have tough skin covered by scales." to Arnosky's visual and description in *All about Sharks* (2008, TL3–5, A, NF). He provides an illustration of a shark from above and below with an inset, or close-up view, and caption noting, "Shark skin is covered with tiny tooth-like scales that make it feel like sandpaper." Another contrast of the detail in visuals and captions can be made with Gibbons's *Coral Reefs* (2007, TL3–5, A, NF) and *Colorful, Captivating Coral Reefs* (2003, TL3–5, I, NF) by Dorothy Hinshaw-Patent. Both authors present the three types of coral reefs: atoll, fringe, and barrier. Hinshaw-Patent uses an illustration divided into three sections with a sentence or two about each type of reef. There are no additional features to support the reader; consequently, the distinction among the three types of reefs is not so clear. The visual to text connection in Gibbons's treatment of the same content is more obvious. She also has a sentence with information about each reef type but she draws out other key terms from the definitions such as *shoreline, channel,* and *lagoon,* and provides those labels with connections to the illustration. Dianna Aston uses a simple poetic line of text in script to introduce a page of facts and detailed illustrations in *An Egg Is Quiet* (2006, TL3–5, A, NF), about fish and bird eggs, and *A Seed Is Sleepy* (2007, TL3–5, A, NF), with basic botany information including charts depicting a seed's growth.

Several examples were cited earlier, *Like People* (Schubert, 2008, TL2–4, A, NF), *Are Trees Alive?* (Miller, 2003, TL2–5, A, NF), and *Have You Ever Seen a Duck in a Raincoat?* (Kaner, 2009, TL1–3, P, NF), of authors using written analogies or comparisons to assist readers to connect with information they may already possess. Visual comparisons may prove even more powerful for some English learners. In *Biggest, Strongest, Fastest* (1995, TL1–5, A, NF) and *Hottest, Coldest, Highest, Deepest* (1998, TL2–5, A, NF), Steve Jenkins provides comparative illustrations and facts to support readers in their understanding of size and proportion. In the first book, an illustration to scale of a blue whale is shown next to one of a human and in the second book, Jenkins pictorially contrasts the deepest lake, Lake Baikal in Russia (5,134 feet deep), with the height of the Empire State Building in New York (1,250 feet). On another two-page spread, the author also compares the length of the Nile, the longest river in the world, to other rivers with a side box.

The end of the nonfiction book is where readers would typically encounter resources such as the index, glossary, list of references, or additional resources to explore. Yet, there are many other informational tools found at the end of the book such as graphic aids, timelines, maps, or additional visuals, as well as author's notes that provide background information about the book's focus or a rationale for why the author wrote the book. The following represent just a few examples. *Beaks* (Collard, 2002, TL2–5, A, NF) has a review at the end to "Test your 'beak-ability.'" Readers are encouraged to match illustrations of the birds' beaks to the task, "What would I eat with this beak?" *Waiting for Wings* (Ehlert, 2001, TL1–3, A, NF) has a butterfly identification chart at the end with large illustrations of several butterflies along with visuals of their appearance as a caterpillar and a chrysalis. On another page, there is also a labeled diagram of the body of a butterfly. *One Watermelon Seed* (Lottridge, 2008, TL2–4, A, NF) has a picture dictionary at the end with illustrations of many of the featured fruits and vegetables along with some common animals the reader might spot in a garden. Many counting books have a visual summary at the end of the numbers and objects presented in the book as in *One Child, One Seed: A South African Counting Book* (Cave, 2003, TL2–5, A, NF). Maps are often placed within the text of a nonfiction book to provide specific information related to text on that page, but they are also placed at the end of nonfiction books as a reference aid when applicable to the entire book. *One Child, One Seed* features a map of South Africa where Nothando, the child in the book, lives, and Ajmera and Ivanko's *Be My Neighbor* (2004a, TL2–5, A, NF) and *To Be an Artist* (2004b, TL2–5, A, NF) have maps to identify the countries mentioned in the photograph captions throughout the book. Timelines as well may be integrated within the text of the book or at the end, depending on the purpose. Gail Gibbons supplies a timeline of "Diving . . . Past and Present" with important dates, an illustration, and an explanatory sentence at the end of *Exploring the Deep, Dark Sea* (1999, TL3–5, A, NF) and Vila uses a timeline at the end of *Building Manhattan* (2008, TL3–5, A, NF) to offer additional information in paragraphs for different time periods, 1850–1950 (immigration), or a specific year, 1609, when the Dutch arrived. DK Publishing even has a series of books, mentioned in the narrow reading resource list in Chapter 3, and the entire text serves as a timeline and each two-page spread moves a street, city, and farm through various time periods.

No space is wasted in a nonfiction book and sometimes, even the endpapers for a book offer information-sharing opportunities. As a case in point, the endpapers of *Surprising Sharks* (Davies, 2003, TL3–5, A, NF) have illustrations of various sharks with their average length listed below. Also, the front endpapers of *Becoming Butterflies* (Rockwell, 2002, TL3–5, A, NF) have illustrations of various caterpillars labeled with their common and scientific name and the back endpapers have illustrations of the butterflies that emerge from those caterpillars.

Whatever the mechanism—visuals on the endpapers, textual author's notes, or organizational format—and wherever they occur in the book—beginning, middle, or end—text support features assist the reader and such scaffolds are particularly important to English learners. In the next section, cultural relevance is explored as another type of support for English learners.

Level of Cultural Fit

When thinking about nonfiction literature, teachers may not immediately consider the genre as a means of introducing a multicultural or global emphasis, but more and more nonfiction has a focus on diversity from alphabet and counting books to biographies of historical figures from different ethnic, geographic, and religious backgrounds and photo essays about different parts of the world. There are even bilingual books that offer an opportunity for readers to experience cultural topics in more than one language or to learn some words of another language in interlingual books. When selecting nonfiction books, teachers should evaluate the fit of the text to learners' cultural or experiential background. For the purposes of this discussion, cultural fit encompasses ethnicity or cultural background, language, geography, religion, socioeconomic status, and gender, and teachers might consider the following guiding questions in their selection process:

- Is the nonfiction text culturally neutral (with general diversity portrayed but no focus on a specific group)? Culturally generic (with a group featured but less specific detail provided)? Culturally specific (with explicit details about a group portrayed)?
- Does the nonfiction text reflect the background and/or experiences of recent immigrants? U.S.-born English learners?
- Are the characters similar or different than English learners in the classroom?
- Have English learners had an experience like one described in the nonfiction text?
- Have English learners lived in or visited places like those in the nonfiction text?
- How far removed is the nonfiction text from current times?
- Do the characters talk like the English learners and their families?
- Is this author/author style familiar to English learners?

As teachers are thinking through issues of cultural fit, they are not trying to limit books to only those that reflect the children in their classrooms although teachers should be concerned about selecting books with a range of cultural representations so that all children can see themselves reflected in literature. Instead, they are making decisions about the cultural accuracy and the depth of cultural detail as well as the type of background knowledge students, in particular English learners, may need to comprehend the text. As teachers examine books for cultural accuracy and detail, they should take into account whether a book is culturally specific with explicit details about a group, culturally generic with a group featured but less specific detail provided, or culturally neutral with general diversity portrayed but without a focus on a specific group. Also, in terms of English learners, teachers can determine whether a book reflects the experiences of recent immigrants or U.S.-born English learners. Too, teachers should not make assumptions about students simply because they are part of a cultural group. All Latino children are not familiar with quinceaneras or posadas celebrations nor are all Asian children acquainted with the lunar New Year festivities. Just as with limited content knowledge, English learners may need additional support to access books with cultural information that is distant from their own experiences.

Counting books including *One Child, One Seed: A South African Counting Book* (Cave, 2003, TL2–5, A, NF) and alphabet books such as *K Is for Korea* (Cheung & Das, 2008, TL3–5, A, NF), *M Is for Mexico* (Cordero, 2008, TL3–5, A, NF), and *D Is for Dragon Dance* (Compestine, 2006, TL2–5, A, NF) offer many opportunities to highlight culturally specific details about different groups. The vocabulary load in the alphabet books, however, may be challenging to English learners who are learning a new language and are unfamiliar with these cultures. Another excellent overview book with different geographic facts for settings around the globe is Laura Ljungkvist's *Follow the Line around the World* (2008, TL3–5, A, NF). Each two-page spread spotlighting a different place could be used as a stand-alone. For instance for Kenya, readers learn, "Kenya is a country located in Africa./ Female elephants and their babies live together in herds. Male elephants usually live alone."

Among the culturally relevant nonfiction books, there are many picture book biographies that depict historical figures: *Pocahontas, Princess of the New World* (Krull, 2007, TL3–5, A, NF), *Harvesting Hope: The Story of Cesar Chavez* (Krull, 2003, TL3–5, A, NF), and *The Bus Ride That Changed History: The Story of Rosa Parks* (Edwards, 2009, TL3–5, A, NF); and sports greats: *Nothing but Trouble: The Story of Althea Gibson* (Stauffacher, 2007, TL3–5, A, NF), *Campy, the Story of Roy Campanela* (Adler, 2007, TL3–5, A, NF), and *Young Pele: Soccer's First Star* (Cline-Ransome, 2007, TL3–5, A, NF) to name just a few. As noted earlier, most picture biographies are suitable for Level 3–5 English learners. However, teachers should not assume that Latino English learners will automatically know Cesar Chavez or Roy Campanela, but they may be familiar with baseball or simply appreciate learning about individuals who have made a contribution. The biographies noted would be either culturally specific or culturally generic depending on the level of detail included. Certainly, the individuals featured in the biography are part of one or more specific groups, but the focus in biography may be more on the individual rather than details about the cultural group.

Photo essays, on the other hand, would be culturally specific as they offer a detailed snapshot of a cultural group. Again, Diane Hoyt-Goldsmith and George Ancona have numerous culturally relevant photo essays to their credit including *Celebrating Ramadan* (Hoyt-Goldsmith, 2001, TL3–5, I, NF), *Cinco de Mayo: Celebrating the Traditions of Mexico* (Hoyt-Goldsmith, 2008, TL3–5, I, NF), *Mayeros: A Yucatec Maya Family* (Ancona, 1997, TL3–5, I, NF), and *Harvest* (Ancona, 2001, TL3–5, I, NF). Add to these excellent examples, *An Elephant in the Backyard* (Sobol, 2004, TL3–5, I, NF), *Hands of the Maya: Villagers at Work and Play* (Crandell, 2002, TL3–5, I, NF), which could be paired with Ancona's book on a Maya family, and *Celebrate Cinco de Mayo with Fiestas, Music and Dance* (Otto, 2008, TL3–5, I, NF), which could be teamed up with Hoyt-Goldsmith's book on this Latino celebration.

Finally, there are many informational picture books that can provide a global view. A few culturally specific examples include *Kamal Goes to Trinidad* (Frederick, 2008, TL3–5, I, NF) about a boy's first trip to his parent's home, *Gervelie's Journey: A Refugee Diary* (Robinson & Young, 2008, TL3–5, I, NF), which chronicles a young Congolese girl and her father as they flee their war-torn homeland and settle in England, *14 Cows for America* (Deedy & Naiyomah, 2009, TL3–5, I, NF), a poignant story of the gift from a Maasai village to a grieving America still remembering September 11, 2001, and *Going to School in India* (Heydlauff, 2003, TL3–5, I, NF), which offers a fascinating glimpse of schooling in India including the many places school is held and the many ways children reach those schools. Each of these books would be suitable for Level 4 and 5 English learners. Three culturally neutral books that feature a wide spectrum of diversity are *Celebrate! Connections among Cultures* (Reynolds, 2006, TL3–5, I, NF), *It's Back to School We Go!: First Day Stories from around the World* (Jackson, 2003, TL3–5, I, NF), and *Children around the World* (Montanari, 2004, TL2–4, A, NF). The latter book could be used with Level 2 English learners but the other examples are more appropriate for Levels 3–5.

Once teachers are convinced about the appeal and the effectiveness of nonfiction literature for English learners, they begin to think about implementing this genre into the classroom. Quite often nonfiction literature finds its way into the classroom first through supplementing content-area textbooks or in interdisciplinary or thematic units. Teachers can begin to create text sets linked by a common theme or topic but written at varying readability levels. This themed emphasis helps English learners encounter the same vocabulary and concepts multiple times.

Conclusion

Nonfiction literature furnishes meaningful input for literacy activities as English learners develop both language and content literacy. Yet, fiction use still surpasses that of nonfiction in elementary classrooms by a wide margin. The critical need for academic language development, however, makes nonfiction a natural choice when working with English learners.

One means of scaffolding English learners with the content and language load of nonfiction text is through read-alouds. Unfortunately, reading aloud nonfiction rarely seems to occur. This may be due to the kinds of nonfiction published in the past or to a general assumption that children prefer stories. Whatever the case, there are some excellent options for reading aloud nonfiction. Cover-to-cover read-alouds are not the typical choice for nonfiction except perhaps for very engaging picture books. Similar to a cover-to-cover read-aloud, however, teachers might try a chapter read-aloud. For additional read-aloud options, teachers might try participatory read-alouds when there is strong repetition in a book, or they might focus on the text features of nonfiction and use caption reading or introducing the structural elements of a nonfiction book through reading aloud. Finally, much nonfiction is filled with fascinating facts, so a read-aloud with believe-it-or-not or not sharing might be an excellent choice.

I'm Learning to Speak English

J. PATRICK LEWIS

Be pashunt please, I don't know how to spell
Or read or write your language. *Por favor,*
I'm learning to speak English—ESL.

And I am getting better, I can tell.
"The bull is mad. Be carefull, matadoor!"
Be payshent please, I don't know how to spell.

For words like *ant* and *aunt* or *bell* and *belle,*
You must know what the extra letter's for.
I'm learning to speak English—ESL.

My teacher said I'm going to excell.
Excell. A word worth 50 cents—or more!
Be paishunt please, I don't know how to spell.

She told me that I'd fall.... I did! I fell
Into meaty words like a ... *carnivore!*
I'm learning to speak English—ESL.

I want to know my nouns and verbs so well
That someday I will get a perfect score.
Be patient (!) with me while I learn to spell
And write and speak in English—ESL.

Copyright by J. Patrick Lewis. This poem appeared on the children's literature blog *Chicken Spaghetti* on Poetry Friday, June 6, 2008.

Books for Learning about Immigrants and English Learners

Picture books for students and teachers	Books for teachers
A Movie in My Pillow/ Una Pelicula en Mi Almohada by Jorge Argueta, poetry, Salvadoran	*A Step from Heaven* by An Na
A Picnic in October by Eve Bunting, Italian American	*American Born Chinese* by Gene Yang, Chinese
Amelia's Road by Linda Altman, Mexican	*American Eyes: New Asian-American Short Stories for Young Adults* by Lori Carlson
Angel Child, Dragon Child by Michele Maria Surat, Vietnamese	*The Arrival*, Shaun Tan, unspecified
Apple Pie 4th of July by Janet Wong, Chinese	*Ask Me No Questions* by Marina Budhos, Muslim/Bangladeshi
The Color of Home by Mary Hoffman, Somalian	*Celebrating Ramadan* by Diane Hoyt-Goldsmith
Coming to America: A Muslim Family's Story by Bernard Wolf, Egyptian/Muslim	*Cool Salsa: Bilingual Poems on Growing Up Latino in the United States* by Lori Carlson
Dear Juno by Soyung Pak, Korean	*Crossing the Wire* by Will Hobbs, Mexican
Dia's Story Cloth by Dia Cha, Hmong	*Does My Head Look Big in This?* by Randa Abdel-Fattah, Muslim Palestinian
Good-Bye, 382 Shin Dang Dong by Frances and Ginger Park, Korean	*Drita, My Homegirl* by Jenny Lombard, Albanian *First Crossing: Stories about Teen Immigrants* by Donald Gallo
How Many Days to America? A Thanksgiving Story by Eve Bunting, unspecified	*The Fold* by An Na, Korean
I Hate English! by Ellen Levine, Hong Kong	*Home of the Brave* by Katherine Applegate, Sudanese
In the Small, Small Night by Jane Kurtz, Ghanaian *La Mariposa* by Francisco Jiménez, Mexican	*In the Year of the Boar and Jackie Robinson* by Bette Lord, Chinese
	La Linea by Ann Jaramillo, Mexican

Picture books for students and teachers	Books for teachers
The Lotus Seed by Sherry Garland, Vietnamese	*Lowji Discovers America* by Candace Fleming, Indian
Marianthe's Story: Painted Words and Spoken Memories by Aliki, unspecified	*Red Hot Salsa: Bilingual Poems on Being Young and Latino in the United States* by Lori Carlson
My Chinatown: One Year in Poems by Kam Mak, Chinese	*Remix: Conversations with Immigrant Teenagers* by Marian Budhos
My Diary from Here to There/ Mi diario de Aqui Hasta by Amada Perez, Mexican	*Something about America* by Maria Testa, Albanian
My Name is Jorge on Both Sides of the River by Jane Medina, Mexican	*The Story of My Life: An Afghan Girl on the Other Side of the Sky* by Farah Ahmedi and Tamim Ansary, Afghanistan
My Name is Yoon by Helen Recorvits, Korean	
The Name Jar by Yangsook Choi, Korean	*Tangled Threads: A Hmong Girl's Story* by Pegi Deitz Shea, Laotian
Three Cheers for Catherine the Great! by Cari Best, Russian	*Ten Things I Hate about Me* by Randa Abdel-Fattah, Muslim Lebanese
The Whispering Cloth: A Refugee's Story by Pegi Deitz Shea, Hmong	*Voices from the Field: Children of Migrant Farmworkers Tell Their Stories* by S. Beth Atkin
Ziba Came by Boat by Liz Lofthouse, unspecified	*Wait for Me* by An Na, Korean

Note. Coding for TESOL proficiency level, grade level, and genre is found in the "Children's Books Cited" section

Guidelines for Matching Literature
to English Learner Proficiency Levels

TESOL proficiency level and learner characteristics	Text matching criteria
TESOL Level 1, Starting **Initially:** Limited or no understanding of English Seldom uses English to communicate Responds nonverbally to simple commands, statements, and questions Visual literacy ("reading") through pictures and environmental print **Later:** Begins to repeat and imitate others by using single words, and simple phrases Begins to use English spontaneously Reads familiar words, phrases, and very simple sentences with support Writing consists of copied letters, words, and phrases	**Level of content familiarity or background knowledge** • The text addresses familiar topics and concepts • Content focused on the concrete and observable • Typical story structure **Level of language** • Vocabulary reflects English learner's oral language • Vocabulary is focused on informal, social language, survival topics, and basic content concepts • Text is at the word, phrase, or simple sentence level • Simple sentence has clear subject and predicate or is in imperative/command form • Text has predictable, repetitive, or rhyming text **Level of textual support** • Limited text per page • Text located in the same location on each page • Illustrations are on each page or directly opposite text on a two-page spread • One-to-one correspondence of text to illustration, photographs, and graphic support **Level of cultural fit** • Text is a close cultural fit or revolves around universal themes (mealtime, play, cooking)

Note. TESOL levels are based on TESOL (2006). The more the material deviates from the criteria at each proficiency level, the more teacher support will be needed to assist English learners with the obvious language and structural difficulties.

TESOL proficiency level and learner characteristics	Text matching criteria
TESOL Level 2, Emerging Understands phrases and short sentences Shares limited information in simple everyday and routine situations Uses memorized phrases, groups of words, and formulaic language Uses simple structures correctly but still produces basic errors Uses general academic vocabulary and familiar everyday expressions Reads familiar phrases and sentences and simple academic vocabulary with support Makes writing errors that often interfere with communication	**Level of content familiarity or background knowledge** • Familiar story or topic • Typical story structure • New topic or academic content presented with limited number of concrete details, and characteristics **Level of language** • General academic vocabulary and familiar everyday expressions • Phrases and short sentences • Predictable and repetitive text • Simple narrative with single setting, clear resolution, and clear problem • Simple language • Phrases and simple or compound sentences **Level of textual support** • Limited text on a two-page spread • Illustrations on a two-page spread • Illustrations support storyline or text or add rich contextualizations to text **Level of cultural fit** • Text is a cultural fit or revolves around universal themes (mealtime, play, cooking)
TESOL Level 3, Developing Understands more complex speech with repetition Uses English spontaneously Has difficulty expressing some thoughts due to limited vocabulary and lack of command of language structure Speaks in simple, comprehensible, and appropriate sentences	**Level of content familiarity or background knowledge** • Texts/topics for which students have some background knowledge require less textual/teacher support • Unfamiliar texts/topics require increased teacher and textual support **Level of language** • High-frequency language of the content areas • Common idioms, figures of speech, and multimeaning words with teacher support • Some literary language related to different genres such as fairytales, e.g., kingdom • Sentences in written paragraphs

TESOL proficiency level and learner characteristics	Text matching criteria
Makes frequent grammatical errors	**Level of textual support**
Proficiency in reading varies considerably	• Less dependence on illustrations with familiar topic
Comprehends texts for which English learner has background knowledge	• Illustrations support storyline or topic with unfamiliar story or text
	• More text on page
	Level of cultural fit
	• Text reflects cultural content that may not be a fit with English learner, so background and support are needed
TESOL Level 4, Expanding	**Level of content familiarity or background knowledge**
Language skills are adequate for most daily communication needs	• More complex, episodic text with multiple settings
Communicates in English in unfamiliar settings	• Narratives with different points of view
	• Parodies and fractured fairytales
Has occasional difficulty with complex structures and abstract academic concepts	• Academic content, both familiar and unfamiliar with support for new concepts
May read with considerable fluency	**Level of language**
	• Specific and some technical language of the content areas
Locates and identifies specific facts within the text	• A variety of sentence lengths of varying linguistic complexity
Has problems with concepts presented in a decontextualized manner	• Compound, complex sentences with dependent phrases and embedded clauses
	• Idioms, figures of speech, sophisticated language, and multimeaning words
Has problems with complex sentence structure, abstract vocabulary, or vocabulary with multiple meanings	**Level of textual support**
	• Fewer illustrations in text
	• Graphs, charts, and figures with academic content
Reads independently	• Needs support with concepts presented in a decontextualized manner, complex sentence structure, or the abstract vocabulary or multimeaning words
Has occasional comprehension problems with grade-level information	**Level of cultural fit**
	• Text reflects cultural content that is often not a fit with English learner, so some background and support may be needed

TESOL proficiency level and learner characteristics	Text matching criteria
TESOL Level 5, Bridging Uses fluent and spontaneous communication on a range of personal, general, academic, or social topics in a variety of contexts Interacts with native-speaking peers with minimal language support or guidance Has good command of technical and academic vocabulary, idiomatic expressions, and colloquialisms Produces clear, smoothly flowing, well-structured texts of differing lengths and degrees of linguistic complexity Makes few errors Can correct errors when they occur	**Level of content familiarity or background knowledge** • Academic content with new concepts • Complex narratives with subplots, flashbacks • Fantasy with invented vocabulary **Level of language** • The technical language of the content areas • A variety of sentence lengths of varying linguistic complexity in extended written discourse, including stories, essays, or reports • Vocabulary representing a wide range of personal, general, academic, or social topics for a variety of contexts • Idiomatic expressions and colloquialisms **Level of textual support** • Limited or no illustrations in text; illustrations for aesthetic purposes • More complex graphs, charts, and figures with academic content • Needs support with some concepts presented in a decontextualized manner, complex sentence structure, or the abstract vocabulary or multimeaning words **Level of cultural fit** • Text represents a variety of cultural backgrounds. Occasional background and support may be needed for unfamiliar information.

Children's Books for Social Language
(Basic "Survival" Topics)

Animals

- *The Zoo* by Suzy Lee
- *My Cat Copies Me* by Yoon Kwon
- *A Tiger Cub Grows Up* by Joan Hewett
- *Hattie and the Fox* by Mem Fox
- *I Love Animals* by Flora McDonald
- *I Went Walking* by Sue Williams
- *Wild Animals of America ABC* by Hope Ryden
- *Yum, Yum! What Fun!* by Mara Bergman

Body

- *My Five Senses* and *My Hands* and *My Feet* by Aliki
- *Here Are My Hands* by Bill Martin
- *If I Didn't Have Elbows* by Sandi Toksvig
- *All of Me! A Book of Thanks* by Molly Bang

Clothing

- *Hats, Hats, Hats* and *Shoes, Shoes, Shoes* by Ann Morris
- *Little Mouse Gets Ready* by Jeff Smith
- *Naked Mole Rat Gets Dressed* by Mo Willems

Colors

- *Red Is a Dragon: A Book of Colors* by Roseanne Thong
- *Growing Colors* by Bruce McMillan
- *Color Zoo* and *Color Farm* by Lois Ehlert
- *Colors Everywhere* by Tana Hoban
- *Color Dance* by Ann Jonas
- *Red Sings from Tree Tops: A Year in Colors* by Joyce Sidman

Days of the Week and Months of the Year

- *Mrs. Muffly's Monster* by Sarah Dyer
- *Today Is Monday* by Eric Carle

- *Cookie's Week* by Cindy Ward
- *Can You Hear the Sea?* by Judy Cumberbatch
- *We're Sailing to the Galapagos: A Week in the Pacific* by Laurie Krebs
- *Snowy, Flowy, Blowy: A Twelve Months Rhyme* by Nancy Tafuri
- *When Lucy Goes Out Walking: A Puppy's First Year* by Ashley Wolf

Family

- *Family Pictures/ Cuadros de Familia* by Carmen Garza
- *Families* by Ann Morris

Foods

- *Bee-Bim Bop!* by Linda Sue Park
- *Let's Eat: What Children Eat around the World* by Beatrice Hollyer
- *What the World Eats* by Faith D'Aluisio
- *The Very Hungry Caterpillar* by Eric Carle
- *Bread, Bread, Bread* by Ann Morris
- *Everybody Cooks Rice* and *Everybody Bakes Bread* by Norah Dooley
- *Feast for 10* by Cathryn Falwell

Homes and Houses

- *Building a House* by Byron Barton
- *Wonderful Houses around the World* by Akira Nishiyama
- *Homes around the World* by Bobbie Kalman
- *A Chair for My Mother* by Vera Williams
- *Houses and Homes* by Ann Morris

Letters of the Alphabet

- *Eating the Alphabet: Fruits & Vegetables from A to Z* by Lois Ehlert
- *The Graphic Alphabet* by David Pelletier
- *Alphabet City* by Stephen Johnson

Manners and Etiquette

- *What Do You Say, Dear?* and *What Do You Do, Dear?* by Sesyle Joslin
- *Do unto Otters: A Book about Manners* by Laurie Keller
- *Perfect Pigs* by Marc Brown and Stephen Krensky
- *It's a Spoon, Not a Shovel* by Caralyn Buehner
- *Manners* by Aliki

Measurement

- *Inch by Inch* by Leo Lionni
- *Measuring Penny* by Loreen Leedy
- *Ton* by Taora Miura

Money

- *26 Letters and 99 Cents* by Tana Hoban
- *The Coin Counting Book* by Rozanne Williams
- *Bunny Money* by Rosemary Wells
- *Monster Money Book* by Loreen Leedy

Movement

- *Go, Go, Go! Kids on the Move* by Stephen Swinburne
- *Monkey and Me* by Emily Gravett

Numbers and Counting

- *We All Went on Safari: A Counting Journey through Tanzania* by Laurie Krebs
- *Feast for 10* by Cathryn Falwell
- *One Is a Drummer: A Book about Numbers* by Roseanne Thong
- *Ten Go Tango* by Arthur Dorros
- *100 Is a Family* by Pam Ryan
- *Mouse Count* by Ellen Walsh

Occupations

- *Tools* by Taoro Miura
- *Tools* by Ann Morris
- *The Piñata Maker/ El Piñatero* by George Ancona
- *Career Day* by Anne Rockwell
- *Sally Gets a Job* by Stephen Huneck

School

- *A School Like Mine* by Smith and Shaley
- *School Bus* by Donald Crews
- *Emily's First 100 Days of School* by Rosemary Wells
- *Where Are You Going, Manyoni?* by Catherine Stock
- *Off to First Grade* by Louise Borden

- *First Grade, Here I Come* by Nancy Carlson
- *School Days around the World* by Francis Chambers

Self

- *ABC I Like Me* and *I Like Me* by Nancy Carlson
- *Whoever You Are* by Mem Fox
- *Me I Am!* by Jack Prelutsky
- *A Life Like Mine* by Dorling Kindersley

Shapes

- *Round Is a Mooncake: A Book of Shapes* by Roseanne Thong
- *Color Farm* and *Color Zoo* by Lois Ehlert
- *Shape by Shape* by Suse MacDonald

Shopping

- *Supermarket* by Kathleen Krull
- *Bebe Goes Shopping* by Susan Elya
- *Shopping with Dad* by Matt Harvey
- *Shopping* by Rosemary Wells

Signs and Symbols

- *City Signs* by Zoran Milich
- *I Read Signs* and *I Read Symbols* by Tana Hoban

Time and Money

- *Time To* by Bruce McMillan
- *Isn't It Time* by Judy Hindley
- *Telling Time: How to Tell Time on Digital and Analog Clocks* by Jules Older
- *Somewhere in the World Right Now* by Stacey Schuett

Weather

- *Weather Forecasting* by Gail Gibbons
- *Weather Words and What They Mean* by Gail Gibbons
- *Weather: Poems for All Seasons* by Lee Hopkins

Narrow Reading Suggestions for Different Formats

Same Author

- **Seymour Simon**, *Storms; Lightning; Autumn Across America; Winter Across America; Volcanoes; Earthquakes*
- **David Harrison**, *Volcanoes: Nature's Incredible Fireworks; Rivers: Nature's Wondrous Waterways; Caves: Mysteries Beneath Our Feet; Oceans: The Vast, Mysterious Deep*
- **Cathryn Sill**, *About Arachnids; About Amphibians*
- **Jim Arnosky**, *All about Sharks; All about Owls; All about Alligators*
- **Sandra Markle**, *Outside and Inside Big Cats; Outside and Inside Giant Squid; Growing Up Wild: Wolves; Growing Up Wild: Penguins*
- **Laurence Pringle**, *Whales! Strange and Wonderful; Crows! Strange and Wonderful*
- **Chris Demarest**, *Hotshots; Firefighters: A to Z; Smoke Jumpers One to Ten*
- **Steve Jenkins**, *Hottest, Coldest, Highest, Deepest; Biggest, Strongest, Fastest*
- **Diane Hoyt-Goldsmith**, *Celebrating Ramadan; Celebrating a Quinceanera: A Latina's 15th Birthday Celebration*

Same Author/Same Topic (Language Study)

- **Brian Cleary**, *To Root, to Toot, to Parachute: What Is a Verb?; Hairy, Scary, Ordinary: What Is an Adjective?; Dearly, Nearly, Insincerely: What Is an Adverb?; Under, over, by the Clover: What Is a Preposition?; I and You and Don't Forget Who: What Is a Pronoun?*

Same Author/Same Format (Cumulative Repetition)

- **Madeleine Dunphy**, *Here Is the Coral Reef; Here Is the Wetland; Here Is the African Savanna; Here Is the Arctic Winter; Here Is the Tropical Rain Forest*

Same Format (Timelines)/Same Publisher (DK)

- *A Street through Time* by Anne Millard
- *A City through Time* by Philip Steele
- *A Farm through Time* by Angela Wilkes

Series Books with Similar Focus

- **Kingfisher Young Knowledge Series**: *Animal Homes* (Wilkes); *Robots* (Gifford); *Rocks and Fossils* (Hynes); *Birds* (Davies)
- **Kingfisher The Best Book of . . .**: *Wolves and Wild Dogs* (Gunzi); *Snakes* (Gunzi)

Similar Subject Matter

Animal Friendships

- *Mama: A True Story in which a Baby Hippo Loses His Mama during a Tsunami but Finds a New Home, and a New Mama* by Jeanette Winter
- *Owen & Mzee: Best Friends* by Isabella Hatkoff, Craig Hatkoff, and Paula Kahumbu (board book)
- *Owen & Mzee: A Day Together* by Craig Hatkoff and Isabella Hatkoff (board book)
- *A Mama for Owen* by Marion Bauer
- *Owen & Mzee: The True Story of a Remarkable Friendship* by Isabella Hatkoff, Craig Hatkoff, and Paula Kahumbu
- *Owen & Mzee: The Language of Friendship* by Isabella Hatkoff, Craig Hatkoff, and Paula Kahumbu

Music

- *M Is for Music* by Kathleen Krull
- *Ah, Music!* by Aliki

Disasters

- *Volcano: The Eruption and Healing of Mount St. Helens* by Patricia Lauber
- *Volcanoes* by Seymour Simon

Holidays/Celebrations

- *Celebrating a Quinceanera: A Latina's 15th Birthday Celebration* by Diane Hoyt-Goldsmith
- *Celebrating Ramadan* by Diane Hoyt-Goldsmith

Evolution

- *Life on Earth: The Story of Evolution* by Steve Jenkins
- *Our Family Tree: An Evolution Story* by Lisa Peters
- *We* by Alice Schertle

Stairstep Apporach/Layering Difficulty Levels (Presented from Simple to More Challenging)

Spiders

- *Spinning Spiders* by Melvin Berger
- *Sneaky, Spinning Baby Spiders* by Sandra Markle

Penguins

- *Penguin Chick* by Betty Tatham
- *Growing Up Wild: Penguins* by Sandra Markle

Wolves

- *Wolves* by Jim Arnosky
- *Growing Up Wild: Wolves* by Sandra Markle
- *Wolves* by Seymour Simon

Animal Friendships

- *Mama: A True Story in which a Baby Hippo Loses His Mama during a Tsunami but Finds a New Home, and a New Mama* by Jeanette Winter
- *Owen & Mzee: Best Friends* by Craig Hatkoff, Isabella Hatkoff, and Paula Kahumbu (board book)
- *Owen & Mzee: A Day Together* by Craig Hatkoff, Isabella Hatkoff, and Paula Kahumbu (board book)
- *A Mama for Owen* by Marion Bauer
- *Owen & Mzee: The True Story of a Remarkable Friendship* by Isabella Hatkoff, Craig Hatkoff, and Paula Kahumbu
- *Owen & Mzee: The Language of Friendship* by Isabella Hatkoff, Craig Hatkoff, and Paula Kahumbu

Music

- *M Is for Music* by Kathleen Krull
- *Ah, Music!* by Aliki

Branching Out: Exploring Different Facets of a Subject

Desert

- *Desert Trek: An Eye-Opening Journey through the World's Driest Places* by Marie-Ange Le Rochais (geography)
- *Dig, Wait, Listen: A Desert Toad's Tale* by April Sayre (animal life)

American Flag

- *Stars and Stripes: The Story of the American Flag* by Sarah Thompson
- *American Flags: Designs for a Young Nation* by Nancy Druckman
- *I Pledge Allegiance* by Bill Martin and Michael Sampson

Wide Angle to Close Up: From General to Specific

Voting/Voting for the President of the United States

- *America Votes: How Our President Is Elected* by Linda Granfield
- *Grace for President* by Kelly Dipucchio
- *Vote!* by Eileen Christelow

Collective Biographies/Biographies

- *Feathers, Flaps, & Flops: Fabulous Early Fliers* by Bo Zaunders
- *Fly High! The Story of Bessie Coleman* by Louise Borden and Mary Kay Kroeger

Overview of Many/Zoom In on One

- *Animals Nobody Loves* by Seymour Simon with *Outside and Inside Rats and Mice* by Sandra Markle
- *Birds* by Nicola Davies (general overview of birds) or *Birds: Nature's Magnificent Flying Machines* by Caroline Arnold with *On the Wing: American Birds in Migration* by Carol Lerner
- *Giant Pandas* by Gail Gibbons with *Little Panda: The World Welcomes Hua Mei at the San Diego Zoo* by Joanne Ryder
- *Bugs Are Insects* by Anne Rockwell with *Army Ant Parade* by April Sayre and *The Life and Times of the Ant* by Charles Micucci
- *About Arachnids* by Cathryn Sill with *Spinning Spiders* by Melvin Berger and *Sneaky, Spinning Baby Spiders* by Sandra Markle
- *About Amphibians* by Cathryn Sill with *Little Green Frogs* by Frances Barry, *Tadpoles* by Betsy James, and *Frogs Sing Songs* by Yvonne Winer

Similar Writing Format

Narrative/Expository

- *It's Back to School We Go! First Day Stories from around the World* by Ellen Jackson
- *Vote!* by Eileen Christelow
- *Grace for President* by Kelly Dipucchio

Letters

- *Dear Alexandra: A Story of Switzerland* by Helen Gudel
- *Ask Dr. K. Fisher about Creepy-Crawlies* by Claire Llewellyn

Journal

- *Antarctic Journal: Four Months at the Bottom of the World* by Jennifer Dewey
- *Antartic Journal: The Hidden Worlds of Antarctica's Animals* by Meredith Hooper
- *Sir Reginald's Logbook* by Matt Hammill
- *Rachel's Journal: The Story of a Pioneer Girl* by Marissa Moss

Question–Answer

- Don't Know Much About . . . Series by Kenneth Davis
  - *Don't Know Much about the Pioneers*
  - *Don't Know Much about History*
  - *Don't Know Much about Geography*
  - *Don't Know Much about the Civil War*
  - *Don't Know Much about Sitting Bull*
  - *Don't Know Much about George Washington*

Alphabet

- *Capital! Washington D.C. from A to Z* by Laura Melmed
- *M Is for Music* by Kathleen Krull

Life Cycle/Timeline/Process

- *A Taste of Honey* by Nancy Wallace
- *Waiting for Wings* by Lois Ehlert
- *The Snowflake: A Water Cycle Story* by Neil Waldman
- *Pick, Pull, Snap! Where a Flower Once Bloomed* by Lola M. Schaefer
- *It's a Hummingbird's Life* by Irene Kelly
- *Flick a Switch: How Electricity Gets to Your Home* by Barbara Seuling

The Story of . . .

- *Popcorn!* by Elaine Landau
- *How Sweet It Is (and Was): The History of Candy* by Ruth Swain
- *Ice Cream Cones for Sale* by Elaine Greenstein

Children's Books Cited

For abbreviations, see "Coding Scheme for Children's Books Cited" on page xiii.

Abdel-Fattah, R. (2005). *Does my head look big in this?* New York: Orchard. TL5, S, F

Abdel-Fattah, R. (2006). *Ten things I hate about me.* New York: Orchard. TL5, S, F

Ada, A. F. (2002). *I love Saturdays and Domingos.* New York: Atheneum. TL2–4, P, F

Adler, D. A. (1992). *A picture book of Jesse Owens.* New York: Holiday House. TL3–5, A, NF

Adler, D. A. (1994). *A picture book of Anne Frank.* New York: Holiday House. TL3–5, A, NF

Adler, D. A. (1995). *A picture book of Rosa Parks.* New York: Holiday House. TL3–5, A, NF

Adler, D. A. (2000). *A picture book of Sacagawea.* New York: Holiday House. TL3–5, A, NF

Adler, D. A. (2007). *Campy, the story of Roy Campanela.* New York: Viking. TL3–5, A, NF

Ahmedi, F., & Ansary, M. T. (2005). *The story of my life: An Afghan girl on the other side of the sky.* New York: Simon & Schuster. TL5, S, NF

Ajmera, M., & Ivanko, J. D. (2004a). *Be my neighbor.* Watertown, MA: Charlesbridge. TL2–5, A, NF

Ajmera, M., & Ivanko, J. D. (2004b). *To be an artist.* Watertown, MA: Charlesbridge. TL2–5, A, NF

Ajmera, M., & Versola, A. R. (1997). *Children from Australia to Zimbabwe: A photographic journey around the world.* Watertown, MA: Charlesbridge. TL3–5, A, NF

Alarcón, F. (1997). *Laughing tomatoes and other spring poems/ Jitomates risueños y otros poemas de primavera.* San Francisco: Children's Book Press. TL3–5, A, P

Alarcón, F. (1998). *From the bellybutton of the moon: And other summer poems/ Del*

215

ombligo de la luna: Y otros poemas de verano. San Francisco: Children's Book Press. TL3–5, A, P

Alarcón, F. (1999). *Angels ride bikes: And other fall poems/ Los angeles andan en bicicleta: Y otros poemas de otoño.* San Francisco: Children's Book Press. TL3–5, A, P

Alarcón, F. (2005a). *Iguanas in the snow: And other winter poems/ Iguanas en la nieve: Y otros poemas de invierno.* San Francisco: Children's Book Press. TL3–5, I, P

Alarcón, F. (2005b). *Poems to dream together/ Poemas para sonar juntos.* New York: Lee & Low. TL3–5, A, P

Alarcón, F. (2008). *Animal poems of the Iguazu/ Animalario del Iguazu.* San Francisco: Children's Book Press. TL3–5, I, P

Aliki. (1991a). *My feet.* New York: HarperCollins. TL1–3, P, NF

Aliki. (1991b). *My five senses.* New York: Harper Festival. TL1–3, P, NF

Aliki. (1997). *Manners.* New York: Greenwillow. TL1–4, A, NF

Aliki. (1998). *Marianthe's story: Painted words and spoken memories.* New York: Greenwillow. TL3–5, A, F

Aliki. (2005). *Ah, music!.* New York: HarperCollins. TL2–5, A, NF

Altman, L. J. (1993). *Amelia's road.* New York: Lee & Low. TL3–5, A, F

Ancona, G. (1994). *The piñata maker/ El piñatero.* San Diego, CA: Harcourt Brace. TL3–5, I, NF

Ancona, G. (1997). *Mayeros: A Yucatec Maya family.* New York: Lothrop, Lee, & Shephard. TL3–5, I, NF

Ancona, G. (1998a). *Barrio: El barrio de José.* San Diego, CA: Harcourt Brace. TL3–5, I, NF

Ancona, G. (1998b). *Fiesta fireworks.* New York: Lothrop, Lee, & Shephard. TL3–5, I, NF

Ancona, G. (2001). *Harvest.* New York: Cavendish. TL3–5, I, NF

Ancona, G. (2003). *Murals: Walls that sing.* New York: Cavendish. TL3–5, I, NF

Andrews-Goebel, N. (2002). *The pot that Juan built.* New York: Lee & Low. TL3–5, I, P

Applegate, K. (2007). *Home of the brave.* New York: Feiwel & Friends. TL5, S, F

Argueta, J. (2001). *A movie in my pillow/ Una pelicula en mi almohada.* San Francisco: Children's Book Press. TL3–5, I, P

Argueta, J. (2006). *Talking with mother earth/ Hablando con madre tierra*, illustrated by L. A. Perez. Toronto, Ontario, Canada: Groundwood. TL3–5, I, P

Argueta, J. (2009). *Sopa de frijoles/ Bean soup.* Toronto, Ontario, Canada: Groundwood. TL2–5, A, P

Arnold, C. (2003). *Birds: Nature's magnificent flying machines.* Watertown, MA: Charlesbridge. TL4–5, I, NF

Arnosky, J. (1999). *All about owls.* New York: Scholastic. TL3–5, A, NF

Arnosky, J. (2001). *Wolves.* Washington, DC: National Geographic. TL1–3, A, NF

Arnosky, J. (2008a). *All about alligators.* New York: Scholastic. TL3–5, A, NF

Arnosky, J. (2008b). *All about sharks.* New York: Scholastic. TL3–5, A, NF

Aston, D. H. (2006). *An egg is quiet.* San Francisco: Chronicle Books. TL3–5, A, NF

Aston, D. H. (2007). *A seed is sleepy.* San Francisco: Chronicle Books. TL3–5, A, NF

Atkin, S. B. (2000). *Voices from the field: Children of migrant farmworkers tell their stories.* New York: Little, Brown. TL3–5, IS, NF

Aylesworth, J. (2009). *Our Abe Lincoln.* New York: Scholastic. TL2–5, A, P

Azarian, M. (2000). *A gardener's alphabet.* Boston: Houghton Mifflin. TL1–5, A, NF

Bae, H. (2007). *New clothes for New Year's Day.* La Jolla, CA: Kane/Miller. TL2–4, A, F

Baker, J. (2002). *Window.* New York: Walker. TL2–5, A, F

Baker, J. (2004). *Home.* New York: Greenwillow. TL2–5, A, F

Bang, M. (2009). *All of me! A book of thanks.* New York: Scholastic. TL1–3, P, NF

Barasch, L. (2007). *Hiromi's hands.* New York: Lee & Low. TL3–5, I, F

Barner, B. (1996). *Dem bones.* San Francisco: Chronicle. TL1–3, A, NF

Barry, F. (2008). *Little green frogs.* Cambridge, MA: Candlewick Press. TL1–2, P, NF

Barton, B. (1990a). *Bones, bones, dinosaur bones.* New York: Crowell. TL1–3, P, NF

Barton, B. (1990b). *Building a house.* New York: Mulberry. TL1–3, P, NF

Bash, B. (2002). *Desert giant: The world of the saguaro cactus.* San Francisco: Sierra Club Books for Children. TL3–5, A, NF

Bates, K. L. (1994). *O beautiful for spacious skies.* San Francisco: Chronicle. TL3–5, A, P

Bauer, M. D. (2007). *A mama for Owen.* New York: Simon & Schuster. TL2–4, A, F

Beake, L. (2007). *Home now.* Watertown, MA: Charlesbridge. TL3–5, A, F

Beck, C. (2008). *Buttercup's lovely day.* Victoria, BC: Orca. TL3–5, A, F

Bell, K. (2008). *If the shoe fits.* Cambridge, MA: Candlewick Press. TL4–5, I, F

Benjamin, F. (2008). *My two grannies.* London: Lincoln. TL3–5, A, F

Berger, M. (2002). *Spinning spiders.* New York: HarperCollins. TL3–5, A, NF

Bergman, M. (2009). *Yum, yum! What fun!* New York: Greenwillow. TL2–3, P, F

Berner, R. S. (2008). *In the town all year 'round.* San Francisco: Chronicle. TL1–5, P, F

Bernier-Grand, C. T. (2006). *César: Sí se puede/ Cesar: Yes, we can!* Tarrytown, NY: Cavendish. TL3–5, I, P

Best, C. (1999). *Three cheers for Catherine the great!* New York: DK. TL3–5, A, F

Blabey, A. (2009). *Sunday chutney.* Honesdale, PA: Front Street. TL2–4, A, F

Blackstone, S. (2005). *My granny went to market: A round-the-world counting rhyme.* Cambridge, MA: Barefoot Books. TL2–4, A, P

Bley, A. (2009). *A friend.* La Jolla, CA: Kane/Miller. TL2–5, A, F

Bonsignore, J. (2001). *Stick out your tongue! Fantastic facts, features, and functions of human and animal tongues.* Atlanta, GA: Peachtree. TL3–5, A, NF

Booth, D. (1990). *Voices on the wind: Poems for all sesasons.* New York: Morrow. TL3–5, A, P

Borden, L. (2005). *America is . . .* New York: Aladdin. TL2–5, A, P

Borden, L. (2008). *Off to first grade.* New York: McEderry. TL2–4, P, P

Borden, L., & Kroeger, M. K. (2001). *Fly high! The story of Bessie Coleman.* New York: McElderry. TL3–5, A, NF

Boston-Weatherford, C. (2007). *Jesse Owens: Fastest man alive.* New York: Walker. TL3–5, A, NF

Boston-Weatherford, C. (2008). *Before John was a jazz giant: A song of John Coltrane.* New York: Holt. TL3–5, I, NF

Boutignon, B. (2009). *Not all animals are blue: A big book of little differences.* New York: Kane/Miller. TL1–4, A, F

Brown, M., & Krensky, S. (1983). *Perfect pigs.* New York: Little, Brown. TL2–5, A, NF

Brown, R. (2001). *Ten seeds.* New York: Knopf. TL1–3, P, NF

Bruel, N. (2005). *Bad kitty.* New York: Roaring Brook. TL2–5, A, F

Bryan, A. (2007). *Let it shine: Three favorite spirituals.* New York: Atheneum. TL1–5, A, P

Budhos, M. T. (1999). *Remix: Conversations with immigrant teenagers.* New York: Holt. TL5, S, NF

Budhos, M. T. (2006). *Ask me no questions.* New York: Atheneum. TL5, S, F

Buehner, C. (1998). *It's a spoon, not a shovel.* New York: Puffin. TL2–4, A, NF

Bunting, E. (1989). *How many days to America? A Thanksgiving story.* New York: Clarion. TL2–4, A, F

Bunting, E. (1999). *A picnic in October.* San Diego, CA: Harcourt. TL2–4, A, F

Bunting, E. (2006). *One green apple.* New York: Clarion. TL3–5, A, F

Burleigh, R. (2007). *Stealing home: Jackie Robinson against the odds.* New York: Simon & Schuster. TL2–5, A, NF

Cabrera, J. (2008). *Old MacDonald had a farm.* New York: Holiday House. TL1–2, P, F

Cali, D. (2009). *The enemy: A book about peace.* New York: Schwartz & Wade. TL3–4, I, F

Campoy, I., & Ada, A. F. (2006). *Tales our abuelitas told: A Hispanic folktale collection.* New York: Atheneum. TL4–5, I, F

Carle, E. (1997). *Today is Monday.* New York: Putnam. TL1–3, P, F

Carle, E. (2008). *The very hungry caterpillar.* New York: Holt. TL1–4, P, F

Carling, A. L. (2005). *Sawdust carpets.* Toronto, Ontario, Canada: Groundwood. TL4–5, I, F

Carlson, L. (1994a). *American eyes: New Asian-American short stories for young adults.* New York: Holt. TL5, S, F

Carlson, L. (1994b). *Cool salsa: Bilingual poems on growing up Latino in the United States.* New York: Holt. TL5, S, P

Carlson, L. (2005). *Red hot salsa: Bilingual poems on being young and Latino in the United States.* New York: Holt. TL5, S, P

Carlson, N. (1990). *I like me.* New York: Puffin. TL1–4, P, F

Carlson, N. (1999). *ABC I like me.* New York: Puffin. TL1–4, P, F

Carlson, N. (2009). *First grade, here I come.* New York: Puffin. TL2–5, P, F

Carter, D. (1997). *If you're happy and you know it, clap your hands!* New York: Cartwheel. TL1–3, P, F

Cave, K. (2003). *One child, one seed: A South African counting book.* New York: Holt. TL2–5, A, NF

Cha, D. (1996). *Dia's story cloth.* New York: Lee & Low. TL3–5, A, F

Chamberlain, M. (2008). *Please don't tease Tootsie.* New York: Dutton. TL1–4, A, F

Chambers, F. E. (2007). *School days around the world.* New York: DK Children. TL2–5, A, NF

Chandra, D., & Comora, M. (2003). *George Washington's teeth*. New York: Farrar, Straus & Giroux. TL2–4, A, NF

Cheney, L. (2002). *America: A patriotic primer*. New York: Simon & Schuster. TL2–5, A, NF

Cheney, L. (2003). *A is for Abigal: An almanac of amazing American women*. New York: Simon & Schuster. TL2–5, A, NF

Chessa, F. (2008). *Holly's red boots*. New York: Holiday House. TL1–2, P, F

Cheung, H., & Das, P. (2008). *K is for Korea*. London: Lincoln. TL3–5, A, NF

Chihiro, N. (2008). *Who made this cake?* Honesdale, PA: Front Street. TL1–2, P, F

Child, L. (2008). *I completely know about guinea pigs*. New York: Dial. TL3–5, A, F

Child, L. (2009). *We are extremely very good recyclers*. New York: Dial. TL3–5, A, F

Chin-Lee, C. (1997). *A is for Asia*. London: Lincoln Children's Books. TL3–5, A, NF

Chin-Lee, C. (2005). *Amelia to Zora: Twenty-six women who changed the world*. Watertown, MA: Charlesbridge. TL3–5, I, NF

Chin-Lee, C. (2006). *Akira to Zoltan: Twenty-six men who changed the world*. Watertown, MA: Charlesbridge. TL3–5, I, NF

Chin-Lee, C., & de la Peña, T. (1999). *A is for the Americas*. London: Lincoln. TL3–5, A, NF

Choi, Y. (2001). *The name jar*. New York: Farrar, Straus & Giroux. TL4–5, A, F

Choi, Y. (2006). *Behind the mask*. New York: Farrar, Straus & Giroux. TL3–5, A, F

Christelow, E. (2008). *Vote!* New York: Sandpiper. TL3–5, A, NF

Church, C. J. (2003). *Do your ears hang low?* New York: Chicken House. TL1–3, P, F

Church, C. J. (2008). *Ping pong pig*. New York: Holiday House. TL2–4, A, F

Clarke, J. (2008). *Stuck in the mud*. New York: Walker. TL2–3, A, F

Cleary, B. P. (2001a). *Hairy, scary, ordinary: What is an adjective?* Minneapolis, MN: Lerner. TL2–5, A, NF

Cleary, B. P. (2001b). *To root, to toot, to parachute: What is a verb?* Minneapolis, MN: Lerner. TL2–5, A, NF

Clearly, B. P. (2003a). *Dearly, nearly, insincerely: What is an adverb?* Minneapolis, MN: Lerner. TL2–5, A, NF

Cleary, B. P. (2003b). *Under, over, by the clover: What is a preposition?* Minneapolis, MN: Lerner. TL2–5, A, NF

Cleary, B. P. (2006). *I and you and don't forget who: What is a pronoun?* Minneapolis, MN: Lerner. TL2–5, A, NF

Cline-Ransome, L. (2007). *Young Pele: Soccer's first star*. New York: Schwartz & Wade. TL3–5, A, NF

Cobb, V. (2002). *I get wet*. New York: HarperCollins. TL3–5, A, NF

Cole, H. (2003). *On the way to the beach*. New York: Greenwillow. TL2–4, A, NF

Cole, J. (1989). *Anna Banana: 101 jump-rope rhymes*. New York: Morrow Junior Books. TL2–5, A, F

Cole, J. (1997). *The magic school bus and the electric field trip*. New York: Scholastic. TL3–5, A, NF

Cole, J. (1999). *The magic school bus explores the senses*. New York: Scholastic. TL3–5, A, NF

Collard, S. B. (2002a). *Beaks.* Watertown, MA: Charlesbridge. TL2–5, A, NF

Collard, S. B. (2002b). *Leaving home.* Boston: Houghton Mifflin. TL1–5, A, NF

Compestine, Y. C. (2006). *D is for dragon dance.* New York: Holiday House. TL2–5, A, NF

Cooling, W. (Ed.). (2004). *Come to the great world: Poems from around the globe.* New York: Holiday House. TL2–5, A, P

Cordero, F. D. M. (2008). *M is for Mexico.* London: Lincoln. TL3–5, A, NF

Cotton, C. (2008). *Rainplay.* New York: Holt. TL2–4, A, P

Cousins, L. (2007). *Maisy's amazing big book of words.* Cambridge, MA: Candlewick. TL1–2, P, NF

Cousins, L. (2009). *Yummy: Eight favorite fairy tales.* Watertown, MA: Candlewick Press. TL3–5, A, F

Crandell, R. (2002). *Hands of the Maya: Villagers at work and play.* New York: Holt. TL3–5, A, NF

Crews, D. (1993). *School bus.* New York: Greenwillow. TL1–3, P, NF

Cumberbatch, J. (2006). *Can you hear the sea?* New York: Bloomsbury. TL2–4, A, F

Cumyn, A. (2008). *Dear Sylvia.* Toronto, Ontario, Canada: Groundwood. TL4–5, I, F

D'Aluisio, F. (2008). *What the world eats.* Berkley, CA: Tricycle Press. TL4–5, I, NF

Daly, N. (2006a). *Happy birthday, Jamela!* London: Lincoln. TL3–5, A, F

Daly, N. (2006b). *Pretty Salma: A Little Red Riding Hood story from Africa.* New York: Clarion. TL3–5, A, F

Davies, N. (2000). *Big blue whale.* Cambridge, MA: Candlewick Press. TL3–5, A, NF

Davies, N. (2001). *One tiny turtle.* Cambridge, MA: Candlewick Press. TL3–5, A, NF

Davies, N. (2003a). *Birds.* New York: Kingfisher. TL3–5, A, NF

Davies, N. (2003b). *Surprising sharks.* New York: Walker. TL3–5, A, NF

Davis, K. (1998). *Who hops?* New York: Harcourt. TL1–3, P, F

Davis, K. (2000). *Who hoots?* New York: Harcourt. TL1–3, P, F

Davis, K. C. (1999). *Don't know much about the Civil War.* New York: HarperCollins. TL4–5, I, NF

Davis, K. C. (2001). *Don't know much about geography.* New York: HarperCollins. TL4–5, I, NF

Davis, K. C. (2002a). *Don't know much about George Washington.* New York: HarperCollins. TL4–5, I, NF

Davis, K. C. (2002b). *Don't know much about Sitting Bull.* New York: HarperCollins. TL4–5, I, NF

Davis, K. C. (2003). *Don't know much about the pioneers.* New York: HarperCollins. TL4–5, I, NF

Davis, K. C. (2004). *Don't know much about history.* New York: HarperCollins. TL4–5, I, NF

Deedy, C. A. (2007). *Martina, the beautiful cockroach: A Cuban folktale.* Atlanta, GA: Peachtree. TL3–5, A, F

Deedy, C. A., & Naiyomah, W. K. (2009). *14 cows for America.* Atlanta, GA: Peachtree. TL3–5, I, NF

Delacre, L. (Ed.). (1989). *Arroz conleche: Popular songs and rhymes from Latin America.* New York: Scholastic. TL2–4, A, F

Demarest, C. L. (2002). *Smoke jumpers one to ten.* New York: McElderry. TL2–4, A, NF

Demarest, C. L. (2003a). *Firefighters A to Z.* New York: McElderry. TL2–4, A, NF

Demarest, C. L. (2003b). *Hotshots!* New York: McElderry. TL2–4, A, NF

Dewdney, A. (2005a). *Llama, llama misses mama.* New York: Viking. TL1–2, P, F

Dewdney, A. (2005b). *Llama, llama red pajama.* New York: Viking. TL1–2, P, F

Dewdney, A. (2007). *Llama, llama mad at mama.* New York: Viking. TL1–2, P, F

Dewey, J. (2001). *Antarctic journal: Four months at the bottom of the world.* New York: HarperCollins. TL4–5, I, NF

Diakite, B. W. (2007). *Mee-An and the magic serpent.* Toronto, Ontario, Canada: Groundwood. TL3–5, I, F

Diakite, P. (2006). *I lost my tooth in Africa.* New York: Scholastic. TL4–5, A, F

Dipucchio, K. (2008). *Grace for president.* New York: Hyperion. TL3–5, A, F

Dodd, E. (2008). *What pet to get?* New York: Bloomsbury. TL2–4, A, F

Donaldson, J. (2008a). *The fish who cried wolf.* New York: Levine. TL2–5, A, F

Donaldson, J. (2008b). *Where's my mom?* New York: Dial. TL3–5, A, F

Dooley, N. (1992a). *Everybody bakes bread.* Minneapolis, MN: Carolrhoda. TL3–5, A, F

Dooley, N. (1992b). *Everybody cooks rice.* Minneapolis, MN: Carolrhoda. TL3–5, A, F

Dorling Kindersley. (2003). *A life like mine.* New York: DK. TL3–5, A, NF

Dorros, A. (2000). *Ten go tango.* New York: HarperCollins. TL1–3, P, F

Dorros, A. (2005). *Julio's magic.* New York: HarperCollins. TL4–5, I, F

Dorros, A. (2008). *Papá and me.* New York: HarperCollins. TL2–4, P, F

Dotlich, R. K. (2001). *When riddles come rumbling: Poems to ponder.* Honesdale, NY: Boyds Mills Press. TL2–5, A, P

Druckman, N. (2003). American flags: Designs for a young nation. New York: Henry N. Abrams. TL4–5, I, NF

Dunphy, M. (2006a). *Here is the African Savanna.* New York: Web of Life. TL3–5, A, NF

Dunphy, M. (2006b). *Here is the coral reef.* New York: Web of Life. TL3–5, A, NF

Dunphy, M. (2006c). *Here is the tropical rain forest.* New York: Web of Life. TL3–5, A, NF

Dunphy, M. (2007a). *Here is the Arctic winter.* New York: Web of Life. TL3–5, A, NF

Dunphy, M. (2007b). *Here is the wetland.* New York: Web of Life. TL3–5, A, NF

DuQuette, Keith. (2002). *They call me woolly: What animal names can tell us.* New York: Putnam. TL2–4, A, NF

Dyer, S. (2008). *Mrs. Muffly's monster.* London: Frances Lincoln. TL2–4, A, F

Edwards, P. D. (2009). *The bus ride that changed history: The story of Rosa Parks.* New York: Sandpiper. TL3–5, A, NF

Ehlert, L. (1989). *Color zoo.* New York: HarperCollins. TL1–2, P, NF

Ehlert, L. (1990). *Color farm.* New York: HarperCollins. TL1–2, P, NF

Ehlert, L. (1996). *Eating the alphabet: Fruits and vegetables from A to Z.* San Diego, CA: Harcourt. TL1–3, A, NF

Ehlert, L. (2001). *Waiting for wings.* San Diego, CA: Harcourt. TL1–3, A, NF

Elvegren, J. R. (2006). *Josias, hold the book*. Honesdale, PA: Boyds Mills Press. TL3–5, A, F

Elya, S. M. (2006). *Bebe goes shopping*. San Diego, CA: Harcourt. TL1–3, P, F

Elya, S. M., & Banks, M. (2007). *N is for Navidad*. San Francisco: Chronicle. TL2–5, A, F

Falwell, C. (1993). *Feast for 10*. New York: Scholastic. TL1–3, P, F

Fanelli, S. (2007). *My map book*. New York: Walker. TL1–3, P, F

Fearnley, J. (2008). *Martha in the middle*. New York: Walker. TL3–5, A, F

Fine, E. H. (2007). *Armando and the blue tarp school*. New York: Lee & Low. TL4–5, I, F

Fitzgerald, J. (2008). *Yum! Yum! Delicious nursery rhymes*. Markham, Ontario, Canada: Fitzhenry & Whiteside. TL2–4, A, F

Fleischman, P. (2007). *Glass slipper, gold sandal: A worldwide Cinderella*. New York: Henry Holt. TL3–5, A, F

Fleming, C. (2005). *Lowji discovers America*. New York: Atheneum. TL5, S, F

Fleming, D. (2000). *The everything book*. New York: Henry Holt. TL1–2, P, F

Florian, D. (2000a). *A pig is big*. New York: Greenwillow. TL1–4, A, P

Florian, D. (2000b). *On the wing*. New York: Voyager Books. TL2–5, A, P

Florian, D. (2001). *In the swim*. New York: Voyager Books. TL2–5, A, P

Florian, D. (2002). *Insectlopedia*. New York: Voyager Books. TL2–5, A, P

Florian, D. (2004). *Mammalibilia*. New York: Voyager Books. TL2–5, A, P

Florian, D. (2005a). *Lizards, frogs, and polliwogs*. New York: Sandpiper Books. TL2–5, A, P

Florian, D. (2005b). *Zoo's who*. San Diego, CA: Harcourt. TL2–5, A, P

Florian, D. (2007a). *Bing bang boing*. San Diego, CA: Harcourt. TL1–5, A, P

Florian, D. (2007b). *Comets, stars, the moon, and Mars: Space poems and paintings*. San Diego, CA: Harcourt. TL2–5, A, P

Foreman, J. & Foreman, M. (2008). *Say hello*. Cambridge, MA: Candlewick Press. TL1–2, P, F

Foreman, M. (2006). *Mia's story: A sketchbook of hopes and dreams*. Cambridge, MA: Candlewick Press. TL2–5, A, F

Forest, H. (2005). *Feathers: A Jewish tale from Eastern Europe*. Little Rock, AR: August House. TL3–5, I, F

Fox, M. (1992). *Hattie and the fox*. New York: Aladdin. TL1–3, A, F

Fox, M. (1997). *Whoever you are*. San Diego, CA: Harcourt. TL1–3, A, F

Franco, B. (2009). *Messing around on the monkey bars: And other school poems for two voices*. Somerville, MA: Candlewick Press. TL1–5, A, P

Fraser, M. A. (2002). *How animal babies stay safe*. New York: HarperCollins. TL2–5, A, NF

Fredrick, M. (2008). *Kamal goes to Trinidad*. London: Lincoln Children's Books. TL3–5, I, NF

Friedman, I. R. (1984). *How my parents learned to eat*. Boston: Houghton Mifflin. TL3–5, A, F

Gallo, G. R. (2004). *First crossing: Stories about teen immigrants*. Cambridge, MA: Candlewick Press. TL5, S, F

Garland, S. (1993). *The lotus seed*. San Diego, CA: Harcourt. TL3–5, A, F

Garza, C. L. (2000). *In my family/ En mi familia*. San Francisco: Children's Book Press. TL3–5, A, NF

Garza, C. L. (2005). *Family pictures/ Cuadros de familia*. San Francisco: Children's Book Press. TL3–5, A, NF

Gay, M.L. (2008). *On the road again! More travels with my family*. Toronto, Ontario, Canada: Groundwood. TL4–5, I, F

Gibbons, G. (1992). *Weather words and what they mean*. New York: Holiday House. TL3–5, A, NF

Gibbons, G. (1993). *Weather forecasting*. New York: Aladdin. TL3–5, A, NF

Gibbons, G. (1996). *Recycle: A handbook for kids*. New York: Little, Brown. TL3–5, A, NF

Gibbons, G. (1999). *Exploring the deep, dark sea*. New York: Little, Brown. TL3–5, A, NF

Gibbons, G. (2001). *Polar bears*. New York: Holiday House. TL3–5, A, NF

Gibbons, G. (2004). *Giant pandas*. New York: Holiday House. TL3–5, A, NF

Gibbons, G. (2005). *Owls*. New York: Holiday House. TL3–5, A, NF

Gibbons, G. (2007a). *Coral reefs*. New York: Holiday House. TL3–5, A, NF

Gibbons, G. (2007b). *Snakes*. New York: Holiday House. TL3–5, A, NF

Gibbons, G. (2007c). *The vegetables we eat*. New York: Holiday House. TL3–5, A, NF

Gibbons, G. (2009). *Hurricanes*. New York: Holiday House. TL3–5, A, NF

Gifford, C. (2003). *Robots*. New York: Kingfisher. TL3–5, A, NF

Gilchrist, J. S. (2007). *My America*. New York: HarperCollins. TL1–5, A, P

Giovanni, N. (2008). *Hip hop speaks to children: A celebration of poetry with a beat*. Naperville, IL: Jabberwocky/Sourcebooks. TL2–5, A, P

Gonzalez, M. C. (2009). *I know the river loves me/ Yo se que el rio me ama*. San Francisco: Children's Press. TL1–3, P, F

Graham, B. (2008). *How to heal a broken wing*. Cambridge, MA: Candlewick Press. TL1–3, P, F

Graham, J. B. (2001). *Splish splash*. New York: Sandpiper. TL2–5, A, P

Graham, J. B. (2003). *Flicker flash*. New York: Sandpiper. TL2–5, A, P

Granfield, L. (2005). *America votes: How our president is elected*. New York: Kids Can. TL3–5, A, NF

Gravett, E. (2008a). *Little mouse's big book of fears*. New York: Simon & Schuster. TL1–5, A, F

Gravett, E. (2008b). *Monkey and me*. New York: Simon & Schuster. TL1, P, F

Greenfield, E. (1991). *Night on neighborhood street*. New York: Dial. TL2–5, I, P

Greenfield, E. (2006a). *The friendly four*. New York: Amistad/HarperCollins. TL1–4, A, P

Greenfield, E. (2006b). *When the horses ride by: Children in the times of war*. New York: Lee & Low. TL2–5, A, P

Greenstein, E. (2003). *Ice cream cones for sale*. New York: Levine. TL3–5, A, NF

Grey, M. (2008). *Traction Man meets Turbo Dog*. New York: Knopf. TL4–5, I, F

Grifalconi, A. (2007) *Ain't nobody a stranger to me*. New York: Jump at the Sun. TL4–5, I, F

Gudel, H. (1999). *Dear Alexandra: A story of Switzerland*. Norwalk, CT: Soundprints. TL2–4, A, F

Gunning, M. (2004). *America: My new home*. Honesdale, PA: Boyds Mills Press. TL3–5, A, P

Gunzi, C. (2003). *Wolves and wild dogs*. New York: Kingfisher. TL3–5, A, NF

Gunzi, C. (2006). *Snakes*. New York: Kingfisher. TL3–5, A, NF

Gurth, P. (2009). *Oh, Canada!* Toronto, Ontario, Canada: Kids Can Press. TL1–2, P, NF

Hächler, B. (2008). *Anna's wish*. New York: NorthSouth. TL3–5, A, F

Hamilton, M., & Weiss, M. (2007). *Priceless gifts*. Little Rock, AR: August House. TL3–5, A, F

Hamilton, R. (2008). *If I were you: A daddy–daughter story*. New York: Bloomsbury. TL2–5, A, F

Hammill, M. (2008). *Sir Reginald's logbook*. Toronto, Ontario, Canada: Kids Can Press. TL4–5, A, F

Harris, P. (1996). *Hot cold bold shy*. Toronto, Ontario, Canada: Kids Can Press. TL1–3, P, NF

Harrison, D. L. (2001). *Caves: Mysteries beneath our feet*. Honesdale, PA: Boyds Mills Press. TL3–5, I, NF

Harrison, D. L. (2002a). *Rivers: Nature's wondrous waterways*. Honesdale, PA: Boyds Mills Press. TL3–5, I, NF

Harrison, D. L. (2002b). *Volcanoes: Nature's incredible fireworks*. Honesdale, PA: Boyds Mills Press. TL3–5, I, NF

Harrison, D. L. (2003). *Oceans: The vast, mysterious deep*. Honesdale, PA: Boyds Mills Press. TL3–5, I, NF

Harvey, M. (2008). *Shopping with dad*. Cambridge, MA: Barefoot Books. TL2–4, A, F

Hatkoff, C., & Hatkoff, I. (2008). *Owen & Mzee: A day together*. New York: Cartwheel Books. TL2–4, A, NF

Hatkoff, I., Hatkoff, C., & Kahumbu, P. (2006). *Owen & Mzee: The true story of a remarkable friendship*. New York: Scholastic. TL3–5, A, NF

Hatkoff, I., Hatkoff, C., & Kahumbu, P. (2007a). *Owen & Mzee: Best friends*. New York: Scholastic. TL2–4, A, NF

Hatkoff, I., Hatkoff, C., & Kahumbu, P. (2007b). *Owen & Mzee: The language of friendship*. New York: Scholastic. TL3–5, A, NF

Hayes, S. (2008). *Dog day*. New York: Farrar, Straus & Giroux. TL2–4, A, F

Heard, G. (2009). *Falling down the page: A book of list poems*. New York: Roaring Brook Press. TL2–5, A, P

Herrera, J. F. (1998). *Laughing out loud, I fly: A carcajadas yo vuelo*. New York: HarperCollins. TL4–5, I, P

Herrera, J. F. (2000). *The upside down boy*. San Francisco: Children's Book Press. TL3–5, A, F

Hewett, J. (2001). *A tiger cub grows up*. Minneapolis, MN: First Avenue Editions. TL2–4, A, NF

Heydlauff, L. (2003). *Going to school in India*. Watertown, MA: Charlesbridge. TL3–5, I, NF

Hindley, J. (2008). *Isn't it time*. New York: Walker. TL1–3, A, F

Hinshaw-Patent, D. (2003). *Colorful, captivating coral reefs*. New York: Walker. TL3–5, I, NF

Hoban, T. (1983). *I read symbols*. New York: Greenwillow. TL1–3, A, NF

Hoban, T. (1987). *I read signs*. New York: Greenwillow. TL1–3, A, NF

Hoban, T. (1995a). *Colors everywhere*. New York: Greenwillow. TL1–3, A, NF

Hoban, T. (1995b). *26 letters and 99 cents*. New York: Greenwillow. TL1–3, A, NF

Hoban, T. (1997). *Exactly the opposite.* New York: Greenwillow. TL1–3, A, NF

Hoban, T. (1998). *More, fewer, less.* New York: Greenwillow. TL1–3, A, NF

Hoban, T. (2008). *Over, under, through.* New York: Aladdin. TL1–3, A, NF

Hobbs, W. (2006). *Crossing the wire.* New York: HarperCollins. TL5, S, F

Hoberman, M. A. (2004). *The eensy-weensy spider.* New York: Little Brown. TL1–3, P, F

Hodge, D. (2008). *Who lives here? Desert animals.* Toronto, Ontario, Canada: Kids Can Press. TL2–4, A, NF

Hoestlandt, J. (2008) *Gran, you've got mail!* New York: Delacorte. TL4–5, I, F

Hoffman, M. (2002). *The color of home.* New York: Fogelman. TL4–5, A, F

Hollyer, B. (2004). *Let's eat: What children eat around the world.* New York: Holt. TL3–5, I, NF

Hooper, M. (2001). *Antarctic journal: The hidden worlds of Antarctica's animals.* London: Lincoln. TL4–5, I, NF

Hopkins, L. B. (1995a). *Weather: Poems for all seasons.* New York: Harcourt. TL2–5, A, P

Hopkins, L. B. (Ed). (1995b). *Small talk: A book of short poems.* San Diego, CA: Harcourt. TL2–5, A, P

Hopkins, L. B. (1996). *Blast off! Poems about space.* New York: HarperCollins. TL2–5, A, P

Hopkins, L. B. (1997). *Marvelous math: A book of poems.* New York: Simon & Schuster. TL3–5, A, P

Hopkins, L. B. (1999a). *Dino-roars.* New York: Golden. TL2–5, A, P

Hopkins, L. B. (1999b). *Spectacular science: A book of poems.* New York: Simon & Schuster. TL3–5, A, P

Hopkins, L. B. (2000). *Sports! Sports! Sports! A poetry collection.* New York: HarperCollins. TL2–5, A, P

Hopkins, L. B. (2003). *Alphathoughts: Alphabet poems.* Honesdale, PA: Boyds Mills Press. TL1–5, A, P

Hopkins, L. B. (2009a). *City I love.* New York: Abrams. TL1–5, A, P

Hopkins, L. B. (2009b). *Sky magic.* New York: Dutton. TL2–5, A, P

Horácek, P. (2008). *Look out, Suzy Goose!* Cambridge, MA: Candlewick Press. TL2–3, P, F

Horse, H. (2008a). *The last cowboys.* Atlanta, GA: Peachtree. TL4–5, I, F

Horse, H. (2008b). *The last gold diggers.* Atlanta, GA: Peachtree. TL4–5, I, F

Howell, F. (2002). *Zoo flakes.* New York: Walker. TL1–3, A, NF

Hoyt-Goldsmith, D. (1998a). *Celebrating Chinese New Year.* New York: Holiday House. TL3–5, I, NF

Hoyt-Goldsmith, D. (1998b). *Lacrosse: The national game of the Iroquois.* New York: Holiday House. TL3–5, I, NF

Hoyt-Goldsmith, D. (1999). *Las Posadas: An Hispanic Christmas celebration.* New York: Holiday House. TL3–5, I, NF

Hoyt-Goldsmith, D. (2000). *Celebrating Passover.* New York: Holiday House. TL3–5, I, NF

Hoyt-Goldsmith, D. (2001). *Celebrating Ramadan.* New York: Holiday House. TL3–5, I, NF

Hoyt-Goldsmith, D. (2002). *Celebrating a Quinceanera: A Latina's 15th birthday celebration.* New York: Holiday House. TL3–5, I, NF

Hoyt-Goldsmith, D. (2004). *Three Kings Day: A celebration at Christmastime.* New York: Holiday House. TL3–5, I, NF

Hoyt-Goldsmith, D. (2008). *Cinco de Mayo: Celebrating the traditions of Mexico.* New York: Holiday House. TL3–5, I, NF

Huneck, S. (2008). *Sally gets a job.* New York: Abrams. TL2–5, A, F

Hynes, M. (2008). *Rocks and fossils.* New York: Kingfisher. TL3–5, I, NF

Ichikawa, S. (2006). *My father's shop.* La Jolla, CA: Kane/Miller. TL2–4, A, F

Isadora, R. (2007a). *The princess and the pea.* New York: Putnam. TL2–4, A, F

Isadora, R. (2007b). *Twelve dancing princesses.* New York: Putnam. TL3–5, A, F

Isadora, R. (2007c). *Yo, Jo!* San Diego, CA: Harcourt. TL1–3, A, F

Iyengar, M. M. (2007). *Romina's rangoli.* Walnut Creek, CA: Shen's Books. TL4–5, I, F

Jackson, E. (2003a). *It's back to school we go! First day stories from around the world.* Brookfield, CT: Millbrook Press. TL3–5, I, NF

Jackson, E. (2003b). *My tour of Europe by Teddy Roosevelt, age 10.* Brookfield, CT: Millbrook Press. TL3–5, I, NF

James, B. (2006). *Tadpoles.* New York: Scholastic. TL4–5, A, F

Janeczko, P. (2001). *A poke in the I: A collection of concrete poems.* Cambridge, MA: Candlewick Press. TL2–5, A, P

Jaramillo, A. (2006). *La linea.* New York: Roaring Brook. TL5, S, F

Jenkins, M. (2001). *Chameleons are cool!* Cambridge, MA: Candlewick Press. TL3–5, A, NF

Jenkins, S. (1995). *Biggest, strongest, fastest.* Boston: Houghton Mifflin. TL1–4, A, NF

Jenkins, S. (2001). *Animals in flight.* Boston: Houghton Mifflin. TL2–5, A, NF

Jenkins, S. (2002). *Life on Earth: The story of evolution.* Boston: Houghton Mifflin. TL4–5, I, NF

Jenkins, S. (2004). *Hottest, coldest, highest, deepest.* New York: Sandpiper. TL2–5, A, NF

Jenkins, S., & Page, R. (2003). *What do you do with a tail like this?* Boston: Houghton Mifflin. TL2–5, A, NF

Jenkins, S., & Page, R. (2006). *Move!* Boston: Houghton Mifflin. TL1–4, A, F

Ji, Z., & Xu, C. (2008). *No! That's wrong!* La Jolla, CA: Kane/Miller. TL1–3, P, F

Jiménez, M. (1998). *La mariposa.* Boston: Houghton Mifflin. TL3–5, P, F

Johnson, A. (2007). *Wind flyers.* New York: Simon & Schuster. TL3–5, I, F

Johnson, S. (1999). *Alphabet city.* New York: Puffin. TL1–5, A, NF

Johnston, T. (1999). *My Mexico/ México mío.* New York: Putnam. TL3–5, I, P

Jonas, A. (1989). *Color dance.* New York: Greenwillow. TL1–3, P, NF

Joslin, S. (1986a). *What do you do, dear?* New York: HarperCollins. TL2–4, P, NF

Joslin, S. (1986b). *What do you say, dear?* New York: HarperCollins. TL2–4, P, NF

Kalman, B. (1994). *Homes around the world.* New York: Crabtree. TL2–5, A, NF

Kaner, E. (2009). *Have you ever seen a duck in a raincoat?* Toronto, Ontario, Canada: Kids Can Press. TL1–3, P, NF

Katz, B. (2006). *Once around the sun.* San Diego, CA: Harcourt. TL2–5, A, P

Katz, B. (2009). *More pocket poems.* New York: Dutton. TL2–5, A, P

Katz, K. (2007). *My first Ramadan.* New York: Holt. TL2–4, A, F

Keller, L. (2007). *Do unto otters: A book about manners.* New York: Holt. TL2–5, A, F

Kelly, I. (2003). *It's a hummingbird's life.* New York: Holiday House. TL3–5, A, NF

Kennemore, T. (2008) *Alice's birthday pig.* Grand Rapids, MI: Erdmans. TL4–5, I, F

Kerley, B. (2006). *A cool drink of water.* Washington, DC: National Geographic. TL1–4, A, NF

Kerley, B. (2007). *A little peace.* Washington, DC: National Geographic. TL1–4, A, NF

Kerrin, J. S. (2008). *Martin Bridge: In high gear.* Toronto, Ontario, Canada: Kids Can Press. TL4–5, I, F

Kerrin, J. S. (2009). *Martin Bridge: Onwards and upwards!* Toronto, Ontario, Canada: Kids Can Press. TL4–5, I, F

Kosaka, F. (2001). *Let's count the raindrops.* New York: Viking. TL2–4, A, P

Krebs, L. (2003). *We all went on safari: A counting journey through Tanzania.* Cambridge, MA: Barefoot Books. TL2–5, A, NF

Krebs, L. (2005). *We're sailing to the Galapagos: A week in the Pacific.* Cambridge, MA: Barefoot Books. TL2–5, A, NF

Krull, K. (2001). *Supermarket.* New York: Holiday House. TL2–4, A, NF

Krull, K. (2003a). *Harvesting hope: The story of Cesar Chavez.* San Diego, CA: Harcourt. TL3–5, A, NF

Krull, K. (2003b). *M is for music.* San Diego, CA: Harcourt. TL2–5, A, NF

Krull, K. (2007). *Pochahontas: Princess of the new world.* New York: Walker. TL3–5, A, NF

Kurtz, J. (2005). *In the small, small night.* New York: Greenwillow. TL2–4, P, F

Kwon, Y. (2007). *My cat copies me.* La Jolla, CA: Kane/Miller. TL1–3, P, F

Landau, E. (2003). *Popcorn!* Watertown, MA: Charlesbridge.TL3–5, I, NF

Lauber, P. (1994). *Volcano: The eruption and healing of Mount St. Helens.* New York: Simon & Schuster. TL3–5, I, NF

Lee, H. Y. (2008). *Something for school.* La Jolla, CA: Kane/Miller. TL2–3, P, F

Lee, M. (2006). *Landed.* New York: Farrar, Straus & Giroux. TL4–5, I, F

Lee, S. (2007). *The zoo.* La Jolla, CA: Kane/Miller. TL1–2, P, F

Lee-Tai, A. (2006). *A place where sunflowers grow.* San Francisco: Children's Book Press. TL3–5, I, F

Leedy, L. (2000a). *Measuring Penny.* New York: Holt. TL2–4, A, NF

Leedy, L. (2000b). *Monster money book.* New York: Holiday House. TL3–5, I, NF

Lehman, B. (2004). *The red book.* Boston: Houghton Mifflin. TL2–5, A, F

Lehman, B. (2006). *Museum trip.* Boston: Houghton Mifflin. TL2–5, A, F

Lehman, B. (2007). *Rainstorm.* Boston: Houghton Mifflin. TL2–5, A, F

Lerner, C. (2005). *On the wing: American birds in migration.* New York: HarperCollins. TL3–5, I, NF

Le Rochais, M. (2001). *Desert trek: An eye-opening journey through the world's driest places.* New York: Walker. TL2–5, A, NF

Lessac, F. (2005). *Island counting 1 2 3.* Cambridge, MA: Candlewick Press. TL1–2, A, F

Lester, A. (2009a). *Horse crazy* (Horse Crazy Series). San Francisco: Chronicle Books. TL4–5, I, F

Lester, A. (2009b). *The silver horse switch* (Horse Crazy Series). San Francisco: Chronicle Books. TL4–5, I, F

Levenson, G. (2004). *Bread comes to life: A garden of wheat and a loaf to eat.* Berkley, CA: Tricycle Press. TL2–5, A, NF

Levine, E. (1995). *I hate English!* New York: Scholastic. TL3–5, A, F

Lewis, E. B. (2005). *This little light of mine.* New York: Simon & Schuster. TL1–5, A, P

Lewis, J. P. (2002). *Doodle dandies: Poems that take shape.* New York: Atheneum. TL2–5, A, P

Lewis, J. P. (2007). *Big is big (and little, little): A book of contrasts.* New York: Holiday House. TL1–4, A, P

Lionni, L. (1995). *Inch by inch.* New York: HarperCollins. TL2–4, P, F

Lipp, F. (2008). *Running shoes.* Watertown, MA: Charlesbridge. TL3–5, A, F

Ljungkvist, L. (2008). *Follow the line around the world.* New York: Viking. TL3–5, A, NF

Llewellyn, C. (2008). *Ask. Dr. K. Fisher about creepy-crawlies.* New York: Kingfisher. TL2–5, A, F

Lofthouse, L. (2007). *Ziba came by boat.* La Jolla, CA: Kane/Miller. TL2–5, A, F

Lombard, J. (2006). *Drita, my homegirl.* New York: Putnam. TL5, S, F

Long, S. (2001). *Twinkle, twinkle little star.* San Francisco: Chronicle. TL1–3, P, F

Look, L. (2004). *Ruby Lu, brave and true.* New York: Atheneum. TL4–5, I, F

Look, L. (2006a). *Ruby Lu, empress of everything.* New York: Atheneum. TL4–5, I, F

Look, L. (2006b). *Uncle Peter's amazing Chinese wedding.* New York: Atheneum. TL3–5, A, F

Lord, B. B. (1984). *In the year of the boar and Jackie Robinson.* New York: Harper & Row. TL5, I-S, F

Lottridge, C. B. (2008). *One watermelon seed.* Markham, Ontario, Canada: Fitzhenry & Whiteside. TL2–4, A, NF

Lujan, J. (2008). *Colors! Colores!* Toronto, Ontario, Canada: Groundwood. TL3–5, A, P

Lunde, D. (2007). *Hello, bumblebee bat.* Watertown, MA: Charlesbridge. TL2–5, A, NF

MacDonald, M. R. (2004). *Three minute tales: Stories from around the world to read or tell when time is short.* Little Rock, AR: August House. TL4–5, I, F

MacDonald, M. R. (2006a). *Conejito: A folktale from Panama.* Little Rock, AR: August House. TL3–5, A, F

MacDonald, M. R. (2006b). *Go to sleep, Gecko! A Balinese folktale.* Little Rock, AR: August House. TL3–5, A, F

MacDonald, M. R. (2007a). *Five minute tales: More stories to read and tell when time is short.* Little Rock, AR: August House. TL4–5, I, F

MacDonald, M. R. (2007b). *The great smelly, slobbery, small-tooth dog: A folktale from Great Britain.* Little Rock, AR: August House. TL3–5, A, F

MacDonald, S. (2009). *Shape by shape.* New York: Simon & Schuster. TL1–3, P, NF

Mado, M. (1992). *The animals.* New York: McElderry. TL3–5, I, P

Mado, M. (1998). *The magic pocket: Selected poems.* New York: McElderry. TL1–5, A, P

Mak, K. (2001). *My Chinatown: One year in poems*. New York: HarperCollins. TL3–5, A, P

Markle, S. (2001). *Growing up wild: Wolves*. New York: Atheneum. TL3–5, A, NF

Markle, S. (2002). *Growing up wild: Penguins*. New York: Atheneum. TL3–5, A, NF

Markle, S. (2003). *Outside and inside big cats*. New York: Atheneum. TL3–5, NF

Markle, S. (2005). *Outside and inside giant squid*. New York: Walker. TL3–5, A, NF

Markle, S. (2008a). *Outside and inside rats and mice*. New York: Aladdin. TL3–5, I, NF

Markle, S. (2008b). *Sneaky, spinning baby spiders*. New York: Walker. TL3–5, A, NF

Martin, Jr., B. (2007). *Here are my hands*. New York: Henry Holt. TL1–3, P, NF

Martin, Jr., B., & Sampson, M. (2004). *I pledge allegiance*. Cambridge, MA: Candlewick. TL2–5, A, NF

Marzollo, J. (1997). *Pretend you're a cat*. New York: Puffin. TL1–2, P, F

Matthews, T. (2007). *Out of the egg*. Boston: Houghton Mifflin. TL2–3, A, F

Mayhew, J. (2008). *Where's my hug?* New York: Bloomsbury. TL2–5, A, F

McClure, G. (2008). *The land of the Dragon King and other Korean stories*. London: Lincoln. TL4–5, I, F

McDonald, F. (1996). *I love animals*. Cambridge, MA: Candlewick Press. TL2–4, P, F

McGrath, B. B. (2003). *Soccer counts!* Watertown, MA: Charlesbridge. TL2–5, A, NF

McKissack, P. C. (2007). *A song for Harlem*. New York: Viking. TL4–5, I, F

McMillan, B. (1989). *Time to*. New York: Lothrop, Lee & Shepard. TL1–3, P, NF

McMillan, B. (1992). *One sun: A book of terse verse*. New York: Holiday House. TL1–3, A, P

McMillan, B. (1994). *Growing colors*. New York: Mulberry. TL1–3, P, NF

Medina, J. (1999). *My name is Jorge on both sides of the river*. Honesdale, PA: Boyds Mills Press. TL3–5, A, P

Melmed, L.K. (2003). *Capital! Washington D.C. from A to Z*. New York: HarperCollins. TL2–5, A, NF

Micucci, C. (2006). *The life and times of the ant*. New York: Sandpiper. TL3–5, I, NF

Milich, Z. (2005). *City signs*. Toronto, Ontario, Canada: Kids Can Press. TL1–5, A, NF

Millard, A. (1998). *A street through time*. New York: DK. TL4–5, I, NF

Miller, D. S. (2003). *Are trees alive?* New York: Walker. TL2–5, A, NF

Miura, T. (2006). *Ton*. San Francisco: Chronicle. TL1–2, P, NF

Miura, T. (2007). *Tools*. San Francisco: Chronicle. TL1–2, P, NF

Mobin-Uddin, A. (2005). *My name is Bilal*. Honesdale, PA: Boyds Mills Press. TL4–5, I, F

Mobin-Uddin, A. (2007). *The best Eid ever*. Honesdale, PA: Boyds Mills Press. TL4–5, I, F

Montanari, D. (2004). *Children around the world*. Toronto, Ontario, Canada: Kids Can Press. TL2–4, A, NF

Moodie, F. (2008). *Noko's surprise party*. London: Lincoln. TL3–5, A, F

Moore, L. (2005). *Mural on second avenue and other city poems.* Cambridge, MA: Candlewick Press. TL2–5, A, P

Mora, P. (1999). *Confetti: Poems for children.* New York: Lee & Low. TL2–5, A, P

Mora, P. (1997). *Tomás and the library lady.* New York: Knopf. TL4–5, A, F

Mora, P. (2007). *Yum! Mmmm! Que rico! America's sproutlings.* New York: Lee & Low. TL3–5, A, P

Mora, P. (2008). *Join hands: The ways we celebrate life.* Watertown, MA: Charlesbridge. TL2–4, P, NF

Morgan, P. (1996). *The turnip.* New York: Putnam. TL2–3, A, F

Morris, A. (1993a). *Bread, bread, bread.* New York: HarperCollins. TL1–4, A, NF

Morris, A. (1993b). *Hats, hats, hats.* New York: HarperCollins. TL1–4, A, NF

Morris, A. (1993c). *Weddings.* New York: HarperCollins. TL1–4, A, NF

Morris, A. (1994). *On the go.* New York: HarperCollins. TL1–4, A, NF

Morris, A. (1998a). *Shoes, shoes, shoes.* New York: HarperCollins. TL1–4, A, NF

Morris, A. (1998b). *Tools.* New York: HarperCollins. TL1–4, A, NF

Morris, A. (2000). *Families.* New York: HarperCollins. TL1–4, A, NF

Morris, A. (2005). *Houses and homes.* New York: HarperCollins. TL1–4, A, NF

Moss, M. (2001). *Rachel's journal: The story of a pioneer girl.* Boston: Houghton Mifflin. TL4–5, I, F

Na, A. (2001). *A step from Heaven.* Honesdale, PA: Front Street. TL5, S, F

Na, A. (2006). *Wait for me.* New York: Putnam. TL5, S, F

Na, A. (2008). *The fold.* New York: Putnam. TL5, S, F

Nayar, N. (2009). *What should I make?* Berkley: Tricycle Press. TL1–3, P, F

Nelson, K. (2005). *He's got the whole world in His hands.* New York: Dial. TL1–5, A, P

Nicholson, C. D. (2008). *Niwechihaw, I help.* Toronto, Ontario, Canada: Groundwood. TL1–2, P, F

Nishiyama, A. (2004). *Wonderful houses around the world.* Bolinas, CA: Shelter. TL3–5, I, NF

Nitto, T. (2006). *The Red rock: The graphic fable.* Toronto, Ontario, Canada: Groundwood. TL2–5, A, F

Nye, N. S. (1997). *Sitti's secrets.* New York: Aladdin. TL3–5, A, F

Okimoto, J. D. (2007). *Winston of Churchill: One bear's battle against global warming.* Seattle, WA: Sasquatch. TL2–5, A, F

Older, J. (2000). *Telling time: How to tell time on digital and analog clocks.* Watertown, MA: Charlesbridge. TL2–4, P, NF

Otto, C. (2008). *Celebrate Cinco de Mayo with fiestas, music and dance.* Washington, DC: National Geographic. TL3–5, I, NF

Pak, S. (1999). *Dear Juno.* New York: Viking. TL3–5, P, F

Paraskevas, B. (1995). *Gracie Graves and the kids from room 402.* San Diego, CA: Harcourt. TL2–5, A, P

Park, F., & Park, G. (2002). *Good-bye, 382 Shin Dang Dong.* Washington, DC: National Geographic. TL4–5, A, F

Park, F., & Park, G. (2005). *The have a good day café.* New York: Lee & Low. TL4–5, I, F

Park, L. S. (2004). *The firekeeper's son.* New York: Sandpiper. TL2–5, A, F

Park, L. S. (2005). *Bee-bim bop!* New York: Clarion. TL2–4, P, F

Parker, T. T. (2005). *Sienna's scrapbook: Our African American heritage trip*. San Francisco: Chronicle. TL4–5, I, F

Patz, N., & Roth, S. (2007). *Babies can't eat kimchee!* New York: Bloomsbury. TL2–3, P, F

Pelletier, D. (1996). *The graphic alphabet*. New York: Scholastic. TL1–5, A, NF

Pennypacker, S. (2008). *Clementine's letter*. New York: Hyperion. TL4–5, I, F

Perez, A. I. (2002). *My diary from here to there/ Mi diario de aqui hasta alla*. San Francisco: Children's Book Press. TL4–5, A, F

Peters, L. W. (2003). *Our family tree: An evolution story*. San Diego, CA: Harcourt. TL3–5, I, NF

Pinchon, L. (2008). *Penguins*. New York: Orchard. TL2–4, P, F

Pinkney, M., & Pinkney, S. (2007). *I am Latino: The beauty in me*. New York: Little, Brown. TL2–4, A, F

Poole, A. (2005). *The pea blossom*. New York: Holiday House. TL3–5, A, F

Porter, P. (2008). *Yellow moon, apple moon*. Toronto, Ontario, Canada: Groundwood Books. TL1–5, P, P

Post, H., & Heij, K. (2008). *Sparrows*. Honesdale, PA: Boyds Mills Press. TL2–5, A, NF

Prelutsky, J. (2007). *Me I am!* New York: Random House. TL2–4, A, P

Prelutksy, J. (2008). *It's Thanksgiving!* New York: HarperCollins. TL2–4, A, P

Pringle, L. (2002). *Crows! Strange and wonderful*. Honesdale, PA: Boyds Mills Press. TL4–5, I, NF

Pringle, L. (2003). *Whales! Strange and wonderful*. Honesdale, PA: Boyds Mills Press. TL4–5, I, NF

Quarmby, K. (2008). *Fussy Freya*. London: Lincoln. TL3–5, A, F

Raschka, C. (1993). *Yo! Yes*. New York: Scholastic. TL1–2, A, F

Ravishankar, A. (2008). *Elephants never forget*. Boston: Houghton Mifflin. TL2–4, A, F

Recorvits, H. (2002). *My name is Yoon*. New York: Foster. TL3–5, P, F

Reynolds, J. (2006). *Celebrate! Connections among cultures*. New York: Lee & Low. TL3–5, I, NF

Rinck, M. (2008). *I feel a foot!* Rotterdam, Netherlands: Lemniscaat. TL2–4, A, F

Rink, C. A. (2002). *Where does the wind blow?* Nevada City, CA: Dawn. TL2–3, A, F

Ritchie, S. (2009). *Follow that map! A first look at mapping skills*. Toronto, Ontario, Canada: Kids Can Press. TL3–5, A, NF

Robinson, A., & Young, A. (2008). *Gervelie's journey: A refugee diary*. London: Lincoln. TL3–5, I, NF

Rockwell, A. (2000). *Career day*. New York: HarperCollins. TL3–5, A, F

Rockwell, A. (2001). *Bugs are insects*. New York: HarperCollins. TL3–5, A, NF

Rockwell, A. (2002). *Becoming butterflies*. New York: Walker. TL3–5, A, NF

Root, P. (2002). *Big mama makes the world*. Cambridge, MA: Candlewick Press. TL2–5, A, F

Ryan, P. M. (1996). *100 is a family*. New York: Hyperion. TL2–5, A, F

Ryden, H. (1988). *Wild animals of America ABC*. New York: Dutton. TL2–5, A, NF

Ryder, J. (2001). *Little panda: The world welcomes Hua Mei at the San Diego Zoo*. New York: Simon & Schuster. TL2–5, A, NF

Rylant, C. (2008). *Alligator Boy*. New York: Harcourt. TL2–4, A, F

Sakai, K. (2009). *The snow day*. New York: Levine. TL1–3, P, F

Say, A. (2005). *Kamichibai man*. Boston: Houghton Mifflin. TL3–5, I, F

Sayre, A. P. (2001). *Dig, wait, listen: A desert toad's tale*. New York: Greenwillow. TL2–4, A, F

Sayre, A. P. (2002a). *Army ant parade*. New York: Holt. TL3–5, A, NF

Sayre, A. P. (2002b). *Shadows*. New York: Holt. TL2–4, A, F

Sayre, A. P., & Sayre, J. (2003). *One is a snail, ten is a crab: A counting by feet book*. Cambridge, MA: Candlewick Press. TL1–4, A, NF

Schaefer, L. M. (2004). *Pick, pull, snap! Where a flower once bloomed*. New York: Greenwillow. TL3–5, A, NF

Schanzer, R. (1998). *How we crossed the west: The adventures of Lewis and Clark*. Washington, DC: National Geographic. TL3–5, I, NF

Schertle, A. (2007). *We*. New York: Lee & Low. TL3–5, A, NF

Schneider, R. M. (1995) *Add it, dip it, fix it: A book of verbs*. Boston: Houghton Mifflin. TL1–2, P, NF

Schubert, I. (2008). *Like people*. Honesdale, PA: Boyds Mills Press. TL2–4, A, NF

Schuett, S. (1997). *Somewhere in the world right now*. Albuquerque, NM: Dragonfly Books. TL2–5, A, F

Schwartz, A. (1992). *And the green grass grew all around: Folk poetry from everyone*. TL2–5, A, F

Sciurba, K. (2007). *Oye, Celia!: A song for Celia Cruz*. New York: Holt. TL2–5, I, F

Seuling, B. (2003). *Flick a switch: How electricity gets to your home*. New York: Holiday House. TL3–5, A, NF

Shahan, S. (2004). *Spicy hot colors/ colores picantes*. Little Rock, AR: August House. TL1–5, A, NF

Shahan, S. (2005). *Cool cats counting*. Little Rock, AR: August House. TL1–5, A, NF

Shannon, G. (2007). *Rabbit's gift*. San Diego, CA: Harcourt. TL2–4, A, F

Shaw, N. (1986). *Sheep in a jeep*. Boston: Houghton Mifflin. TL1–2, P, F

Shaw, N. (1989). *Sheep on a ship*. Boston: Houghton Mifflin. TL1–2, P, F

Shaw, N. (1991). *Sheep in a shop*. Boston: Houghton Mifflin. TL1–2, P, F

Shaw, N. (1992). *Sheep out to eat*. Boston: Houghton Mifflin. TL1–2, P, F

Shaw, N. (1994). *Sheep take a hike*. Boston: Houghton Mifflin. TL1–2, P, F

Shaw, N. (1997). *Sheep trick or treat*. Boston: Houghton Mifflin. TL1–2, P, F

Shaw, N. (2003). *Raccoon tune*. New York: Holt. TL1–2, P, F

Shaw, N. (2008). *Sheep blast off*. Boston: Houghton Mifflin. TL1–2, P, F

Shea, P. D. (1996). *The whispering cloth: A refugee's story*. Honesdale, PA: Boyds Mills. TL2–5, I, F

Shea, P. D. (2003). *Tangled threads: A Hmong girl's story*. New York: Clarion. TL4–5, S, F

Sheth, K. (2007). *My dadima wears a sari*. Atlanta, GA: Peachtree. TL4–5, A, F

Shields, G. (2008). *Dogfish*. New York: Atheneum. TL2–4, A, F

Shore, D. Z., & Alexander, J. (2006). *This is the dream*. New York: HarperCollins. TL2–5, I, P

Showers, P. (1994). *Where does the garbage go?* New York: HarperCollins. TL2–4, A, NF

Sidman, J. (2009). *Red sings from tree tops: A year in colors.* Boston: Houghton Mifflin. TL3–5, A, P

Siebert, D. (1992). *Mojave.* New York: HarperCollins. TL3–5, I, P

Siebert, D. (1996). *Sierra.* New York: HarperCollins. TL3–5, I, P

Siebert, D. (2000). *Cave.* New York: HarperCollins. TL3–5, I, P

Siebert, D. (2001). *Mississippi.* New York: HarperCollins. TL3–5, I, P

Sill, C. P. (1991). *About birds.* Atlanta, GA: Peachtree. TL2–4, A, NF

Sill, C. P. (1997). *About mammals.* Atlanta, GA: Peachtree. TL2–4, A, NF

Sill, C. P. (1999). *About reptiles.* Atlanta, GA: Peachtree. TL2–4, A, NF

Sill, C. P. (2000a). *About amphibians.* Atlanta, GA: Peachtree. TL2–4, A, NF

Sill, C. P. (2000b). *About insects.* Atlanta, GA: Peachtree. TL2–4, A, NF

Sill, C. P. (2001). *About amphibians: A guide for children.* Atlanta, GA: Peachtree. TL2–4, A, NF

Sill, C. P. (2002). *About fish.* Atlanta, GA: Peachtree. TL2–4, A, NF

Sill, C. P. (2003). *About arachnids.* Atlanta, GA: Peachtree. TL2–4, A, NF

Sill, C. P. (2008a). *About deserts.* Atlanta, GA: Peachtree. TL2–4, A, NF

Sill, C. P. (2008b). *About rodents.* Atlanta, GA: Peachtree. TL2–4, A, NF

Sill, C. P. (2008c). *About wetlands.* Atlanta, GA: Peachtree. TL2–4, A, NF

Sill, C. P. (2009). *About penguins.* Atlanta, GA: Peachtree. TL2–4, A, NF

Silverstein, S. (2000). *Where the sidewalk ends.* New York: HarperCollins. TL1–5, A, P

Silverstein, S. (2001). *A light in the attic.* New York: HarperCollins. TL1–5, A, P

Simon, S. (1992). *Storms.* New York: HarperCollins. TL4–5, I, NF

Simon, S. (1994a). *Autumn across America.* New York: HarperCollins. TL4–5, I, NF

Simon, S. (1994b). *Winter across America.* New York: HarperCollins. TL4–5, I, NF

Simon, S. (1995a). *Volcanoes.* New York: HarperCollins. TL4–5, I, NF

Simon, S. (1995b). *Wolves.* New York: HarperCollins. TL4–5, I, NF

Simon, S. (2002). *Animals nobody loves.* San Francisco: Chronicle. TL3–5, I, NF

Simon, S. (2006a). *Earthquakes.* New York: HarperCollins. TL4–5, I, NF

Simon, S. (2006b). *Lightning.* New York: HarperCollins. TL4–5, I, NF

Simon, S. (2006c). *Sharks.* New York: HarperCollins. TL3–5, A, NF

Simon, S. (2006d). *Whales.* New York: HarperCollins. TL3–5, A, NF

Simon, S. (2009). *Wolves.* New York: HarperCollins. TL3–5, A, NF

Simon, S., & Fauteux, N. (2003a). *Let's try it out in the air: Hands-on early-learning science activities.* New York: Aladdin. TL3–5, A, NF

Simon, S., & Fauteux, N. (2003b). *Let's try it out in the water: Hands-on early-learning science activities.* New York: Aladdin. TL3–5, A, NF

Simon, S., & Fauteux, N. (2003c). *Let's try it with towers and bridges: Hands-on early-learning science activities.* New York: Simon & Schuster. TL3–5, A, NF

Smith, J. (2009). *Little mouse gets ready.* New York: Raw Junior. TL1–2, P, F

Smith, P., & Shaley, Z. (2007). *A school like mine.* New York: DK. TL2–5, A, NF

Sobol, R. (2004). *An elephant in the backyard.* New York: Dutton. TL3–5, I, NF

Soto, G. (1994). *Too many tamales.* New York: Putnam. TL3–4, A, F

Soto, G. (1996). *Que monton de tamales!* New York: PaperStar. TL3–4, A, F

Spanyol, J. (2003). *Carlos likes colors.* Cambridge, MA: Candlewick Press. TL1, P, F

Stanton, K. (2007). *Papi's gift*. Honesdale, PA: Boyds Mills Press. TL3–5, A, F

Stauffacher, S. (2007). *Nothing but trouble: The story of Althea Gibson*. New York: Knopf. TL3–5, A, NF

Steele, P. (2004). *A city through time*. New York: DK. TL4–5, I, NF

Steffensmeier, A. (2008). *Millie in the snow*. New York: Walker. TL2–4, A, F

Steggal, S. (2008). *The life of a car*. New York: Holt. TL1–2, P, NF

Stewart, M. (2008). *When rain falls*. Atlanta, GA: Peachtree. TL3–5, A, NF

Stock, C. (1993). *Where are you going, Manyoni?* New York: HarperCollins. TL2–5, A, F

Stockdale, S. (2008). *Fabulous fishes*. Atlanta, GA: Peachtree. TL2–4, A, NF

Surat, M. M. (1989). *Angel child, dragon child*. New York: Scholastic. TL3–5, A, F

Swain, R. F. (2003). *How sweet it is (and was): The history of candy*. New York: Holiday House. TL3–5, A, NF

Swinburne, S. R. (2000). *What's opposite?* Honesdale, PA: Boyds Mills Press. TL1–3, P, NF

Swinburne, S. R. (2002a). *Go go go! Kids on the move*. Honesdale, PA: Boyds Mills Press. TL1–2, P, NF

Swinburne, S. R. (2002b). *What color is nature?* Honesdale, PA: Boyds Mills Press. TL1–2, P, NF

Symes, H. (2008). *Harriet dancing*. New York: The Chicken House. TL2–4, A, F

Taback, S. (1997). *There was an old lady who swallowed a fly*. New York: Dutton. TL2–4, A, F

Taback, S. (2002). *This is the house that Jack built*. New York: Putnam. TL2–4, A, F

Tafuri, N. (2000). *Snow, flowy, blowy: A twelve months rhyme*. New York: Scholastic. TL1–5, A, F

Tan, S. (2006). *The arrival*. New York: Levine. TL4–5, IS, F

Tatham, B. (2001). *Penguin chick*. New York: HarperCollins. TL3–5, A, NF

Taylor, S. (2008). *The great snake: Stories from the Amazon*. London: Frances Lincoln. TL4–5, I, F

Testa, M. (2005). *Something about America*. Cambridge, MA: Candlewick Press. TL4–5, S, P

Thompson, H. (2007). *The Wakame gatherers*. Walnut Creek, CA: Shen's Books. TL4–5, I, F

Thompson, S. (2003). *Stars and stripes: The story of the American flag*. New York: HarperCollins. TL3–5, I, NH

Thong, R. (2000). *Round is a mooncake: A book of shapes*. San Francisco: Chronicle. TL2–4, A, F

Thong, R. (2008). *One is a drummer: A book about numbers*. San Francisco: Chronicle. TL2–4, A, F

Thong, T. (2008). *Red is a dragon: A book of colors*. San Francisco: Chronicle. TL2–4, A, F

Toksvig, S. (1998). *If I didn't have elbows*. New York: Kingfisher. TL2–4, P, NF

Tougas, C. (2008). *Art's supplies*. Victoria, BC: Orca. TL3–5, A, F

Uegaki, C. (2008). *Rosie and Buttercup*. Toronto, Ontario, Canada: Kids Can Press. TL3–5, A, F

Vila, L. (2008). *Building Manhattan*. New York: Viking. TL3–5, A, NF

Voake, J. (2008). *Tweedle-dee-dee*. Cambridge, MA: Candlewick Press. TL2–5, A, P

Voake, S. (2008). *Daisy Dawson is on her way!* Cambridge, MA: Candlewick Press. TL4–5, I, F

Voake, S. (2009). *Daisy Dawson and the secret pond.* Watertown, MA: Candlewick Press. TL4–5, I, F

Waldman, N. (2003). *The snowflake: A water cycle story.* Brookfield, CT: Millbrook Press. TL3–5, A, NF

Walker, A. (2007). *Why war is never a good idea.* New York: HarperCollins. TL3–5, I, P

Wallace, N. E. (2005). *A taste of honey.* New York: Cavendish. TL2–4, P, NF

Walsh, E. S. (1995). *Mouse count.* New York: Voyager Books. TL1–3, P, F

Walsh, M. (2008). *Ten things I can do to help my world.* Cambridge, MA: Candlewick Press. TL1–4, A, NF

Ward, C. (1997). *Cookie's week.* New York: Putnam. TL1–3, P, F

Waring, G. (2008).*Oscar the bat: A book about sound.* Cambridge, MA: Candlewick Press. TL2–3, A, F

Watt, M. (2006). *Scaredy squirrel.* Toronto, Ontario, Canada: Kids Can Press. TL3–5, A, F

Watt, M. (2007). *Scaredy squirrel makes a friend.* Toronto, Ontario, Canada: Kids Can Press. TL3–5, A, F

Watt, M. (2008). *Scaredy squirrel at the beach.* Toronto, Ontario, Canada: Kids Can Press. TL3–5, A, F

Watt, M. (2009). *Scaredy squirrel at night.* Toronto, Ontario, Canada: Kids Can Press. TL3–5, A, F

Webb, S. (2000). *My season with penguins: An Antarctic journal.* Boston: Houghton Mifflin. TL4–5, I, NF

Weeks, S. (2006). *Counting ovejas.* New York: Atheneum. TL1, P, F

Wells, R. (2000). *Bunny money.* New York: Puffin. TL2–3, P, F

Wells, R. (2005). *Emily's first 100 days of school.* New York: Hyperion. TL1–3, P, F

Wells, R. (2008). *Yoko writes her name.* New York: Hyperion. TL2–3, P, F

Wells, R. (2009). *Shopping.* New York: Viking. TL1–3, P, F

Wiesner, D. (1991). *Tuesday.* New York: Clarion. TL2–5, A, F

Wiesner, D. (2006). *Flotsam.* New York: Clarion. TL2–5, A, F

Wiesner, D. (2008). *Free fall.* New York: HarperCollins. TL2–5, A, F

Wilkes, A. (2002). *A farm through time.* New York: DK. TL4–5, I, NF

Wilkes, A. (2007). *Animal homes.* New York: Kingfisher. TL3–5, I, NF

Willems, M. (2009). *Naked mole rat gets dressed.* New York: Hyperion. TL2–4, A, F

Williams, K. L., & Mohammad, K. (2007). *Four feet, two sandals.* Grand Rapids, MI: Eerdmans. TL3–5, A, F

Williams, M. (2005). *Brothers in hope: The story of the lost boys of Sudan.* New York: Lee & Low. TL4–5, I, F

Williams, M. (2007). *Archie's war: My scrapbook of the first world war, 1914–1918.* Cambridge, MA: Candlewick Press. TL4–5, I, F

Williams, R. L. (2001). *The coin counting book.* Watertown, MA: Charlesbridge. TL1–3, A, NF

Williams, S. (1990). *I went walking.* San Diego, CA: Gulliver Books. TL1–3, P, F

Williams, V. (1984). *A chair for my mother.* New York: Greenwillow. TL2–4, P, F

Willis, J. (2008). *Cottonball Colin.* Grand Rapids, MI: Eerdmans. TL2–4, A, F

Wilson, K. (2007). *How to bake an American pie*. New York: McElderry. TL3–5, I, F

Winer, Y. (2003). *Frogs sing songs*. Watertown, MA: Charlesbridge. TL3–5, I, P

Winter, J. (2006). *Mama: A true story in which a baby hippo loses his mama during a tsunami but finds a new home, and a new mama*. San Diego, CA: Harcourt. TL1–2, P, NF

Winter, J. (2007). *Angelina's island*. New York: Farrar, Straus & Giroux. TL2–4, A, F

Winters, K. (2008). *Colonial voices: Hear them speak*. New York: Dutton. TL4–5, I, NF

Wolf, A. (2009). *When Lucy goes out walking: A puppy's first year*. New York: Holt. TL2–4, P, F

Wolf, B. (2003). *Coming to America: A Muslim family's story*. New York: Lee & Low. TL4–5, I, NF

Wolff, F. (2008). *The story blanket*. Atlanta, GA: Peachtree. TL2–4, A, F

Wong, J. (2000). *The trip back home*. San Diego, CA: Harcourt. TL2–5, A, F

Wong, J. (2002). *Apple pie 4th of July*. San Diego, CA: Harcourt. TL2–4, A, F

Wong, J. (2007a). *Good luck gold*. Seattle: BookSurge. TL3–5, I, P

Wong, J. (2007b). *Night garden: Poems from the world of dreams*. New York: Aladdin. TL3–5, I, P

Wong, J. (2008a). *The rainbow hand*. Seattle, WA: BookSurge. TL3–5, I, P

Wong, J. (2008b). *A suitcase of seaweed and other poems*. Seattle, WA: BookSurge. TL3–5, I, P

Wong, J. S. (2000). *This next new year*. New York: Foster. TL2–4, A, F

Yang, B. (2004). *Hannah is my name*. Cambridge, MA: Candlewick Press. TL4–5, A, F

Yang, G. L. (2007). *American born Chinese*. New York: First Second. TL5, S, F

Yim, S. (2002). *Ruby's wish*. San Francisco: Chronicle. TL4–5, I, F

Yolen, J. (1992). *Street rhymes around the world*. Honesdale, PA: Wordsong/Boyds Mill Press. TL2–5, A, F

Yolen, J. (2005). *Snow, snow: Winter poems for children*. Honesdale, PA: Boyds Mills Press. TL3–5, A, P

Zaunders, B. (2001). *Feathers, flaps, & flops: Fabulous early fliers*. New York: Dutton. TL3–5, A, NF

Zelinksy, P. O. (1990). *The wheels on the bus*. New York: Dutton. TL1–3, P, F

Zelinksy, P. O. (2002). *Knick knack paddywhack*. New York: Dutton. TL1–3, P, F

References

Allen, V. G. (1994). Selecting materials for the reading instruction of ESL children. In K. Spangenberg-Urbschat & R. Pritchard (Eds.), *Kids come in all languages: Reading instruction for ESL students* (pp. 108–131). Newark, DE: International Reading Association.

Allington, R. L. (2009a). *What really matters in fluency: Research-based practices across the curriculum.* Boston: Allyn & Bacon.

Allington, R. L. (2009b). *What really matters in response to intervention: Research-based designs.* Boston: Allyn & Bacon.

Anderson, J., Anderson, A., Lynch, J., & Shapiro, J. (2003). Storybook reading in a multicultural society: Critical perspectives. In A. van Kleek, S. A. Stahl, & E. B. Bauer (Eds.), *On reading books to children: Parents and teachers* (pp. 203–230). Mahwah, NJ: Erlbaum.

Anderson, T. H., & Armbruster, B. B. (1986). Readable textbooks: Or, selecting a textbook is not like buying a pair of shoes. In J. Orasanu (Ed.), *Reading comprehension: From research to practice* (pp. 151–162). Hillsdale, NJ: Erlbaum.

Angus, C. (2007). Keys to global understanding: Notable books for a global society text sets. In N. L. Hadaway & M. J. McKenna (Eds.), *Breaking boundaries with global literature: Celebrating diversity In K–12 classrooms* (pp. 131–140). Newark, DE: International Reading Association.

Armbruster, B., & Anderson, T. H. (1985). Producing "considerate" expository text: Or easy reading is damned hard writing. *Journal of Curriculum Studies, 17,* 247–263.

Arreaga-Mayer, C., & Perdomo-Rivera, C. (1996). Ecobehavioral analysis of instruction for at-risk language-minority students. *Elementary School Journal, 96*(3), 245–258.

Asher, J. (1982). *Learning another language through actions: The complete teachers' guidebook.* Los Gatos, CA: Sky Oaks.

Association of Library Services for Children. (2005). Bilingual books for children booklist. Retrieved June 7, 2006, from *www.ala.org/ala/alsc/alscresources/booklists/bilingualbooks.htm.*

August, D., Beck, I. L., Calderón, M., Francis, D. J., Lesaux, N. K., Shanahan, T., et al. (2008). Instruction and professional development. In D. August & T. Shanahan (Eds.), *Developing reading and writing in second-language learners: Lessons from the report of the National Literacy Panel on language-minority children and youth* (pp. 131–250). New York: Routledge.

Beaty, J. J. (1997). *Building bridges with multicultural picture books: For children 3–5.* Upper Saddle River, NJ: Prentice-Hall.

Beck, I. L., McKeown, M., Omanson, R., & Pople, M. (1984). Improving the comprehensibility of stories: The effects of revisions that improve coherence. *Reading Research Quarterly, 19*, 263–277.

Beck, I. L., McKeown, M. G., & Kucan, L. (2002). *Bringing words to life: Robust vocabulary instruction.* New York: Guilford Press.

Bermúdez, A. B. (1994). *Doing our homework: How schools can engage Hispanic communities.* Culturally and Linguistically Appropriate Services, Early Childhood Research Institute. Retrieved July 8, 2007, from *clas.uiuc.edu/fulltext/cl00136/chapter1.html.*

Bishop, R. S. (1997). Selecting literature for a multicultural curriculum. In V. J. Harris (Ed.), *Using multiethnic literature in the K–8 classroom* (pp. 1–20). Norwood, MA: Christopher-Gordon.

Bridge, C. (1986). Predictable books for beginning readers and writers. In M. R. Sampson (Ed.), *The pursuit of literacy: Early reading and writing* (pp. 50–66). Dubuque, IA: Kendall/Hunt.

Brozo, W. G., & Flynt, E. (2008). Motivating students to read in the content classroom: Six evidence-based principles. *The Reading Teacher, 62*, 172–174.

Buhrow, B., & Garcia, A. U. (2006). *Ladybugs, tornadoes, and swirling galaxies: English language learners discover their world through inquiry.* Portland, ME: Stenhouse.

Capellini, M. (2005). *Balancing reading & language learning: A resource for teaching English language learners, K–5.* Newark, DE: International Reading Association.

Cassidy, J., & Cassidy, D. (2004–2005). What's hot, what's not for 2005. *Reading Today, 22*, 1.

Center for the Improvement of Early Reading Achievement (CIERA). (2003). *Put reading first: The building blocks of reading instruction, kindergarten through grade 3* (2nd ed.). Retrieved September 9, 2009, from *www.nifl.gov/partnershipforreading/publications/Cierra.pdf.*

Chamot, A. U., & O'Malley, J. M. (1987). The cognitive academic learning approach: A bridge to the mainstream. *TESOL Quarterly, 21*, 227–249.

Chatton, B. (2009). *Using poetry across the curriculum: Learning to love language.* Santa Barbara, CA: Libraries Unlimited.

Christian, D. (2004). *Advancing the achievement of English language learners.* Paper presented at the Fourth Annual Claiborne Pell Education Policy Seminar. Retrieved October 31, 2004, from *www.alliance.brown.edu/pubs/IS2000/downloads/christian.pdf.*

Christison, M. A., & Bassano, S. (1995). *Purple cows & potato chips: Multisensory language acquisition activities.* Provo, UT: Alta Book Center.

Collier, V. P. (1989). How long? A synthesis of research on academic achievement in a second language. *TESOL Quarterly, 23*, 509–531.

Colorín Colorado. (2007). Capitalizing on similarities and differences between Spanish and English. Retrieved April 2, 2008, from *www.colorincolorado.org/educators/background/capitalizing*.

Cornell, E. H., Sénéchal, M., & Brodo, L. S. (1988). Recall of picture books by 3-year-old children: Testing and repetition effects in joint reading activities. *Journal of Educational Psychology, 80*(4), 537–542.

Crago, H., & Crago, M. (1976). The untrained eye? A preschool child explores Felix Hoffman's "Rapunzel." *Children's Literature in Education, 22*, 135–151.

Cullinan, B. E. (1993). *Fact and fiction across the curriculum*. Newark, DE: International Reading Association.

Cullinan, B. E., Scala, M. C., & Schroder, V. C. (1995). *Three voices: An invitation to poetry across the curriculum*. York, ME: Stenhouse.

Cummins, J. (1980). The construct of language proficiency in bilingual education. In J. E. Alatis (Ed.), *Georgetown University roundtable on languages and linguistics* (pp. 76–93). Washington, DC: Georgetown University Press.

Cummins, J. (1981). The role of primary language development in promoting educational success for language minority students. In *Schooling and language minority students: A theoretical framework*. Sacramento: California State Department of Education.

Cummins, J. (2001). *Negotiating identities: Education for empowerment in a diverse society*. Los Angeles: California Association for Bilingual Education.

Cummins, J. (2003). Reading and the bilingual student: Fact and friction. In G. Garcia (Ed.), *English learners: Reaching the highest levels of English literacy* (pp. 2–33). Newark, DE: International Reading Association.

Cummins, J., & Schecter, S. (2003). School-based language policy in culturally diverse contexts. In S. Schecter & J. Cummins (Eds.), *Multilingual education in practice: Using diversity as a resource* (pp. 1–16). Portsmouth, NH: Heinemann.

Cunningham, P. M. (2007). Best practices in teaching phonological awareness and phonics. In L. B. Gambrell, L. M. Morrow, & M. Pressley (Eds.), *Best practices in literacy instruction* (pp. 159–177). New York: Guilford Press.

Dorfman, L. R., & Cappelli, R. (2007). *Mentor texts: Teaching writing through children's literature, K–6*. Portland, ME: Stenhouse.

Duke, N. K. (2000). 3.6 minutes per day: The scarcity of informational texts in first grade. *Reading Research Quarterly, 35*, 202–224.

Duke, N. K. (2003). Informational text? The research says, "Yes!" In L. Hoyt, M. Mooney, & B. Parkes (Eds.), *Exploring informational texts: From theory to practice* (pp. 2–7). Portsmouth, NH: Heinemann.

Duke, N. K., & Bennett-Armistead, V. S. (2003). *Reading and writing informational text in the primary grades: Research-based practices*. New York: Scholastic.

Dulay, H. C., & Burt, M. K. (1974). Errors and strategies in child second language acquisition. *TESOL Quarterly, 8*, 129–136.

Echevarria, J., Vogt, M. E., & Short, D. (2008). *Making content comprehensible for English learners: The SIOP model*. Boston: Pearson/Allyn & Bacon.

Ehmann, S., & Gayer, K. (2009). *I can write like that! A guide to mentor texts and craft studies for writer's workshop, K–6*. Newark, DE: International Reading Association.

Elley, W. B. (1989). Vocabulary acquisition from listening to stories. *Reading Research Quarterly, 24*, 174–187.

Ernst-Slavit, G., & Mulhern, M. (2003, September/October). Bilingual books: Promoting literacy and biliteracy in the second-language and mainstream classroom. *Reading Online, 7*(2). Available at *www.readingonline.org/articles/art_index.asp?HREF=ernst-slavit/index.html.*

Ervin-Tripp, S. (1974). Is second language learning like the first? *TESOL Quarterly, 8,* 111–127.

Evers, A. J., Lang, L. F., & Smith, S. V. (2009). An ABC literacy journey: Anchoring in text, bridging literacy, and creating stories. *The Reading Teacher, 62,* 461–470.

Fagin, L. (1991). *The list poem: A guide to teaching and writing catalog verse.* New York: Teachers and Writers Collaborative.

Fillmore, L. W. (2002). *Issues of language differences and literacy development: What do language minority students need?* Paper presented at the Spicola Forum, Texas Woman's University, Denton, TX.

Fillmore, L. W., & Snow, C. E. (2002). *What teachers need to know about language.* Washington, DC: Center for Applied Linguistics, ERIC Clearinghouse on Languages and Linguistics. Retrieved December 12, 2002, from *www.cal.org/ericcll/teachers/teachers.pdf.*

Fisher, D., Flood, J., Lapp, D., & Frey, N. (2004). Interactive read-alouds: Is there a common set of implementation practices? *The Reading Teacher, 58,* 8–17.

Freeman, D. E., & Freeman, Y. S. (2006). Teaching language through content themes: Viewing our world as a global village. In T. A. Young & N. L. Hadaway (Eds.), *Supporting the literacy development of English learners: Increasing success in all classrooms* (pp. 61–78). Newark, DE: International Reading Association.

Freeman, D. E., & Freeman, Y. S. (2007). *English language learners: The essential guide.* New York: Scholastic.

Freeman, Y., & Freeman, D. (2004). Connecting students to culturally relevant texts. *Talking Points, 15,* 7–11.

García, G. E. (2000). Bilingual children's reading. In M. L. Kamil, P. B. Mosenthal, P. D. Pearson, & R. Barr (Eds.), *Handbook of reading research, Volume III* (pp. 813–834). Mahwah, NJ: Erlbaum.

Gardner, D. (2008). Vocabulary recycling in children's authentic reading materials: A corpus-based investigation of narrow reading. *Reading in a Foreign Language, 20,* 92–122.

Gersten, R., & Baker, S. (2002). What we know about effective instructional practices for English-language learners. *Exceptional Children, 55,* 454–471.

Gill, S. (1996). Shared book experience with poetry. *The State of Reading: Journal of the Texas State Reading Association, 3*(1), 27–30.

Giorgis, C., & Glazer, J. I. (2009). *Literature for young children: Supporting emergent literacy, ages 0–8.* Boston: Pearson/Allyn & Bacon.

Goodman, K., Shannon, P., Freeman, Y., & Murphy, S. (1988). *Report card on basal readers.* New York: Owen.

Gottlieb, M., Cranley, M. E., & Cammilleri, A. (2007). *Understanding the WIDA English Language Proficiency Standards: A resource guide.* Madison: Board of Regents of the University of Wisconsin System, on behalf of the WIDA Consortium. Retrieved September 27, 2009, from *www.wida.us/standards/Resource_Guide_web.pdf.*

Grabe, W. (2009). *Reading in a second language: Moving from theory to practice.* New York: Cambridge.

Guthrie, J. T. (2002). Preparing students for high-stakes test taking in reading. In A. E. Farstrup & S. J. Samuels (Eds.), *What research has to say about reading instruction* (pp. 370–391). Newark, DE: International Reading Association.

Guthrie, J. T. (2003). Concept-oriented reading instruction: Practices of teaching reading for understanding. In A. P. Sweet & C. E. Snow (Eds.), *Rethinking reading comprehension* (pp. 115–140). New York: Guilford Press.

Guthrie, J. T., Schafer, W. D., VonSecker, C., & Alban, T. (2000). Contributions of instructional practices to reading achievement in a statewide improvement program. *Journal of Educational Research, 93,* 211–225.

Hadaway, N. L. (2009, April). A narrow bridge to academic reading. *Educational Leadership,* 38–41.

Hadaway, N. L., Vardell, S. M., & Young, T. A. (2001). Scaffolding oral language development through poetry for students learning English. *The Reading Teacher, 54,* 796–806.

Hadaway, N. L., Vardell, S. M., & Young, T. A. (2002a). Highlighting nonfiction literature: Literacy development and English language learners. *New England Reading Association Journal, 38*(2), 16–22.

Hadaway, N. L., Vardell, S. M., & Young, T. A. (2002b, October/November). Linking science and literature for ESL students. *Book Links, 12*(2), 31–36.

Hadaway, N. L., Vardell, S. M., & Young, T. A. (2002c). *Literature-based instruction for English language learners: K–12.* Boston: Allyn & Bacon/Longman.

Hadaway, N. L., Vardell, S. M., & Young, T. A. (2006). Language play, language work: Using poetry to develop oral language. In T. A. Young & N. L. Hadaway (Eds.), *Supporting the literacy development of English learners: Increasing success in all classrooms* (pp. 168–184). Newark, DE: International Reading Association.

Hamayan, E. V. (1990). Preparing mainstream classroom teachers to teach potentially English proficient students. In *Proceedings of the First Research Symposium on Limited English Proficient Student Issues.* Washington, DC: U.S. Department of Education, Office of Bilingual Education and Minority Languages Affairs. Retrieved December 12, 2002, from *www.ncela.gwu.edu/ncbe-pubs/symposia/first/preparing.htm.*

Harper, C., & de Jong, E. (2004). Misconceptions about teaching English-language learners. *Journal of Adolescent and Adult Literacy, 48,* 152–162.

Hass, B. (2002). How equitable is U.S. education for English language learners? *Stanford Educator.* Retrieved April 2, 2008, from *ed.stanford.edu/suse/news-bureau/educator/fall2002/pages/article-us-education-fall02.html.*

Helman, L. (2009). Emergent literacy: Planting the seeds for accomplished reading and writing. In L. Helman (Ed.), *Literacy development with English learners: Research-based instruction in grades K–6.* New York: Guilford Press.

Helman, L. A. (2004). Building on the sound system of Spanish: Insights from the alphabetic spellings of English-language learners. *The Reading Teacher, 57,* 452–460.

Hiebert, E. H. (1998). Selecting text for beginning readers. In T. E. Raphael & K. H. Au (Eds.), *Literature-based instruction: Reshaping the curriculum* (pp. 195–218). Norwood, MA: Christopher-Gordon.

Hopkins, L. B. (1993). Poetry—practically. In M. K. Rudman (Ed.), *Children's literature: Resource for the classroom* (pp. 201–210). Norwood, MA: Christopher-Gordon.

Jett-Simpson, M. (1986). *Reading resource book.* Lake Worth: FL: Humanics.

Johnson, P. (1981). Effects on reading comprehension of language complexity and cultural background of a text. *TESOL Quarterly, 15,* 169–181.

Juel, C. (1991). Beginning reading. In R. Barr, M. L. Kamil, P. B. Mosenthal, & P. D. Pearson (Eds.), *Handbook of reading research* (pp. 759–788). New York: Longman.

Kamil, M. L., & Hiebert, E. H. (2005). The teaching and learning of vocabulary: Perspectives and persistent issues. In E. H. Hiebert & M. L. Kamil (Eds.), *Teaching and learning vocabulary: Bringing research to practice* (pp. 1–23). Mahwah, NJ: Erlbaum.

Kindler, A. (2002). *Survey of the states' limited English proficient students and available educational programs and services, 2000–2001 summary report.* Washington, DC: National Clearinghouse for English Language Acquisition and Language Instruction Educational Programs.

Kletzien, S. B., & Dreher, M. J. (2004). *Informational text in K–3 classrooms: Helping children read and write.* Newark, DE: International Reading Association.

Klingner, J. K., & Vaughn, S. (1996). Reciprocal teaching of reading comprehension strategies for students with learning disabilities who use English as a second language. *The Elementary School Journal, 96,* 275–293.

Krashen, S. (1987). *Principles and practices in second language acquisition.* Englewood Cliffs, NJ: Prentice-Hall International.

Krashen, S. (2003). The (lack of) experimental evidence supporting the use of Accelerated Reader. *Journal of Children's Literature, 29,* 16–30.

Krashen, S. (2004). The case for narrow reading. *Language Magazine, 3*(5), 17–19. Retrieved September 13, 2009, from *www.sdkrashen.com/articles/narrow/all.html.*

Krashen, S. D. (1985). *The input hypothesis: Issues and implications.* New York: Longman.

Krashen, S. D., & Terrell, T. D. (1983). *The natural approach.* San Francisco: Alemany Press.

Kutiper, K., & Wilson, P. (1993). Updating poetry preferences: A look at the poetry children really like. *Reading Teacher, 47,* 28–34.

Lehman, B. A., & Crook, P. R. (1998). Doubletalk: A literary pairing of *The Giver* and *We Are All in the Dumps with Jack and Guy. Children's Literature in Education, 29,* 69–78.

Lesaux, N. K., Geva, E., Koda, K., Siegel, L. S., & Shanahan, T. (2008). Development of literacy in second-language learners. In D. August & T. Shanahan (Eds.), *Developing reading and writing in second-language learners: Lessons from the report of the National Literacy Panel on language-minority children and youth* (pp. 27–59). New York: Routledge.

Lesaux, N., Koda, K., Siegel, L., & Shanahan, T. (2006) Development of literacy. In D. August & T. Shanahan (Eds.), *Developing literacy in second-language learners: Report of the National Literacy Panel on language-minority children and youth* (pp. 75–122). Mahwah, NJ: Erlbaum.

Lightbown, P. M., & Spada, N. (1990). Focus on form and corrective feedback in communicative language teaching. *Studies in Second Language Acquisition, 12*, 429–448.

Linan-Thompson, S., & Vaughn, S. (2007). *Research-based methods of reading instruction for English language learners, grades K–4.* Alexandria, VA: Association for Supervision and Curriculum Development.

McGee, L. M., & Schickedanz, J. A. (2007). Repeated interactive read-alouds in preschool and kindergarten. *The Reading Teacher, 60*, 742–751.

McGill-Franzen, A., Allington, R., Yokoi, L., & Brooks, G. (1999). Putting books in the classroom seems necessary but not sufficient. *Journal of Educational Research, 93*(2), 67–74.

Meeks, L. L., & Austin, C. J. (2003). *Literacy in the secondary English classroom: Strategies for teaching the way kids learn.* Boston: Allyn & Bacon.

Mesmer, H. A. E. (2008). *Tools for matching readers to texts.* New York: Guilford Press.

Meyer, L. (2000). Barriers to meaningful instruction for English learners. *Theory into Practice, 39*, 228–236.

Milon, J. (1974). The development of negation in English by a second language learner. *TESOL Quarterly, 8*, 137–143.

Mitchell, D. (2003). *Children's literature: An invitation to the world.* Boston: Allyn & Bacon.

Mooney, M. E. (2004). *A book is a present: A resource for intentional teaching.* Katonah, NY: Owens.

Mora, J. K. (2004). NCLB's Reading First and multilingual, multicultural learners. In K. Goodman, P. Shannon, Y. Goodman, & R. Rapoport (Eds.), *Saving our schools: The case for public education* (pp. 229–231). Berkeley, CA: RDR Books.

Morrow, L. M. (2004). Methods of research on teaching English language arts. In J. Flood, D. Lapp, J. R. Squires, & J. M. Jensen (Eds.), *Handbook of research on teaching the English language arts* (pp. 857–867). Mahwah, NJ: Erlbaum.

Morrow, L. M., & Brittain, R. (2003). The nature of storybook reading in the elementary school: Current practices. In A. van Kleek, S. A. Stahl, & E. B. Bauer (Eds.), *On reading books to children: Parents and teachers* (pp. 140–158). Mahwah, NJ: Erlbaum.

Moss, B. (1992). Children's nonfiction trade books: A complement to content area texts. *The Reading Teacher, 45*, 26–32.

Moustafa, M., & Land, R. (2002). The reading achievement of economically-disadvantaged children in urban schools using Open Court vs. comparably disadvantaged children in urban schools using non-scripted reading programs. *American Educational Research Association (AERA) Urban Learning, Teaching and Research 2002 Yearbook*, 44–53.

Multilingual Resources for Children Project. (1995). *Building bridges: Multilingual resources for children.* Clevedon, UK: Multilingual Matters.

Muñiz-Swicegood, M. (1994). The effects of metacognitive reading strategy training on the reading performance and student reading analysis strategies of third grade bilingual students. *Bilingual Research Journal, 18*, 83–97.

Nagy, W. (1988). *Teaching vocabulary to improve comprehension.* Newark, DE: International Reading Association.

Nash, R. (1997). NTC's dictionary of Spanish cognates thematically organized. *TESOL Quarterly, 8*, 137–143.

Natalicio, D. S., & Natalicio, L. F. S. (1971). A comparative study of English pluralization by native and non-native English speakers. *Child Development, 42,* 1302–1306.

National Council of Teachers of English. (2009). English language learners: A policy research brief. Retrieved September 12, 2009, from *www.ncte.org/library/files/Publications/Newspaper/Chron0308PolicyBrief.pdf.*

No Child Left Behind Act of 2001 (Public Law 107-110, 115 Stat. 1425, enacted January 8, 2002).

Odlin, T. (1989). *Language transfer: Cross-linguistic influence in language learning.* Cambridge, MA: Cambridge University Press.

Olmedo, I. M. (2003). Language mediation among emergent bilingual children. *Linguistics and Education, 14,* 143–162.

Olsen, L. (2006). Ensuring academic success for English learners. *University of California Linguistic Minority Research Institute Newsletter, 15,* 1–8.

Ovando, C. J., Collier, V. P., & Combs, M. C. (2003). *Bilingual and ESL classrooms: Teaching in multicultural contexts* (3rd ed.). Boston: McGraw-Hill.

Paivio, A. (1968). A factor-analytic study of word attributes and learning. *Journal of Verbal Learning and Verbal Behavior, 7,* 41–48.

Pellegrini, A. D., & Galda, L. (1982). The effects of thematic-fantasy play training on the development of children's story comprehension. *American Educational Research Journal, 19,* 443–452.

Pica, T. (1994). Research on negotiation: What does it reveal about second-language learning, conditions, processes, and outcomes? *Language Learning, 44,* 493–527.

Pilgreen, J. (2006). Supporting English learners: Developing academic language in the content area classroom. In T. A. Young & N. L. Hadaway (Eds.), *Supporting the literacy development of English learners in all classrooms* (pp. 41–60). Newark, DE: International Reading Association.

Ramírez, J. D. (1992). Executive summary. *Bilingual Research Journal, 16,* 1–62.

Ranker, J. (2009). Learning nonfiction in an ESL class: The interaction of situated practice and teacher scaffolding in a genre study. *The Reading Teacher, 62,* 580–589.

Rasinski, T. V. (2000). Speed does matter in reading. *The Reading Teacher, 54,* 146–151.

Rasinski, T. V. (2003). Reading first: Fluency is fundamental. *Instructor, 113*(4), 15–20.

Rasinski, T. V. (2006). Reading fluency instruction: Moving beyond accuracy, automaticity, and prosody. *The Reading Teacher, 59*(7), 704–706.

Ravem, R. (1968). Language acquisition in second language environment. *International Review of Applied Linguistics, 6,* 175–185.

Reed, B., & Railback, J. (2003). Strategies and resources for mainstream teachers of English language learners. Northwest Regional Laboratory. Retrieved August 12, 2009, from *www.nwrel.org/request/2003may/index.html.*

Reese, E., & Cox, A. (1999). Quality of adult book reading affects children's emergent literacy. *Developmental Psychology, 35*(1), 20–28.

Richard-Amato, P. A. (2003). *Making it happen: From interactive to participatory language teaching.* White Plains, NY: Longman.

Rosenshine, B., Meister, C., & Chapman, S. (1996). Teaching students to generate questions: A review of the intervention studies. *Review of Educational Research, 66,* 181–221.

Routman, R. (2003). *Reading essentials: The specifics you need to teach reading well.* Portsmouth, NH: Heinemann.

Rowe, D. W. (1998). The literate potentials of book-related dramatic play. *Reading Research Quarterly, 33,* 10–35.

Savage, J. F. (1994). *Teaching reading using literature.* Madison, WI: Brown & Benchmark.

Scarcella, R. (1990). *Teaching language minority students in the multicultural classroom.* Upper Saddle River, NJ: Prentice-Hall Regents.

Scarcella, R. C., & Oxford, R. L. (1992). *The tapestry of language learning: The individual in the communicative classroom.* Belmont, CA: Heinle ELT/Cengage.

Schon, I. (2004, June). *Caveat emptor/Inferior translations.* Presentation at the Summer Institute, Barahona Center for the Study of Books in Spanish for Children and Adolescents, San Marcos, California.

Schrank, F. A., Fletcher, T. V., & Alvarado, C. G. (1996). Comparative validity of three English oral language proficiency tests. *Bilingual Research Journal, 20,* 55–68.

Sénéchal, M., Lefevre, J., Thomas, E. M., & Daley, K. E. (1998). Differential effects of home literacy experiences on the development of oral and written language. *Reading Research Quarterly, 33,* 96–116.

Short, K. G., & Harste, J. C. (with Burke, C.). (1996). *Creating classrooms for authors and inquirers* (2nd ed.). Portsmouth, NH: Heinemann.

Snow, C. E., Burns, M. S., & Griffin, P. (1998). *Preventing reading difficulties in young children.* Washington, DC: National Academy Press.

Snow, C. (1993). Bilingualism and second language acquisition. In J. B. Gleason & N. B. Ratner (Eds.), *Psycholinguistics* (pp. 392–416). Ft. Worth, TX: Harcourt Brace.

Snow, C. (2008). Cross-cutting themes and future research directions. In D. August & T. Shanahan (Eds.), *Developing reading and writing in second-language learners: Lessons from the report of the National Literacy Panel on language-minority children and youth* (pp. 275–300). New York: Routledge.

Solari, E. (2007). Improving reading comprehension of English learners through listening comprehension instruction. *University of California Linguistic Minority Research Institute Newsletter, 16,* 1.

Spada, N., & Lightbown, P. M. (1993). Instruction and the development of questions in L2 classrooms. *Studies in Second Language Acquisition, 15,* 205–224.

Stahl, S., & Nagy, W. (2006). *Teaching word meanings.* Mahwah, NJ: Erlbaum.

Stanley, N. (2004). A celebration of words. *Teaching Pre-K–8, 34*(7), 56–57.

Stanovich, K. (1985). Matthew effects in reading: Some consequences of individual differences in the acquisition of literacy. *Reading Research Quarterly, 21,* 360–407.

Stein, N. L., & Glenn, C. G. (1979). An analysis of story comprehension in elementary children. In R. Freedle (Ed.), *New directions in discourse processing* (pp. 53–120). Norwood, NJ: Ablex.

Suárez-Orozco, C., & Suárez-Orozco, M. M. (2001). *Children of immigration*. Cambridge, MA: Harvard University Press.

Swain, M. (1985). Communicative competence: Some roles of comprehensible input and comprehensible output in its development. In S. Gass & C. Madden (Eds.), *Input in second language acquisition* (pp. 235–253). Rowley, MA: Newbury House.

Swain, M. (1995). Three functions of output in second language learning. In G. Cook & B. Seidlhofer (Eds.), *Principle and practice in applied linguistics: Studies in honour of H. G. Widdowson* (pp. 125–144). Oxford, UK: Oxford University Press.

Teale, W. H. (2003). Reading aloud to young children as a classroom instructional activity: Insights from research and practice. In A. van Kleek, S. A. Stahl, & E. B. Bauer (Eds.), *On reading books to children: Parents and teachers* (pp. 114–139). Mahwah, NJ: Erlbaum.

TESOL. (2006). Pre-K–12 English language proficiency standards in the core content areas. Retrieved April 4, 2008, from *www.tesol.org/s_tesol/bin. asp?CID=1186&DID=3461&DOC=FILE.PDF*.

Thomas, W., & Collier, V. (1995). Language minority student achievement and program effectiveness. *California Association for Bilingual Education Newsletter, 17*(5), 19, 24.

Tompkins, G. E. (2007). *Teaching writing: Balancing process and product*. Upper Saddle River, NJ: Prentice-Hall.

Trelease, J. (2006). *The read-aloud handbook*. New York: Penguin.

van der Veur, B. (1975). Imagery rating of 1,000 frequently used words. *Journal of Educational Psychology, 67*, 44–56.

Vardell, S. M. (2007). *Poetry people: A practical guide to children's poets*. Santa Barbara, CA: Greenwood.

Vardell, S. M., Hadaway, N. L., & Young, T. A. (2002, April/May). Choosing and sharing poetry with ESL students. *Book Links, 11*(5), 51–56.

Vardell, S. M., Hadaway, N. L., & Young, T. A. (2006). Matching books and readers: Selecting books for English learners. *The Reading Teacher, 59*, 734–741.

Vogel, M., & Tilley, J. (1993). Story poems and the stories we've been waiting to tell. *English Journal, 82*, 86–89.

Vygotsky, L. (1978). *Mind and society*. Cambridge, MA: Harvard University Press.

Walker, S., Edwards, V., & Blacksell, R. (1996). Designing bilingual books for children. *Visible Language, 30*, 268–283.

Wasik, B. A., & Bond, M. A. (2001). Beyond the pages of a book: Interactive book reading and language development in preschool classrooms. *Journal of Experimental Psychology, 93*, 243–250.

Wells, C. G. (1986). *The meaning makers: Children learning language and using language to learn*. Portsmouth, NH: Heinemann.

WIDA Consortium. (2007). World-Class Instructional Design and Assessment Consortium. *Understanding the WIDA English Language Proficiency Standards: A Resource Guide*. Retrieved June 24, 2008, from *www.wida.us/standards/ Resource_Guide_web.pdf*.

Yang, A. (2001). Reading and the non-academic learner: A mystery solved. *System, 29*(4), 451–466.

Yokota, J. (1993). Issues in selecting multicultural children's literature. *Language Arts, 70,* 156–167.

Yopp, H. K. (1998). Read aloud books for developing phonemic awareness: An annotated bibliography. In R. Allington (Ed.), *Teaching struggling readers: Articles from The Reading Teacher* (pp. 217–225). Newark, DE: International Reading Association.

Young, T. A. (2006). Weaving the magic together: Threads of student success and engagement. In M. E. Mooney & T. A. Young (Eds.), *Caught in the spell of writing and reading: Grade 3 and beyond* (pp. 173–190). Katonah, NY: Owen.

Young, T. A., & Moss, B. (2006). Nonfiction in the classroom library: A literacy necessity. *Childhood Education, 82,* 207–212.

Index